STORYTELLING IN MUSEUMS

AMERICAN ALLIANCE OF MUSEUMS

The American Alliance of Museums has been bringing museums together since 1906, helping to develop standards and best practices, gathering and sharing knowledge, and providing advocacy on issues of concern to the entire museum community. Representing more than 35,000 individual museum professionals and volunteers, institutions, and corporate partners serving the museum field, the Alliance stands for the broad scope of the museum community.

The American Alliance of Museums' mission is to champion museums and nurture excellence in partnership with its members and allies.

Books published by AAM further the Alliance's mission to make standards and best practices for the broad museum community widely available.

STORYTELLING IN MUSEUMS

Edited by Adina Langer

ROWMAN & LITTLEFIELD
Lanham • Boulder • New York • London

Published by Rowman & Littlefield
An imprint of The Rowman & Littlefield Publishing Group, Inc.
4501 Forbes Boulevard, Suite 200, Lanham, Maryland 20706
www.rowman.com

86-90 Paul Street, London EC2A 4NE

British Library Cataloguing in Publication Information Available

Library of Congress Cataloging-in-Publication Data

Names: Langer, Adina, author. | American Alliance of Museums.
Title: Storytelling in museums / [edited by] Adina Langer.
Description: Lanham : Rowman & Littlefield, [2022] | Publication supported by the American Alliance of Museums. | Includes bibliographical references and index.
Identifiers: LCCN 2022011995 (print) | LCCN 2022011996 (ebook) | ISBN 9781538156933 (cloth) | ISBN 9781538156940 (paperback) | ISBN 9781538156957 (ebook)
Subjects: LCSH: Museums—Social aspects. | Storytelling. | Museum techniques. | Communication in museums. | Museums and community. | Museums—Educational aspects. | Museums and minorities.
Classification: LCC AM7 .S77 2022 (print) | LCC AM7 (ebook) | DDC 069—dc23/eng/20220317
LC record available at https://lccn.loc.gov/2022011995
LC ebook record available at https://lccn.loc.gov/2022011996

∞™ The paper used in this publication meets the minimum requirements of American National Standard for Information Sciences—Permanence of Paper for Printed Library Materials, ANSI/NISO Z39.48-1992.

CONTENTS

PREFACE

Adina Langer

In 2001, as museums worried about their relevance at the dawn of the digital age, Leslie Bedford advocated strongly for a trend she was beginning to witness in her *Curator* article "Storytelling: The Real Work of Museums." In it she wrote,

> Stories are the real thing. Stories are the most fundamental way we learn. They have a beginning, a middle, and an end. They teach without preaching, encouraging both personal reflection and public discussion. Stories inspire wonder and awe; they allow a listener to imagine another time and place, to find the universal in the particular, and to feel empathy for others. They preserve individual and collective memory and speak to both the adult and the child.[1]

Two decades after Bedford's assessment, it is no longer controversial to think of storytelling as essential work in museums. We delight in showcasing stories that teach and inspire and in weaving together fragments to build a more complete whole. In the 2020s, museums are in the business of telling stories from as many perspectives as possible to bring people closer to a vision of the truth that accounts for complexity and contradiction. The storytelling paradigm has come of age, and this book is the first to explore it holistically. The eighteen essays that comprise this edited volume represent a conversation among a diverse set of professionals for whom storytelling connotes their daily museum practice. As educators, collectors, curators, designers, researchers, planners, and collaborators, the authors of this book consider the "real work" of storytelling from every angle. From the inclusion of personal stories in educational programs to the meta-narratives on display in exhibitions, this book balances practical examples with ethical considerations, placing the praxis of storytelling within the larger context of the twenty-first-century museum.

But what do we mean when we say "storytelling?" The term has become so ubiquitous in recent years as to risk losing its meaning. Rather than relegating the word to empty jargon, this book seeks to illuminate its use in situ, allowing common themes to emerge from the experience of practitioners in the field. This book is not a prescriptive manual based on a singular definition of storytelling, but it does recognize that there are some common elements of storytelling that ground the discussion. As an interpretive focus, storytelling is about the people behind the art, artifacts, and history on display. As a communication method, storytelling relies on rhetorical devices that shape the relationship between the "teller" and the "listener," clearly defining their roles and perspectives. As a design approach, storytelling intentionally plans for audience engagement with a varying assortment of story elements, often including characters, narrative tension, the arc of events across time (plot), and the interplay of the familiar and the unexpected. Finally, as a community engagement strategy, storytelling connects people with the larger social, or even political, narratives that help them make sense of the world and their place in it.[2] Recognizing both the challenge and importance of understanding what we mean by storytelling, the contributors to this volume tease out the definition and role of storytelling in their own work and in their experiences as museum professionals. Some essays focus primarily on storytelling's philosophical underpinnings, while others offer more concrete advice for practitioners.

This book begins with a big idea: Storytelling in museums gains its relevance through the primacy of mission-driven audience engagement. This primacy can be traced through the methodological literature. For example, Beverly Serrell's *Exhibit Labels: An Interpretive Approach*[3] has come to be viewed by curators, educators, and exhibit designers as a kind of contemporary bible for museum practice. Its insights go beyond label writing, and the second edition, published by Rowman and Littlefield in 2015, includes research from evaluators and visitor-studies experts that affirms the importance and effectiveness of taking a visitor-centered approach to storytelling within museums. Audience-engagement is the watchword of museum practice, and Serrell reminds us that audiences respond best to clearly articulated "big ideas" in our exhibits. If label text must always support the big idea of an exhibit, then it follows that all museum content—from exhibits, to programs, to collections access and marketing—should support the "big idea" of the museum as well. The most clearly articulated big idea of any museum is its mission. Modern museums embrace educational missions, often imagining an audience of curious non-experts, eager to learn about people, places, and ideas that may be unfamiliar to them, but whose humanity is universally recognizable. The inclusion of personal stories—whether testimony from war veterans, scientists, artists, cultural creators, laborers, witnesses, family members, or survivors of trauma—supports this educational mission by evoking an emotional response in visitors.

Museums have come to rely on storytelling to support their missions because visitors identify with personal narratives. Emotional connection, that feeling of resonance, is a hook that can lead to deeper and broader curiosity. And curiosity is the lifeblood of the museum in its current form.[4] We seek to foster lifelong learning and to create situations in which our visitors are challenged, perspectives are broadened, and people feel safe to discuss the big questions that underpin human civilization: How do we know what we know? How do people gain and use power? What motivates people to care for each other and for the planet? What are the larger narratives that give our lives meaning?[5]

Thus, an important concept for ethical consideration in museum storytelling is the role of visitors' emotional response in fulfilling educational missions. Are we providing an honest appraisal of our subject matter? Are we providing a depth and breadth of evidence in support of conclusions that can be drawn through informal learning? Are we encouraging reasoning by anecdote, or emphasizing emotional connection at the expense of other forms of reasoning? Are we challenging visitors to take responsibility for their engagement, to be more than mere consumers of stories? The authors of the chapters that follow consider these questions in settings ranging from living history demonstrations to exhibits about dinosaurs.

Museums seek to use their power as educational institutions to foster prosocial missions. Storytelling, woven around art, artifacts, images, and documents, has become a primary tool for fostering that mission. But curatorial ethics apply in storytelling as they do in the stewardship and use of art and artifacts.

As museum professionals, our responsibilities are not only to our visitors, but also to our collections, and to the sources of those collections. When human stories take their place alongside more traditional art objects and artifacts in our collections and educational toolkits, the imperative to consider the ethics of stewardship and representation grows ever stronger. This is true whether those stories are embedded in provenance or recorded through oral history.[6] Are we acting in accordance with best practices of consent, even if our narrators have passed on and are no longer able to speak for themselves? Are we tokenizing? Are we using individuals as stand-ins for entire groups? Are we honoring the complexity and contradictions embedded in the human experience? Are we using people to make a point? Museum professionals have long navigated among stakeholders in their practice, but the use of personal stories in museums requires a special ethics of care.

In a Twitter presentation hosted by the National Council on Public History on July 8, 2020, Aleia Brown shared her understanding[7] of the idea of an ethic of care[8] for Black life as it applies to public history projects. The idea of an ethic of care is rooted in Black feminist theory and has gained traction recently within the archives literature as exemplified in Michelle Caswell and Marika Cifor's "From Human Rights to Feminist Ethics: Radical Empathy in the Archives."[9] Brown's presentation challenged public historians to shift their thinking beyond the concept of "shared authority"[10] when imagining partnerships and projects focused on communities that have suffered from marginalization, dispossession, and one-sided "representation" at the hands of people and institutions that have long held power in American society.

Brown's analysis is relevant to the work of storytelling in museums because it challenges us to think more broadly about our missions and the imperative to balance a broad audience-centered educational outlook with considerations related to the people—individuals and communities—whose stories we share through our exhibitions, programs, marketing platforms, and research portals.

In thinking about the perspective that results from this approach, it is also helpful to consider the work of artist and theorist David Koh. In the 2020 *Medium* article "The 4th Person Perspective: The Emergence of the Collective Subjective," Koh wrote about the effect of digital technology on narrative storytelling and identity, both individual and group. He described the paradox of "narrative impressionism" that can result from seeing only a single image within a whole comprised of an abundance of images produced from multiple perspectives, the result of a multitude of slightly different camera angles capturing the scene.

> We then realize we live within the sight of all cameras and thus the narrative itself. There is no existing behind a camera or outside the narrative when there are cameras, and eyes everywhere . . . Because we only see one perspective of things

> that are far away, our views skew to the extreme. This is called one dimensionality. Metaphorically, this applies towards many things: vilifying people from exotic cultures, romanticizing unreachable celebrities, vilifying lower or higher class people, even unhealthily romanticizing a romantic partner. Image is not solely the fiction we consume in entertainment but also the fiction we experience in real life.[11]

Demonstrated in the essays that follow, museums that emphasize storytelling from multiple angles can serve as a kind of counterpoint to our tendency to fixate on singular images of things we know little about. Through multivalent storytelling, museums can help illuminate the reality of an emergent fourth-person perspective.

This "collective subjective" creates a kind of paradox for museums as traditional sites of cultural power: at the same time that they must acknowledge that they cannot control the narrative, they must also embrace their power to contribute to it through the multivalent, multivocal stories that they choose to share. Despite the anxiety induced by the advent of the internet, the past three decades have not led to a diminishment of the special gravity at the core of the museum. Time has only honed our understanding of how that gravity results from the trust placed in the institution by its constituents.

Thus, an exploration of the praxis of telling stories in museums is especially relevant as we reflect on the events of 2020, a year in which we were called upon to examine our assumptions in almost every sphere of our personal and professional lives. The COVID-19 pandemic placed tremendous stress on our institutions, forcing us to consider what we value the most as we balance the needs of staff and stakeholders. It also encouraged us to embrace an expanded definition of the museum, encompassing digital platforms in addition to physical spaces. Likewise, the summer of racial reckoning spurred by the police killings of George Floyd, Breonna Taylor, and others prompted us to think more deeply about equity and belonging.[12] Questions have been raised at every level about power and privilege, racism and anti-racism, agency and use.

This book moves beyond advocacy for storytelling as an essential part of the museum's toolkit. It provides a diverse set of critical reflections on the use of personal stories, and multiple storytelling techniques, to support the larger public narratives embedded in museums' missions. The idea for this book was born from the collaborative engagement begun with the planning of the 2016 AAM session "Out of Many, One: Personal Stories to Public Narratives." Four of the contributors to that session are joined by nineteen additional authors representing perspectives from different regions of the United States and around the world and from across the museum field, to provide both a snapshot of this popular practice at the beginning of the third decade of the twenty-first century as well as a review of important questions for practitioners to consider as they move forward with this methodology. Although the majority of the essays are rooted in the discipline of public history, this volume also includes contributions representing art museums, science museums, and children's museums. The book's contributors represent a spectrum of ages, gender identities, and sexual orientations, and racial, religious, and ethnic identities within the museum field. They offer insights from the point of view of their lived experiences. Thus, we hope this book will resonate with museum professionals at every stage of their careers as well as students, educators, and innovators in related fields such as public history, archives, nonprofit management, journalism, and higher education.

The eighteen chapters that follow are divided into two parts. Part One: Storytelling Methods consists of essays focused on the structure and function of storytelling in museums. Part Two: Storytelling in the Community consists of analyses of museums' community engagement as it relates to the stories they tell. There are many ways in which the content in these two sections overlaps, but the grouping is intended to provide some scaffolding for engagement with the volume. The following summary can help guide you through your reading of this book.

PART ONE: STORYTELLING METHODS

In chapter 1, Benjamin Filene interrogates what museums mean by "storytelling" in exhibitions and provides examples of best practices from across the field and around the world. Designer Corey Timpson follows in chapter 2 by discussing his approach to dialogically rich and inclusive storytelling through his work in the United States, Canada, and Asia. In chapter 3, Amy Weinstein describes how artifacts and oral histories work together to tell stories at the National September 11 Memorial & Museum in New York City. In chapter 4, Anna Tucker describes how the Museum of the Southern Jewish Experience used the storytelling paradigm as the basis for the design and curation of their new museum in New Orleans, Louisiana. Written by educators Marcy Breffle and Mary Margaret Fernandez, chapter 5 digs into interpretation at Oakland Cemetery in Atlanta, Georgia, and provides insights into how cemeteries can best serve as inclusive sites for public history by sharing the diverse and interrelated stories of their "residents." Chapter 6 examines how personal stories expand public narratives through two case studies involving digital and distributed projects overseen by educator Miriam Bader. In chapter 7, I explore the mobilization of personal narratives at higher-education-based Holocaust museums and provide insights from an evaluation of traveling exhibits. Deitrah Taylor follows in chapter 8 with an exploration of dramaturgy as a storytelling methodology for public history and the realization of the West African concept of *sankofa*. In chapter 9, Rebecca Melsheimer and Jose Santamaria describe best practices for storytelling in science museums with a focus on label text. Finally, in chapter 10, Lois Carlisle provides insights into the craft of effective digital storytelling and marketing strategy gleaned from her experiences at the Atlanta History Center.

PART TWO: STORYTELLING IN THE COMMUNITY

Chapter 11 begins this section with the evolution of museology in Morocco through Samir El Azhar's chronicling of the introduction of story-collecting at the Ben M'sik Community Museum in Casablanca. In chapter 12, Judy Goldberg and Meredith Schweitzer describe the multisite collaboration that led to storytelling workshops associated with the *Voices of Counterculture in the Southwest* exhibit at the New Mexico History Museum. In chapter 13, independent designer Margaret Middleton advocates for centering queer stories for family audiences in museums and provides practical advice for doing so effectively. In chapter 14, Sarah Litvin describes how the single story of the Reher family of Kingston, New York, gives way to multiple community connections on the interlocking themes of immigration, community, work, and bread, rooted in the preservation of the Reher family's bakery in the Rondout neighborhood. Chapter 15 shifts to New York City with an exploration of the collaboration between Chinese medicine specialist Donna Mah and the Museum of the Chinese in America to produce a temporary exhibit about Chinese medicine focused on stories of "ideas, people, and practices." In chapter 16, Elysia Poon returns to New Mexico to chart the implementation of the School for Advanced Research's *Guidelines for Collaboration* through the case study of the Indian Arts Research Center and the way that its artifact review process re-centers Indigenous perspectives and changes the stories people learn from objects. Chapter 17, written by Michelle Grohe, describes the use of transformative inclusion in exhibit planning through the case study of the *Boston's Apollo* exhibit, which explores the story of the relationship between the white American painter John Singer Sargent and Thomas McKeller, a Black man who worked as his model. Chapter 18 closes out the book with a three-voice case study focused on the story of the decades-long relationship and emerging partnership between James Madison's

Montpelier and the Montpelier Descendant Community, which resulted in the award-winning exhibit *The Mere Distinction of Colour* and is actively shaping the future of the museum site. The chapter is written by Iris Carter Ford, Patrice Preston-Grimes, and Christian Cotz.

As this book goes to press, museums are continuing to define and refine themselves in response to the needs and desires of their communities. Even as we seek to understand this process, we remain forever in the middle of the story.

NOTES

1. Leslie Bedford, "Storytelling: The Real Work of Museums," *Curator: The Museum Journal* 44, no. 1 (2001): 27–34, https://doi.org/10.1111/j.2151-6952.2001 tb00027.x.

2. For a gateway into the academic discourse of narrative theory on which this characterization is based, see "What Is Narrative Theory? | Project Narrative," accessed January 7, 2022, https://projectnarrative.osu.edu/about/what-is-narrative-theory. Also useful to consider when thinking about rhetoric in museums is: George Lakoff and Mark Johnson, *Metaphors We Live By* (first edition) (Chicago: University of Chicago Press, 2003).

3. Beverly Serrell, *Exhibit Labels: An Interpretive Approach* (second edition) (Lanham, MD: Rowman and Littlefield, 2015), https://rowman.com/ISBN/9781442249028/Exhibit-Labels-An-Interpretive-Approach-Second-Edition.

4. Wilkening Consulting, "Curiosity: A Primer," American Alliance of Museums, October 13, 2020, http://www.wilkeningconsulting.com/uploads/8/6/3/2/86329422/curiosity_primer_ds.pdf.

5. For more on the use of personal stories to tell larger narratives, see: Shawn M. Rowe, James V. Wertsch, and Tatyana Y. Kosyaeva, "Linking Little Narratives to Big Ones: Narrative and Public Memory in History Museums," *Culture & Psychology* 8, no. 1 (March 1, 2002): 96–112, https://doi.org/10.1177/1354067X02008001621.

6. The oral history literature is a rich source of discourse on ethical considerations around collecting and presenting narrative. For an excellent perspective on contemporary oral history theory, see Robert Perks, ed., *The Oral History Reader* (third edition) (London; New York: Routledge, 2015).

Although a number of the essays in this book discuss oral history practices, the book's premise goes beyond oral history to examine story collection and storytelling in other contexts as well.

7. "Thread by @CollardStudies: Thank You! I'm Glad to Present and Discuss What an #EthicofCare Could Look like Doing Black Public History. Preface // Drawing from a Differ. . . .," accessed November 13, 2020, https://threadreaderapp.com/thread/1281000986358755328.html.

8. Twitter, "(20) #EthicofCare—Twitter Search / Twitter," accessed November 13, 2020. https://twitter.com/hashtag/ethicofcare.

9. Michelle Caswell and Marika Cifor, "From Human Rights to Feminist Ethics: Radical Empathy in the Archives," n.d., 22.

10. This concept was first popularized in Michael H. Frisch, *A Shared Authority: Essays on the Craft and Meaning of Oral and Public History* (Albany: State University of New York Press, 1990).

11. David Koh, "The 4th Person Perspective: The Emergence of the Collective Subjective," *Medium*, February 20, 2020, https://medium.com/@CellestialStudios/the-4th-person-perspective-the-emergence-of-the-collective-subjective-5bb10302dd14.

12. Ailsa Chang, Rachel Martin, and Eric Marrapodi, "Summer of Racial Reckoning," NPR, August 16, 2020, https://www.npr.org/2020/08/16/902179773/summer-of-racial-reckoning-the-match-lit.

I

STORYTELLING METHODS

1

THE WHY, WHAT, AND HOW OF THE BEST STORYTELLING IN MUSEUM EXHIBITIONS

Benjamin Filene

The museum field has embraced storytelling as the way to describe what we do in our exhibitions. But are we fooling ourselves? Usually, we're not using the term in the way that most people (including our visitors) do. In our exhibitions, we don't expect people to sit still and listen to a yarn. Even the most rigid design efforts can't force a linear progression through a beginning, middle, and end. Rarely do our topics lend themselves to neat endings anyway. And how can you develop characters in a 100- (or 75- or 35-) word label?

So, why do we keep turning to storytelling to describe our aspirations? And if we *are* in the storytelling business, what does it look like when we get it right? These questions apply to all our public offerings, but they have particular centrality to exhibitions. Although museums use all kinds of in-person and online programming formats to engage audiences, exhibitions remain key attractions and central to the institutional identities of most museums.

The storytelling turn in museums has been a half century or more in the making, shaped by new ways of understanding knowledge and learning. Postmodernism undercut the notion of a finite, unchanging, or even fully knowable body of knowledge. Encyclopedic or definitive histories became untenable.

Storytelling in part became a way to pull back: we're not giving the *only* take on this subject; we're telling a *story*, making an interpretation—one of many that could be told.

The postmodernist philosophical insight about knowledge translated directly into a new understanding of learning: constructivism. If knowledge is not fixed and eternal, the ways in which people acquire that knowledge are likewise shaped by their backgrounds, predilections, and contexts. So our visitors aren't all trudging up the same knowledge mountain: they are building the structures they need out of the materials that seem useful to them. If, under constructivist learning principles, visitors "make meaning," then museums must find ways to meet visitors where they are and build bridges to their experiences.[1] Personal connection becomes essential to successful museum learning; and emotional engagement—so central to effective storytelling—becomes not a distraction but a powerful tool for encouraging exploration and meaning-making.

Critics have found that emotional engagement to be a source of worry, particularly in the realm of history.[2] Will emotion taint historical analysis and lead to presentist or pandering renditions of the past? But good storytelling is not at odds with solid research or facts. It does not mean embellishing or making up history. Rather, the attention to story works from the building blocks of good historical practice—people, tensions and uncertainties, change over time—and connects them to the foundation of good public history: there is an audience out there, with needs and interests that we must address if we want our work to have impact. Storytelling offers a framework through which to pursue audience engagement because it invites attention not just to what is said—the content—but to how and to what effect. It pushes museums to move past a singular focus on the information or ideas we are sharing and to consider, too, the strategies through which we share them and what visitors actually do with them. Storytelling encourages craftsmanship and intentionality as we build rich, multilayered visitor experiences.

So, what does effective storytelling look like in a gallery setting? Much like in fiction or film, any attempt at a rigid definition of exhibition-based storytelling quickly collapses under the weight of its exceptions. Instead of seeking a fixed formula, I offer a list of common attributes—ingredients to be considered when baking the storytelling cake, even if the creative baker may ultimately choose, with intentionality, to experiment with others. So, with that culinary *caveat emptor*, here are some elemental attributes of storytelling in exhibitions.

IN AN EXHIBITION,

. . . the best stories are about people.

This seemingly simple observation is still not universally understood. Too often, we museum professionals build exhibitions around abstract ideas and illustrate them with mute objects: "Industrialism was powerful; look at this powerful machine." But to grasp and wrestle with the implications of an idea, visitors need a human connection that invites emotional engagement and empathy. Presidential speechwriters know that the story of a single unemployed autoworker carries more weight than a raft of unemployment statistics. Exhibition developers need to ask human-scaled questions: What was it like to work behind that powerful machine? How much noise did it make? How hot was it? What did it smell like? In what posture did one need to stand behind it? For how many hours for what paycheck did one work to buy how much food for one's family?

I think of the National Museum of American History's 2020 exhibition *Girlhood (It's Complicated)*, which brought to life issues of gender identity, conformity, and resistance by showcasing Isabella Aiukli Cornell's 2018 prom dress, bright red. The label text notes that Cornell, a citizen of the Choctaw Nation of Oklahoma, chose red to express solidarity with Indigenous women and their struggle against "systemic violence and abuse." The display prominently features a personal plea from Cornell: "Today and always we remember and honor our Missing and Murdered Indigenous Women. They are not forgotten. Bring them justice. Bring them home."[3]

Of course, not every story is literally about people. But I submit that when they are not, successful stories are about forces with which people identify: A story about birds migrating thousands of miles resonates with people's pull to home; stories about DNA work better when connected to questions about the essence of life.

. . . the best stories have tension.

It's a stretch to say that all of our exhibition stories, down to the object labels, have a beginning, middle, and end. Some do, certainly. I'm partial to Larry Borowsky's "Telling a Story in 100 Words" and to the sometimes-lyrical tales that win AAM's Excellence in Exhibition Label Writing Competition.[4] Many in-gallery media pieces and "object theaters" are short, sit-down pieces with narrative arcs. I think of the Minnesota History Center's 1990s-era *Homeplace Minnesota* and its ongoing *To the Basement* piece about a tornado event. But exhibitions as a medium tend not to have a fixed path or a set start time. Visitors graze or meander, even in shows that do have fixed linear paths.

So, what aspects of narrative storytelling can apply to individual exhibition components? Most centrally, story-driven exhibitions seek out tensions. Even at the level of individual objects and identification labels, they push beyond basic illustration and simple fact. The story is how these objects—and the people they illuminate—relate to each other, to imagined alternatives, or to what came before and after. I think of the National Museum of American History's exhibition *In Sickness and in Health* (opening 2023).[5] It plans to show the first artificial heart—the actual device that, "tethered to a console the size of a washing machine," was implanted into an Illinois printing estimator named Haskell Karp in 1969, to keep him alive as he waited for a human heart transplant. Instead of simply treating the device as a technological miracle, the draft exhibition text introduces tensions. It adds that the forty-seven-year-old Karp died less than two days after receiving a human heart. It notes that the device was untested when implanted and that the surgeon, Denton Cooley, was deemed "reckless" by colleagues for taking such risks. The label mentions that the federal government dedicated millions of dollars to help develop the artificial heart. The device becomes not only a miracle but a question, a locus for multiple competing forces that come together across time—a story. I think of Fred Wilson's exhibition *Mining the Museum*. Through the power of juxtaposition, Wilson managed to tell stories largely without words. When his display paired slave shackles and fine silver, all he needed to animate tension and bring the story to life was a title: "Metalwork." His juxtaposition of a KKK hood in a baby carriage didn't even need that.

. . . the best stories are particular.

Great stories are about specific people, rooted in time and place, not generic types. The singularity of the story is what makes it resonant and human. While a composite picture can be deeply researched, it also flattens. Lacking the irregular details of individual lives, it somehow feels less true. For generations, historic houses and historic sites have depended on this-happened-here specificity, but museum exhibitions sometimes short-circuit the particularity of their stories, succumbing to a desire to "cover" the topic at hand and pursue more "serious" interpretation by reaching for generalities.

By contrast, I think of the Lower East Side Tenement Museum (LESTM) in New York, whose power, since its founding in 1988, has been rooted in the particular. Instead of talking about immigration in general, the LESTM tells you stories of the actual people who lived right there at 97 Orchard Street—the seamstresses, saloonkeepers, newlyweds, and deadbeat dads. As a simple but striking example of the power of specificity, I think of how the Arktikum in Rovaniemi, on the edge of the Arctic Circle in Finland, depicts its Indigenous people, the Sami.[6] Instead of relying on general depictions of native traditions and vague assertions of the tenacity of their culture, the exhibition shares the stories of two particular Sami people, interviewed in three moments in their lives. Through photos and oral history excerpts, we see and hear from "Salla" as a girl in 1992, doing chores with her family; as a young adult in 2001, trying out new identities in the big city of Helsinki; and again in 2014, as a farmer with a family of her own. Is Salla a typical Sami? Certainly not. But her story says more about the richness and complexity of contemporary Indigenous people's lives in the region than would a dozen carefully honed labels of generalizations.

. . . the best stories connect to something bigger.

For all their specificity, good stories resonate beyond themselves. They animate broader ideas or tensions. I think of how the Swedish History Museum in Stockholm explains class divisions through a series of five-second videos and pithy labels: "The king eats off a silver plate" (video of hands digging into meat on a shiny platter); "The nobility eat off a tin plate" (another video; not quite as much meat on the plate); "Burghers share a wooden plate" (video of unidentifiable brown mushy material on plate). With hardly a word, mealtime becomes a story that makes class inequities hit home.

I think of the Minnesota History Center's exhibition *Sounds Good to Me*. In a section on music-making in the home, it brought to life the power of the phonograph by featuring 1909 letters that Minnesotans James and Mary Scofield exchanged with their grown daughter Mayme in Wisconsin. Over the sound of Caruso singing in the background, visitors heard actors reading excerpts from the letters, chronicling how the phonograph changed the Scofields' relationship to music. James expresses his astonishment at being able to hear Caruso "at the drop of a needle." At one point, Mayme explains sheepishly, "Owing to having a phonograph in the house, I didn't write last night." "We are wild for the phonograph."[7] To set the stage for the Caruso example, the museum provided context—showing how middle-class Minnesotans heard music in the home before and after the phonograph, from parlor pianos to garage bands. Such contextual information provides background and framing, but strong stories bring these ideas to life.

In the best exhibitions, stories build upon each other to create a sense of an overarching narrative. This dynamic is perhaps easiest to see in a chronologically organized exhibition. I think of the Museum of the American Revolution in Philadelphia, which across a linear layout tells a series of stories about the "ordinary" people who supported the Revolutionary cause and shaped its success. By the end of the exhibition, one's traditional understandings of who founded the country have shifted, with women and Black and Indigenous peoples becoming much more central to the story.

The notion of an overarching story applies equally to non-chronological exhibitions. Here is where the power of Beverly Serrell's "big idea" especially comes into play—the statement that identifies the exhibition's "fundamental meaningfulness that is important to human nature."[8] With a big idea, freestanding vignettes coalesce around an overarching framework. For *ToyBoom!* (opened 2019) at the North Carolina Museum of History, it was that "Cold War toys reflect the abundance and anxieties of their time." An exhibition about the segregated African American village of Terra Cotta in Greensboro, North Carolina, was built around the idea that "Terra Cotta residents built community through constraints." With the most effective big ideas, disparate exhibition components resolve into a bigger picture that a visitor can carry with them beyond the gallery, like a quilt design that connects patchwork pieces into a whole. I think of an exhibition that inspired me at the very outset of my career, *Dream and Reality: Vienna, 1870–1900* (1985), which charted how modernism shaped the arts, intellectual life, and visions of the future among European urbanites before World War I. By connecting Sigmund Freud, Gustav Klimt, and Gustav Mahler; dinnerware, graphic design, and public buildings; the exhibition didn't just teach me about Vienna but changed how I understood how culture (and cultural history) works.[9]

. . . the best stories are purposeful about voice.

As with any story, it matters greatly who is doing the telling. The best exhibition stories are attuned both to perspective and tone. *Down Home: Jewish Life in North Carolina* (a traveling exhibition that opened at the North Carolina Museum of History) conveyed the challenges of a religious minority in the South through a series of quotations whose matter-of-factness conveyed the mix of acceptance and enduring pain that interviewees carried with them. Muriel Offerman, of Wallace, North Carolina, recalled that "We did have Christian prayers and Bible readings in school. I always felt that I was being left out, but I managed it by just keeping my eyes open. It was like I wasn't praying that prayer if I didn't close my eyes." Leonard Kaplan of High Point, North Carolina, recounted,

> When I was in second grade, we were having a Christmas play, and I was very little, so they designated me to be baby Jesus, the lead role. I came home all excited and told my father, "Guess what? I got the lead role! I'm going to be baby Jesus!" He said, "You're not going to be baby Jesus." So I went back the next day to tell the teacher I couldn't be baby Jesus.

Labels in third person can be equally attentive to voice. I think of *Collecting Carolina*, a series of installations at the North Carolina Museum of History designed to convey how objects tell stories. To illustrate the skill involved in creating a tobacco-twine coverlet, curator Diana Bell-Kite used highly visual language that conveyed motion, like the voiceover in a film narrating a scene:

> A tireless twiner
>
> Elma McCormick's fingers could *fly*.
> On sweltering August days, they flew over the tobacco
> stick, coarse twine taut in one sweaty hand, green stems
> sticky in the other. Around, under, flip over, around,
> tighten—19 times per stick, 500 sticks to fill the barn.
>
> When the pungent leaves cured golden and the air
> turned brisk, Elma's fingers flew with a crochet hook,
> too. Same rough twine, same resolve. Work into
> the loop, chain stitch, three loops on the hook. Finally, her
> fingers alighted, motionless atop her completed star-
> wheel coverlet.

. . . the best stories don't mind showing that they *are* stories.

Even as the best exhibition stories are transporting, they aren't closed machines: they invite visitors to consider how they have been assembled. They encourage visitors to weigh evidence, are open about gaps in existing research, and invite multiple interpretations. I think of *Vasa's Women*, a companion exhibition to the massive reconstruction of a seventeenth-century shipwreck in Stockholm. The exhibition begins with a question about historical omission: "Where are the women?" It notes that women are largely absent from the museum's massive and beautifully detailed story of the reconstruction of the excavated ship. But actually, women played important roles on and around the ship. The label explains how the curators began to realize that women were absent from the exhibition because their stories were hard to access, not because they were peripheral. Through a series of stirring examples, the exhibition details how the curators brought women's stories to the surface. The curators had to learn to think differently—to ask different historical questions, use different research tools, and allow themselves more freedom to focus on individual lives and to speculate.

Art museums traditionally have privileged connoisseurship and expertise in their storytelling, but some museums are challenging the assumptions built into that approach by inviting new voices to join in with their own interpretations. I think of Ars Nova, a contemporary art museum in Turku, Finland. It highlighted the constructed nature of stories by showcasing different storytellers. The labels in its exhibition *Young Curators* (2018–2019) were written by eighth graders, who expressed their fascination ("Dark as the night before Monday") and mystification ("It's pretty, and really colourful, but it kind of looked like a tree at first") with the modern art on the walls.[10]

Being transparent about the process of storytelling doesn't mean we turn every exhibition into a self-referential "meta" exercise. Often it just involves asking questions and resisting easy answers. I think of *Reading, Writing, and Race: One Children's Book and the Power of Stories*, a traveling exhibition (2018–2019) that focused on *Tobe*, a pioneering photobook about rural African American life.[11] One section, "Close Reading," highlighted the book's racial and class-based assumptions by juxtaposing photographs featured in the book with alternative archival images that had not been chosen for publication. "Can you spy five differences between [these two images]?" asked a text panel. "Why might [the photographer] have chosen to publish this image instead of the alternate scene?" The exhibition went on to point to details in the chosen image that might have made the people in the photo seem more accessible and appealing to middle-class white families. Such simple "think with me" invitations position visitors as active learners, encouraging them to recognize that they, too, can analyze and construct stories.[12]

. . . the best stories connect us.

In dissecting the elements of a museum story, we can't lose track of their impact when they come together. Stories in exhibitions can encourage personal reflection but also connection—among family members and, sometimes, among strangers. I think of the Oakland Museum of California's 2014 exhibition *Vinyl: The Sound and Culture of Records*. It was hardly a tightly structured storytelling venture; more it was a grab bag of listening stations, record bins, and beanbag couches. But at every turn it invited the sharing of opinions and memories, through "curated crates" of albums, top-ten lists, summer song recollections, shared listening experiences, and chalkboard talk-backs ("Did we forget your favorite record? Tell us what it is!"). It became the kind of experience that prompted one to turn to a fellow visitor and say, "What do you make of that?" The sharing of stories was contagious and became part of visitors' experience of the exhibition.

Of course, there is no one way to tell a story: the best ones break the mold. But the elements above can perhaps serve as starting points—questions to be asked—as one sets out to do the ineffable work of in-gallery storytelling. If we approach storytelling in museum exhibitions with intentionality, a spirit of experimentation, and a determination to listen and respond to how our audiences experience our efforts, then "storytelling" can become more than a postmodern metaphor. It can guide us in our efforts to make museums the relevant, transformative gathering places that we want them to be.

NOTES

1. I explore this historical arc in a different context in "History Museums and Identity: Finding 'Them,' 'Me,' and 'Us' in the Gallery," in *The Oxford Handbook of Public History*, eds. James B. Gardner and Paula Hamilton (New York: Oxford University Press, 2017), 330–31.

See George E. Hein and Mary Alexander, *Museums: Places of Learning* (Washington, DC: American Association of Museums, 1998) and George E. Hein, *Learning in the Museum* (New York: Routledge, 2000 [1998]).

2. Alexander Freund depicts storytelling, as exemplified by StoryCorps, as a threat to the professional field of oral history and as a sign of a wider (and dangerous) "emergence of a crass hyperindividualism": "The storytelling industry thrives on sympathy but fails to create empathy or understanding" [Freund, "Under Storytelling's Spell? Oral History in a Neoliberal Age," *The Oral History Review* 42 (2015): 97, 108]. While I agree that public storytelling *can* be used in ways that divert attention from collective or systemic power dynamics, I don't feel that this dynamic is inherent to the approach. I explore what museums can learn from StoryCorps and analyze the power and limits of its approach to history in "Listening Intently: Can StoryCorps Teach Museums How to Win the Hearts of New Audiences?" in *Letting Go? Sharing Historical Authority in a User-Generated World*, eds. Bill Adair, Benjamin Filene, and Laura Koloski (Philadelphia: Pew Center for Arts & Heritage/Left Coast Press, 2011), 174–93.

3. *Girlhood (It's Complicated): Prom*, https://americanhistory.si.edu/girlhood/fashion/prom.

4. Larry Borowsky, "Telling a Story in 100 Words: Effective Label Copy," *History News* 62 (Autumn 2007), Technical Leaflet #240: 1–8.; American Alliance of Museums, "Excellence in Label Writing Competition," https://www.aam-us.org/programs/awards-competitions/excellence-in-exhibition-label-writing-competition/.

5. Since the time of drafting this chapter, the exhibition has been reworked and will open in fall 2023 under the title *Do No Harm*.

6. I am grateful to the Fulbright Foundation for a 2019 fellowship to Finland that allowed me to explore the rich public history practice of the Nordic-Baltic region. Some of these examples I cite in "What Finland Taught Me about Doing History in Public," in *Museum Studies: Bridging Theory and Practice*, ed. Nina Robbins (ICOM International Committee for Museology, 2021).

7. Minnesota Historical Society, "Mary Scofield and Family Papers" (finding aid), http://www2.mnhs.org/library/findaids/00696.xml. (Without archival access due to the pandemic, I cannot give citations for the particular letters quoted here.)

8. Beverly Serrell, *Exhibit Labels: An Interpretive Approach* (second edition) (Lanham, MD: Rowman and Littlefield, 2015), 7.

9. The original exhibition that I saw in 1985 was *Traum und Wirklichkeit: Wien, 1870–1930* (*Dream and Reality: Vienna*), at the Kunstlerhaus in Vienna. In 1986, the Museum of Modern Art opened its version, *Vienna 1900: Art, Architecture & Design*, accompanied by a book-length exhibition catalogue [Kirk Varnedoe, *Vienna 1900: Art, Architecture & Design* (New York: Museum of Modern Art, 1986)].

10. "Young Curators," Aboa Vetus & Ars Nova, https://www.aboavetusarsnova.fi/en/exhibitions/young-curators.

11. The exhibition first opened in 2014 at the North Collection Gallery at the University of North Carolina with the title *Where Is Tobe? Unfolding Stories of Childhood, Race, and Rural Life in North Carolina*.

12. I am eternally grateful to David Carr for the language and spirit behind this invitation. See Beverly Sheppard, Marsha Semmel, and Carol Bossert, "'Think with Me': David Carr's Enduring Invitation," *Curator: The Museum Journal* 59 (April 2016): 113–19.

2

STORYTELLING BY DESIGN

Inclusive Museum Experiences

Corey Timpson

Stories have the power to inspire; storytelling has the power to engage. My responsibility as a designer working in the museum field is to ensure the storytelling I craft respects and does justice to the stories being told. This is my maxim. It guides my approach to creating meaningful, rich, and inclusive museum experiences.

ENGAGEMENT

I largely think of storytelling as one of the principal tactics museums employ as they attempt to inform, educate, and engage their audiences. Programs aimed at school groups, stakeholders, and remote and on-site audiences all aim to deliver an outcome that has most often been contextualized, dressed up, and wrapped in a story. Even service offerings, such as the self-service buying of tickets, have some contextualization that is story-based—providing rationale, incentive, or explanation. Like anything that is designed, storytelling in museums is both a strategic and creative discipline. I consider this use of storytelling deliberately and carefully, structured and implemented to achieve a strategic outcome. That outcome is engagement. An engaged audience is more likely to care, to try, to learn, and to realize the intended result of the scenario—this can be to laugh, it can be to purchase a ticket, it can also be to build rapport and trust, and/or to reflect, consider, and learn.

Museums, built upon their collections, irrespective of the nature of the collection, have a wealth of stories to tell. The careful consideration of how to tell those stories is critical in ensuring relevance with intended audiences, ensuring appropriateness in relation to the audiences, and building and fostering trust with the audiences. Once trust between the museum and the audience exists, learning and experiential objectives may be achieved.

INCLUSIVE DESIGN

All of my work adheres to a strict inclusive design methodology that I have developed, in partnership with Sina Bahram, over the past ten-plus years of our collaboration working on cultural projects in the United States of America, Canada, Europe, and Asia. When it comes to storytelling for in situ experiences, for remote audiences, or for blended audiences, no matter the program type, the inclusive design methodology realizes several outputs. The most prominent output is accessibility. Given that one in four people has a disability in the United States,[1] and this is a massive percentage of the population, it is critical that museums consider exactly who the public is that they serve, who their target audience is for their program development, and how they are going about attempting to engage that audience. Crafting storytelling experiences inclusively is largely about making informed, deliberate decisions early in the design development process and informing design decisions along the way. Other outputs of the methodology include scalability, interoperability, and greater return on investment. There is no greater barrier to a good story than inaccessible storytelling. It is really that simple.

Storytelling must consider both the development of affordances and the surfacing of those affordances. To emphasize the distinction, the development of captions, signed interpretation, or visual description are all examples of developing an affordance. Placing the captions on the bottom of the video screen, or on a companion mobile device, are examples of how the caption affordance gets surfaced. The distinction is important when considering how we develop our storytelling to ensure we don't avoid producing an affordance because we haven't yet determined how best to surface it.

When strategizing how to develop an engaged audience, how to nurture the trust of the intended audience, and how to achieve these objectives through storytelling, there is no single tactic more critical that using an inclusive design methodology across all aspects of the concept, design, development, and final execution of the program.

RELEVANCE

Relevance has become something of a key word the past few years in the museum field.[2] Across Europe, the United States, and Canada, conferences list multiple sessions on "relevance"; articles and papers are published on relevance; curators, educators, and interpreters speak of relevance; and the term has worked its way into museum marketing as well as strategic and corporate planning. And yet the concept of relevance-building has been a simple design tactic for generations. If something is personally or collectively relevant it is more likely to attract attention. If the design goal is to help sell a product and the channel is a poster, when the poster is relevant to the viewer, they are more likely to read it. The more people read the poster the more likely it is to build brand awareness and trust, so that ultimately more products will be sold. If the storytelling I am crafting can be personally or collectively relevant to the audience, then it is more likely to realize the strategic objectives it is being designed and crafted to help achieve.

Years ago, "participation" was a key word.[3] For good reason. Participation allows for co-creation and shared ownership. If I have created something, if I own something, I am more likely to care about it and to engage with it. Likewise with the concept of personalization, if something is personal to an individual, then it is more likely relevant to them. Again, a greater potential is created to capture attention, to develop caring, and to cultivate engagement.

When developing exhibitions, educational programs, or public events, a critical variable in the design of storytelling is to strategically consider opportunities for participation (and collaboration) and personalization. These design strategies, perhaps no longer the popular industry key words they once were, nevertheless build relevance within audiences, fostering opportunities for engagement and positioning programming to better achieve the strategic objectives of the organization.

In 2009 as I was crafting the experience design strategy for the Canadian Museum for Human Rights (CMHR), I developed a multilayered strategy.

In most museums, the predominant experience design scenario is: the museum informs the visitor. Rooted in the line "encouraging reflection and dialogue" from the museum's mandate, the experience design framework of the CMHR included four layers:

- the museum informs the visitor
- the visitor informs the museum
- visitors inform one another (museum as venue/facilitator)
- visitor types inform visitor types (such as remote visitors, on-site visitors, students, educators, members, casual visitors, etc.)[4]

When dealing with the subject matter of human rights, vulnerable to competing interpretations, the participatory nature of programming was critical to enabling the pluralism necessary to develop, nurture, and maintain trust.

Core exhibition installations at the CMHR include a "Share Your Story" booth allowing visitors to contribute their thoughts and perspectives on curated topics, to hear from other visitors, and to engage in a facilitated dialogue. In another example, the "Imagine Wall" installation allows visitors to draw, write, and express a sentiment related to key human rights topics on colored and themed cards and then put the cards on display. This not only shares individual and collective expression but affects the gallery's mood and style given the themed cards have different subjects and bright, highly contrasting colors. When an environmental news story is at its popular apex, for example, and more visitors offer an environmentally themed sentiment over another topic, there are more green cards being used and mounted, and the gallery's visual mood and aesthetic is affected and responds, which in turn affects the gallery experience for all visitors.

PLURALITY AND PERSPECTIVES

With over 90 percent of the population in the United States using smartphones,[5] and similar ratios in Canada, Europe, and Asia, museum visitors today are more digitally enabled and have direct access to more information than ever before. Given the ubiquity of information, the opportunity for museums to be questioned, challenged, or even discredited is substantial.

Each of the United Nations' seventeen sustainable development goals addresses ensuring global equity and humanizing globalization.[6] Museums, as trusted knowledge institutions, holding an enormous amount of soft power[7] and influence and playing prominent roles within communities, can play a critical role in contributing to a more equitable society, now and in the future. Crafting storytelling tactics and techniques must reflect and respond to this reality as a basic tenet of engaging a diverse audience.

Given the role of museums to collect heritage, to steward (in many cases) the public's collections, and to provide access to this knowledge, the current scenario of mobile-enabled information ubiquity, competition for audience attention, rapidly evolving behavioral expectations, and increased diversity of audiences, museums need to carefully and deliberately consider what they collect, how they collect, how they manage collections, and furthermore how they express and provide access to their collections through programming. When storytelling is used as a tactic of program delivery, it must be designed and developed within this fundamental reality. In practical terms, storytelling must ensure that entry points to the stories, and therefore the programs and the museum's content, are available to everyone.

To be relevant and achieve success, all the storytelling tactics employed, including those of participation, collaboration, and personalization, must be initiated within this context and inclusively designed.

Within the "Civil Liberties" installation at the Canadian Museum for Human Rights, the visitor's image is captured (but not stored) by a camera hidden in the scenography of a tossed apartment. There is a barred prison door at the front of the scene. The visitor appears on a monitor included in the scene, and superimposed over the live feed of the visitor are questions provoking one to think about how much of their civil liberties they would consider compromising in order to feel protected by the government. This installation personalizes the experience for the visitor by literally placing their image, via a live, black-and-white grainy feed, at the center of the installation they are looking at, behind what appear to be prison bars, as their image is overlaid with questions. A visitor can revisit the installation and see different provocative questions overlaying their image each time.

INTERACTION DESIGN

Interaction design (IxD) is a critical design facet when developing storytelling for exhibitions and installations. Interaction design can play an important role in ensuring the audience—composed of people with various general preferences, learning styles, abilities and disabilities, cultural perspectives and beliefs, and even more vectors of difference—can be individually and collectively motivated and empowered to engage. Most museum exhibition experiences are dominated by passive interaction design. People read, watch, and listen—they view artifacts in cases, art hung on walls or positioned on plinths, sculptures and objects free-standing and stanchioned off. They read the associated labels, didactic panels, and interpretive text and view and listen to audio-visual materials. Diversifying the interaction design to include instances of active and interactive IxD provides varied experiential opportunities, allows for diversity in learning methods, and also surfaces opportunities for greater inclusive design and accessibility. Active interaction design scenarios allow the audience to perform a task, to do something, while interactive opportunities allow visitors an opportunity to contribute, to exchange, and to affect the outcome of the task they and/or others are involved in. Both active and interactive interaction design scenarios enable visitors to be a determining factor in defining their own experiential outcomes. Storytelling that is designed to feature a mix of passive, active, and interactive IxD scenarios provides greater opportunities for audience members to find entry points to the stories that are most comfortable or accessible to them, to build emotional and cognitive rapport with the content, and to develop relevance and be engaged.

When digitally enabled, active and interactive design scenarios (and some passive design scenarios such as dwell-time tracking via mobile devices or kiosks) also allow museums to capture important usage data. This data can be integrated into analytics and evaluation and contribute valuable insights to data-informed decision-making processes, further allowing storytellers to tune their design intent and ultimately their engagement tactics.

The "Posters for Freedom" installation in the *Mandela: Struggle for Freedom* exhibition developed for the Canadian Museum for Human Rights, and now travelling across North America, allows both on-site and remote audience members to compose protest posters which are then projected into one of three blank protest signs, aggregated with other static protest sign replicas, from the Sowetto Uprising. The poster-making activity is available for anyone to participate at https://PostersForFreedom.ca and facilitates not only an active and interactive experience among audiences but extends the reach of the exhibition to remote audiences, while capturing important data. As this exhibition travels and via the web interface, analytics can be compiled and interpreted based on geolocation and many other insightful data points that can inform the evolution of design tactics and future decision making overall.

PRESENTATION AND STYLE

As with interaction design, strategically varying graphic design and presentation styles can also be used in building relevance for diverse audiences. Varying the stylistic approach—from editorial photo to art directed, from composed to illustration, from photorealism to cartoon, from documentary film to animation—can attract different sectors of the audience with different preferences, interests, and tastes. Style can really affect visual interpretation, and for this reason great care must always be taken to ensure appropriateness between the graphic and presentation stylings and the content being presented. One would not want difficult or upsetting information, for example, to be presented in an unintended manner and to provoke trauma within the audience. Applying strong inclusive design standards in graphic design, interface design, and presentation will help ensure that content is not only accessible to the widest possible audience but also that the audience spends more of its cognitive energy on content and experience and less on trying to access or process the content and experience. Strong storytelling carefully applies congruent stylistic differences across content presentation and media in ways that help deliver storytelling efficiently and effectively to wide audiences.

MEDIA AND TECHNOLOGY

The role of digital media and technology in museums has increased exponentially in virtually all aspects of museum practice. Facilities management, museums services, collections management, communication and marketing, interpretation and programming are, today, all digitally enabled to some extent to create efficiency, leverage data, be scalable, and create interoperable outputs. Storytelling also benefits from the strategic use of various media and technologies. Many interactive techniques in museum storytelling are surfaced through digital means, while remote audience engagement today is largely facilitated via web, mobile, social media, and digital conferencing technologies. Digital media and technology can provide unique and scalable instances of interactivity, personalization, remote audience engagement, and prolonged audience engagement (beyond the on-site visit).

When strategizing relevance-building with audiences, museum storytellers need to consider exploiting the advantages that digital media and technology provide, but they must also address the barriers. Not everyone is comfortable using technology, and even for those who are comfortable there is a learning curve that often needs to be accommodated. While reading an artifact label might be straightforward, using an Augmented Reality (AR) application may not be. There is also an increasing sensitivity to the privacy implications the use of digital media and technology brings with it. Leveraging personal mobile technology can open many possibilities for personalized, dialogic storytelling, yet the devices themselves, in particular the most recent releases with more advanced functionality, can create cost barriers to participation. Yet space constraints, personal preference setting like volume control and size of text, responsive environments, digital augmentation, social integration, and immersion can all effectively be facilitated (or mitigated) through the use of digital media and technology.

Transmedia storytelling holds enormous potential for immersion, interactivity, and fostering personalized experience design. Its greatest attribute is that as a material composition of storytelling, it can provide many different entry points and increase the ability for more people to engage. Virtual Reality (VR), for example, remains a fairly novel technology. It can create rich audio, visual, and vibrotactile experiences and be an excellent component within transmedia installations. Yet in most instances, it (virtually) removes visitors from the gallery and from the people they came to the museum with (there are very few virtual reality applications in museums where visitors share virtual space). VR can also be difficult to make accessible. As with many storytelling tactics, relevance can be won or lost in the application of design intent, and the use of emerging technology in museum storytelling needs to be carefully designed for the context in which it will be applied and the goals it is attempting to attain.

The changeability of both content and experience within an exhibition setting, a typically arduous and complex task, can be made nimble through digital means. Imagine the changing of content through a digital content management system and never having to perpetually refabricate labels or text panels. Or projected scenography that can be turned off when the space is used for a secondary purpose. Or content and its presentation that can be themed, or spotlit and prioritized based on target audiences, special tours, or visitation patterns. These are practical operational examples, and yet for storytelling purposes, the digital environment or digital presentation might appeal to a different audience segment than the print or analogue, it can enable rapid or even dynamic responsiveness to programming initiatives, it can facilitate greater inclusivity and accessibility, and it can deliver blended (digital-physical) experiences that museum audiences won't find at home or in other, non-museum settings. Emerging technology like mixed reality and sensor-based responsive environments can be far more than novel attractions, even if experiential novelty is of storytelling value.

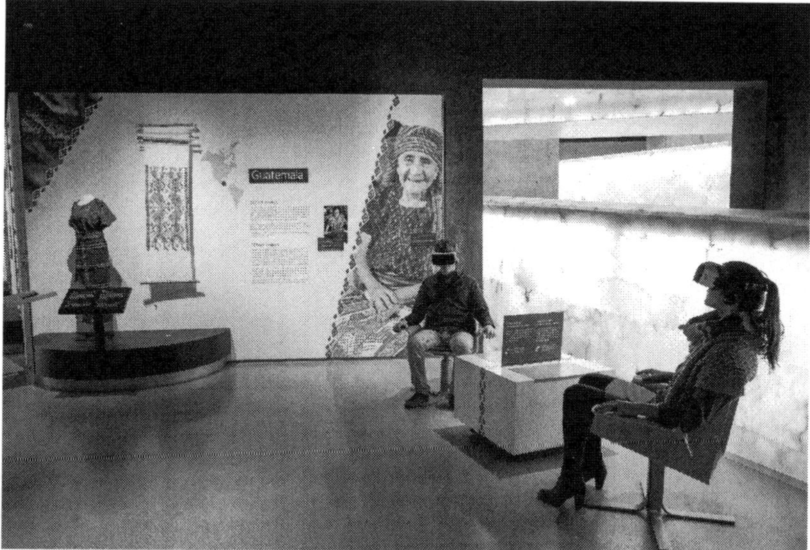

Figure 2.1. This transmedia installation includes the physical artifacts (the dress and the loom) from Guatemala to North America and transports the visitor (via Virtual Reality) to Guatemala to hear the digital artifact—first-person testimony from the women at TRAMA Textiles Cooperative. The transmedia experience is completed by paring the 3D artifacts with touch samples and the digital VR experience with documentary photograph and interpretive text screened onto the wall. Courtesy of Jessica Sigurdson/CMHR.

Digital media and technology can deepen storytelling by providing a plurality of voices and perspectives in a scalable, physically space-saving, and cost-effective manner and can enhance artifact exploration and collections access by making use of the virtual z-axis or through many other digital design techniques.

THE ARTIFACT

The artifact is the root of the museum. Some museums may be non-collecting organizations, but this doesn't mean they operate without artifacts. Expanding the concept of what the artifact truly is can be a prerequisite of good storytelling. Many museums have positioned the 3D object, or more recently the piece of intangible heritage, as the artifact. They are exhibited. Stories are told about these artifacts giving them significance, conveying knowledge, and attempting to develop relevance and engagement with audiences. This is a tried, tested,

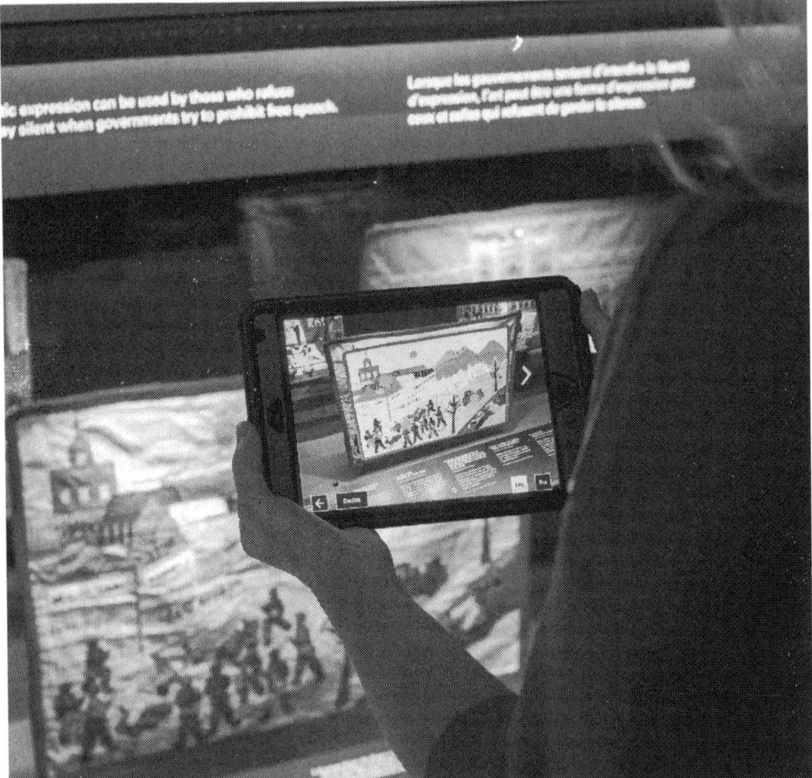

Figure 2.2. The use of Augmented Reality in this installation allows users to better explore the details of the arpilleras which are presented under strict environmental controls including low lighting in climate-controlled cases. This allows for not only pinch and zoom, but also visual description for visitors who are blind or low vision, supplemental interpretation (that wouldn't otherwise fit on the label rail), oral history overlays, and remote audience engagement. It also facilitates social sharing, expanded audience reach, and prolonged visitor engagement. Courtesy of Aaron Cohen/CMHR.

and true method of exhibiting heritage and cultural discourse. For strategic storytelling purposes, if we flip the scenario and consider the story to be the artifact and the 3D object to be an asset that helps deliver the story (along with other assets that include media, technology, didactic panels and labels, scenography, and more), then we're truly positioning the story as the focal point of the learning and experiential ecosystem, and the elements being exhibited are the multisensory and multifaceted delivery system—the storytelling. This alternate positioning lends itself well to providing space for a plurality of perspectives, to enabling the application of inclusive design and accessibility tactics, to communicating with both on-site and remote audiences, to dialogic (interactive) experience design scenarios, and to the strategic goal of building relevance and ultimately engagement.

EVALUATION, TESTING, AND PROTOTYPING

Critical to ensuring engaging, inclusive, and meaningful storytelling is a robust evaluation process. This includes front-end evaluation to inform program development, formative evaluation during design and development phases complete with prototyping and testing, and summative evaluation. During the development of the *Mandela: Struggle for Freedom* exhibition for the Canadian Museum for Human Rights, front-end evaluation revealed a majority of one of the primary target audiences did not recognize the term "apartheid." Determining how to unpack and convey this knowledge greatly impacted the crafting of our narrative and the storytelling tactics and devices we were designing. Without that key insight informing the design development of the exhibition, we likely would have struggled to engage this target audience.

Validating and invalidating concepts and design tactics, especially in multisensory storytelling, is not only a path to trust-building with the intended audiences of the final product, but also informs inclusion and access and leads to innovation. Derivative stories might even be yielded from prototyping and testing sessions that can enhance membership benefits (behind the scenes, making of), while involving diverse testers within evaluation can further trust-building with the public, especially when collaborating with historically marginalized communities.

PUTTING IT ALL TOGETHER

Storytelling is more than simply reciting a story. Undertaken strategically, storytelling can enable museums to efficiently and effectively accommodate pluralism, inclusion, and accessibility. Storytelling can offer museum audiences relevant and meaningful experiences by providing rich, multisensory, and multifaceted programming. A museum without relevant connections to the public is simply a repository of things. A museum that evolves its practices in concert with the public, that maintains and evolves its relevance with its audience, that nurtures trust, will remain a knowledge institution. Museum stories can inspire.

Museum storytelling can engage. My responsibility as a designer is to develop storytelling that respects the stories being told and the audiences they serve.

NOTES

1. "Disability Impacts All of Us," Centers for Disease Control and Prevention, last updated September 16, 2020, https://www.cdc.gov/ncbddd/disabilityandhealth/infographic-disability-impacts-all.html.

2. Elisabeth Nevins, "On Relevance," November 2016, http://www.museumedu.org/on-relevance/.

3. C. Heath and D. vom Lehn, "Interactivity and Collaboration: New Forms of Participation in Museums, Galleries and Science Centres," in Ross Parry (ed.), *Museums in a Digital Age* (Milton Park: Routledge, 2009), 266–80.

4. Corey Timpson, "Intangible Museum Collections and Dialogic Experience Design," in Gregory Chamberlain (ed.), *Museum-iD*, Issue 20 (2017): 67–75.

5. "Number of Smartphone Users in the United States from 2018 to 2025 (in millions)," Statistica, last updated March 19, 2021, https://www.statista.com/statistics/201182/forecast-of-smartphone-users-in-the-us/.

6. "The 17 Goals," United Nations, adopted by all United Nations Member States in 2015, https://sdgs.un.org/goals.

7. Gail Lord and Ngaire Blankenberg, *Cities, Museums, and Soft Power* (Washington, DC: American Alliance of Museums, 2016).

3

TELLING STORIES AT THE NATIONAL SEPTEMBER 11 MEMORIAL & MUSEUM

Amy Weinstein

The notion that storytelling is universal to humans across time and cultures, helping us to make sense of the world and share our experiences with others, hardly merits citation. A bronze plaque embedded into a New York City sidewalk known as Library Way declares, "The universe is made of stories not of atoms," a line from the poem "The Speed of Darkness" by Muriel Rukeyser. Objects and oral histories commingle within the collection of the 9/11 Memorial Museum, collectively providing raw material for a kaleidoscope of perspectives about the terrorist attacks that occurred on September 11, 2001, and their multifaceted repercussions. The stories embedded in those materials encompass the people who were killed, those who knew and loved them, those who survived or witnessed what occurred, and those who came to their aid. Authenticity through artifacts, personal testimony, and first-person narrative are the bedrock upon which the museum sits, metaphorically as well as literally. The museum is situated at the site of the attack in New York City, seventy feet below ground, bounded in part by the Slurry Wall, an archeological in situ relic of the World Trade Center which itself holds many stories about the building of the complex, its significance on 9/11, and its enduring symbolic meaning for many in the 9/11 community. Remnants of steel box columns, still outlining the subterranean remnant footprints of the Twin Towers of the World Trade Center, shape the narrative presentation of the historical exhibition in the North Tower and the bittersweet poignancy of the memorial exhibition in the South Tower.

Cavernous interstitial spaces outside and between the tower footprints hold monumental relics that offer prelude, transition, and opportunity for reflection. Those massive artifacts include the Last Column, a thirty-seven-foot-tall piece of structural steel which assumed such symbolic and emotional meaning at the disaster site that it merits its own digital storytelling platform, offering visitors the opportunity to scroll up and down its four faces to learn about the photographs, memorial cards, and signatures plastering its length. More traditionally, an exhibition case nearby holds artifacts related to the Last Column and its historical significance. A single damaged fire truck, Ladder Co. 3, stands in for all the emergency vehicles carrying responders to the scene who never returned home. The stories behind that firetruck and the Ladder 3 firefighters alone are so numerous and riveting that museum docents are stationed near the firetruck to share some of those stories, answer questions, and set the stage for the historical exhibition, whose entrance is immediately opposite.

Nonetheless, at 110,000 square feet, with ceilings soaring as high as 70 feet, the archeological void filled by the museum is miniscule in comparison to the multitude of stories and memories attached to the approximately 73,000 artifacts, photographs, and oral histories that comprise the museum's holdings.

In the first years after 9/11, it often seemed that everyone wanted to tell one another where they were when they learned about the attacks, whether they were in New York; Washington, DC; or halfway around the world from the epicenters of the crashes of the four hijacked planes. Today, and since the museum's opening in 2014, visitors walk through a soundscape filled with the voices of people recalling just that moment. Walking slowly through the soundscape, even pausing for a moment, the voices of strangers almost seem to be in conversation with each other, simultaneously sharing a mutual experience and describing the unbelievable to one who wasn't there. Supplementing this multilingual audio experience are projected images of eyewitnesses to the disaster struggling with the horrific events playing out before their eyes and segments of a fragmented map of the world. Yet even for those who might be described as natural-born storytellers, speaking about 9/11 and its impact on them in the context of an oral history setting is far from easy.

The museum's collection of approximately twelve hundred oral histories, and an equivalent number of other recorded interviews and conversations, reveals a common struggle to tell a comprehensive story in a narrative arc that can be understood by those unfamiliar with the difficult history that is still being written. Emerging from that struggle to find the right words are oral history recordings that reveal a depth of sensory memory and insight into what was experienced.

In the museum's historical exhibition, titled *September 11, 2001*, thematic audio alcoves enable visitors to hear some of those stories and voices. Short programs, each under five minutes long, were stitched together from thousands of hours of audio. In each program, visitors hear a few words from a multiplicity of individuals, one following the next. The voices of survivors and responders mingle seamlessly, the threads forming a complete "story" told by no single person. Woven into the tapestry are voices of those who were killed, recorded on telephone calls made to 9-1-1 operators, home answering machines, and on a "repeater" device that captured certain radio transmissions made by firefighters as they communicated with each other. Words build upon each other to offer a more detailed view of events as witnessed by many individuals from their own vantage point. Visitors experience the impact of the highjacked aircraft through the words of office workers vividly recalling what they saw and heard; they learn about the rescue and evacuation by hearing from police officers and firefighters who describe the conditions they saw as they walked up the stairs in search of those who were trapped or in need of assistance. Other occupants of the Towers describe what it was like to cross paths with uniformed responders making their way up as they walked down toward safety, through dark, smoke-filled stairwells made slick by jet fuel and water released by sprinkler heads. Unheard in the alcoves, but recorded in the collection's oral histories, are deep reflections by survivors and responders alike about decisions they made that morning, their views on the roles played by fate and faith in their own actions, and memories of coworkers who made other choices.

Many of those narrators also share their stories with the museum through the gift of seemingly ordinary objects that assumed new meaning for them on and after 9/11. Shoes, hats, and other articles of clothing are among their most frequently chosen narrative devices. Fashionable stiletto heels that impossibly stayed on during a harrowing escape down sixty-two flights of stairs and beyond until their owner reached Brooklyn, never once coming off. Chunkier-heeled pumps removed in a South Tower stairwell and carried down in the pockets of a coworker while their owner made her way home to Long Island without them. Utilitarian brown house slippers given to a downtown resident after he ran from smoke and flames without stopping to put on his shoes. Purple flip-flop sandals slipped on hastily by a woman who stepped outside her apartment to investigate and remained on the streets for hours, helping those in need. New patent leather pumps stained by trickles of blood from blisters that went unnoticed for hours. A pair of sneakers given by one survivor to another whose feet blistered while running from danger in leather loafers without socks. Each pair of footwear carries stories of life in and around the World Trade Center before, during, and after 9/11. Visitors to the museum may see them studded throughout different parts of the historical exhibition, punctuating a moment in the densely packed timeline of events. The shoes are telegraphic, conveying important information about who was there that day; their display and accompanying label text leave curious visitors wanting to know more.

This full inventory of shoes is matched by a host of hard hats and helmets worn by responders. Bearing visible evidence of damage inflicted at the hazardous World Trade Center and Pentagon disaster sites or having assumed sentimental value by association with having been worn there, most of these utilitarian head coverings were retired from use long before their donation to the museum. A rotating selection of hard hats in the historical exhibition suggests the diversity of responders, occupations, and branches of service represented at Ground Zero, not all of them expected. Those who want to know more about the person who wore the shoes or helmet, and why they were saved, may delve more deeply into the museum's online collections catalogue or request access to relevant oral histories.[1] Doing so will uncover nuanced, intimate testimony about what it meant to become swept up into the cataclysm of 9/11. The museum's online collections catalogue offers such in-depth examinations into nearly one thousand objects, with notes about the historical or personal significance of each.

Ambient audio and audio wands are additional methods of storytelling employed in the historical exhibition. One unusual presentation technique is the projection of artifactual video onto a piece of structural steel salvaged from the wreckage of the World Trade Center. Projected onto the still-recognizable remains of a trident, an iconic architectural feature of the Twin Towers, the video is accompanied by the voices of responders recalling the devastating scene, their commitment to searching for survivors, and their alternating hope and despair. The audio and video do not directly correspond, but each evokes the other. It was not self-evident that such a fragmented method of delivering emotionally charged content would be effective for visitors or true to the whole story from which each audio moment was extracted. For firefighters and police officers, whether veterans who had seen it all or new to the job, talking about their time at Ground Zero and their search for missing relatives and friends was especially challenging. It was no less difficult for the ironworkers, sanitation workers, crane operators, and others who labored at the site in support of that search. But their memories offer clear and vivid insight into their experience for those who stand before the trident projection. Observing the rapt attention of visitors or standing in the company of those whose voices are shared in this way suggests that authenticity was not lost in the creation of the experience.

The nature of the stories about what happened on September 11, 2001, at all three attack sites is different from the tone of stories about the people who were killed that day and the lives they lived. The museum acknowledges that difference by physically separating the two and environmentally cuing that difference to visitors at the point of entry. Visitors to *September 11, 2001*, the historical exhibition bounded by the footprint of the North Tower, move through a revolving glass door to a world on the brink of change. The silence is punctuated for those who listen carefully by the sounds of the morning news audible on television monitors just out of sight. Visitors to *In Memoriam* cross the box column–delineated threshold into the South Tower to the ambient sound of 9/11 family members saying the names of those who were killed, much as they would hear those voices at the annual commemoration of September 11 held on the Memorial Plaza above at street level. That auditory experience gives way to one that is visual: portraits of each person killed cover the walls from floor to ceiling, surrounding the visitor with faces.

Even a cursory or sweeping glance at those faces reveals a heartbreaking diversity of age, race, and ethnicity. Enveloped by those faces are a changing selection of artifacts that say something about a particular aspect of their lives. A black belt, boxing gloves, golf tees and shoes, hockey and lacrosse sticks, and autographed baseballs represent a love of sport shared by many of the victims, whether they played in college or in intramural corporate leagues with others who worked in the World Trade Center, or they were fans. When on view, the golf tees were displayed as they had been stored by the young man who used them—inside a functional red metal tin for monosodium glutamate ornamented with gold Japanese lettering. The artifact does double duty, addressing his Japanese heritage as well as his love of golf. A chef's toque, model rockets, and drumsticks symbolize other hobbies and careers. A prayer shawl and rosaries testify to devotion and faith. A brown-skinned Barbie smiling on a beach towel belonged to one of the tragedy's youngest victims, an eleven-year-old Black girl killed aboard Flight 77 while on a field trip with the National Geographic Society. These and thousands of other objects in the museum's collection reflect the passions and pursuits that occupied the days and dreams of those who were killed on September 11, 2001, and on February 26, 1993, when the World Trade Center was bombed.

Visitors see only a small number of such artifacts on view at any one time, accompanied by text labels that aim to convey the essence of the relationship between victim and artifact. Curious visitors who want to learn more about a particular victim, and why these objects were held dear, may engage with touchscreen tables situated nearby. By touching the face of one of the nearly three thousand victims of the attacks or querying the table by key word, a more robust story takes shape. Revealed are photographs taken at home, in the office, on vacation, and on birthdays and holidays, all capturing moments in the lives of individuals swept into the victim toll. Images of funeral programs, mass cards, and other memorial items contrast with images of favorite stuffed animals, ties, necklaces, and earrings.

Audio wands provide the opportunity to hear about the chosen victim from those who knew them. Visitors may opt to learn more by selecting longer audio segments that can be experienced in an "inner chamber" a few steps away. Making that choice activates the playing of a recorded remembrance and the projection of photographs. As though listening to the narration of a silent home movie, visitors sitting on benches or standing on the threshold can hear stories about the person they selected and stay as other remembrances and pictures play on screen. Visitors may linger to a seemingly endless array of stories chosen by others. The darkness that enhances the legibility of the projected images seems to encourage the flow of tears.

As a curator and oral historian at the 9/11 Museum, I have acquired objects and oral histories, seeing the storytelling potential in both mediums. Acquisition is sometimes concurrent, at other times the telling of a story suggests the existence of an artifact that the narrator has carefully set aside, often in the back of a closet or in a box under the bed with other artifacts and ephemera that remain too dear to part with. Nearly twenty years after September 11, 2001, new objects and new stories continue to come to light.

Upon occasion, it seems that a single artifact can convey the entire history of 9/11 on its face, on its own merits, without the intervention of significant museum interpretation. For me, one of those is the Chelsea Jeans Memorial, the preserved, dust-coated remains of a thriving retail store located a block away from the World Trade Center. The memorial was seen and photographed by those who ventured into Lower Manhattan following the attacks and acquired by the New-York Historical Society not long after the first anniversary of 9/11. Today it is installed in the museum as it existed in the streetscape of Lower Manhattan, accompanied by no more interpretive text than the brief statement printed on computer paper by the store's owner, who had the foresight to preserve and present the evidence of the attack that infiltrated his premises. In the museum, it is surrounded by a profound silence that encourages contemplation and awe, without accompanying audio or video to explain the nuances of its creation or its impact on those who saw it long before it became a museum artifact. Filled with jeans, T-shirts and sweaters, many of them eerily, ironically red, white, and blue or adorned with motifs emblematic of the American flag, the memorial simultaneously represents life before and after 9/11. Its casual clothing, price tags still attached, recalls the idyllic days of late summer 2001. Words failed on every level the first time I stopped in front of the Chelsea Jeans store, trying to take in the storefront memorial standing shoulder to shoulder with others who came to pay their respects. Looking at the memorial over the years, the words blanketing, smothering, thick, heavy, textured, silent, never seemed sufficient. The best I can do is quote Firefighter Dan Potter, who was engulfed in the dust cloud unleashed by the fall of the North Tower. Recalling the sensation of swallowing the smoke, he said "it was like those gray woolen socks. . . . You just felt that gray wall going down your throat." The object label does not tell visitors that the dust symbolizes all that was destroyed, both human and man-made. In a narrative twist that could not have been anticipated, nor intended by the memorial's creator, the dust brings the history of the attacks into the present day and silently points to the toll its toxins have taken on the lives of those who were exposed to it. That story has not yet been fully told and is still being written twenty years after the attacks.

A much smaller artifact, private and intimate in nature, recently entered the collection and also can be said to carry the full narrative arc of 9/11. That artifact is a prayer bench used for many years by Father Mychal Judge, a chaplain for the Fire Department of New York (FDNY) who was killed while responding to the terrorist attack at the World Trade Center. Judge's body was carried from the disaster scene by responders seeking to place his body away from the danger of further harm. Hours later, Judge was deemed the first homicide victim of the day's attack by New York City's Office of Chief Medical Examiner. Father Judge was revered by many in the FDNY, counseling firefighters and their families as they faced life's issues, and he was recognized outside the department for his work with those affected by AIDS and addiction. When vacationing, Father Judge would often visit his twin sister, who kept a prayer bench for him in a dedicated guest bedroom. The story of the prayer bench's preservation in her home for years after her twin's death, and later in the Episcopal Carmel of Saint Teresa, is a circuitous tale filled with narrative detail. The creased and worn leather kneeling pad is a silent testimonial to Father Judge's faith and devotion to prayer; one of the nuns who safeguarded the prayer bench before transferring it to the museum speculated that its wear reveals Father Judge's internal struggles during long hours of prayer. Its potential interpretive power is vast. As Father Judge's impact continues to be felt two decades after his death, the prayer bench will help tell many stories to those interested in the history of the terrorist attacks, of those who responded, and those whose memories are kept alive in the 9/11 Memorial Museum.

NOTE

1. https://collection.911memorial.org/.

4

BUILDING A NEW MUSEUM ON THE PERSONAL STORIES PARADIGM

How Design, Content, and Technology Come Together to Make a Museum Based on Storytelling

Anna E. Tucker

On May 27, 2021, the Museum of the Southern Jewish Experience opened in New Orleans, Louisiana. It was an institution nearly forty years in the making: Beginning at Henry S. Jacobs Camp in Utica, Mississippi, the original Museum of the Southern Jewish Experience (MSJE) served as a repository for artifacts from closing synagogues and Jewish-owned businesses in the American South.[1] Founding director Macy Hart established MSJE at Jacobs Camp in 1986 and exhibited a selection of these items for summer campers, their families, and a small number of museum visitors. By 2012, MSJE closed in anticipation of moving the collection from rural Mississippi to a location with the potential for far greater visitation. In 2016, the planning committee selected New Orleans as the new site for the Museum of the Southern Jewish Experience. In addition to a different physical location, the board determined MSJE should be reconceptualized in its totality, from audiences to exhibitions.

The board hired executive director Kenneth Hoffman in 2017 and project coordinator and curator Anna Tucker, the author of this chapter, in 2019. Following the relocation of the four thousand–piece artifact collection from Jackson, Mississippi, to New Orleans, Louisiana, I moved directly into the task of curating the opening exhibitions with the support of our exhibit designers, Gallagher & Associates, and digital exhibitions team, Cortina Productions; the executive director and the board of directors; and a team of over thirty historical advisors and scholars.

From the beginning of this initiative, the board, staff, and historical team built the Museum of the Southern Jewish Experience within the art and science of storytelling. The storytelling method that emerged is based on a conversation model, wherein MSJE's design, content, and technology are focused on the rhythms of questions and answers and of building a dialogue between visitors, historical actors, and contemporary events. This specific case study focuses on how the opening museum teams integrated this model of storytelling into three fundamental aspects of the museum: design, content, and technology.

MSJE: MISSION AND SCOPE

The mission of the Museum of the Southern Jewish Experience is to investigate "the many ways that Jews in the American South influenced and were influenced by [their region's] distinct cultural heritage." This approach emphasizes the two-way relationship between Southern Jews and their neighbors, and it highlights the social, political, cultural, and economic changes effected by Southern Jews while also exploring how these same environments influenced Southern Jews' own actions and experiences.

Context is at the forefront of our curatorial scope. MSJE pushes back on the myopia of niche history by studying not only the actions of Southern Jews, but also the other communities with whom they interacted and the regional, national, and international events they experienced. Through this method of examining the milieu of the broader Southern landscape, we move closer to how Southern Jewish experiences both were similar to and different from others in the American South.

Importantly, this approach of contextual study increases the relevance of the museum to audience members outside of the Southern Jewish community. By studying the experiences of an underrepresented group within the context of the American South, we provide the opportunity to explore diverse experiences that challenge simplistic historical narratives. This supports the museum's mission of inclusion, which states, "the Museum encourages new understanding and appreciation for identity, diversity, and acceptance." In addition to the content of the museum, this emphasis also is reflected in the composition of the historical advisory committee and focus groups, with contributors representing diversity across ethnicity, gender, region, religion, and age.[2]

MSJE's thirteen thousand square feet is too limited to contain the entirety of Southern Jewish history spanning three hundred years and thirteen states. Rather than attempt a comprehensive history, we prioritize themes within a basic chronological structure. The themes are organized by a series of archways, each inviting visitors to view Southern Jewish life through a new perspective. The content within each archway is specific to Southern Jewish experiences, but the themes themselves are broad enough to be relevant to visitors who are neither Southern nor Jewish, including themes of immigration, internal migration, imposed racial hierarchies, social inclusivity and exclusivity, and civil rights. This approach prompts visitors to consider other groups and individuals who influenced and were influenced by these same themes, intertwining the experiences of Southern Jews with those of their neighbors.

Just as MSJE seeks to incorporate diverse perspectives from outside the Southern Jewish community, a key aspect of MSJE's scope is also to emphasize the diversity found *within* the Southern Jewish experience. In addition to a range of ages, genders, ethnicities, languages, and cultures incorporated throughout the museum, for almost every "type" of experience presented, a variation is also introduced. Alongside examples of Sam Stein laying the foundation of the Stein Marts of America, we also introduce Southern Jews who failed at their enterprises or experienced antisemitism that hindered their efforts. Storytelling that spans decades and regions is therefore an essential component of this approach, as circumstances and experiences differ not only from person to person, but also within an individual's lifetime.

EXPERIENCE VERSUS HISTORY IN A MUSEUM SETTING

The founding members of the Museum of the Southern Jewish Experience in Utica, Mississippi, made a bold decision as they crafted the new museum in the 1980s: Rather than calling their institution the "Museum of Southern Jewish History," they opted for "Museum of the Southern Jewish Experience." The founding board of the museum's new location in New Orleans, Louisiana, had the opportunity to change the name, but opted, once again, to prioritize "experience" over "history."

Rather than being at odds with each other, "experience" and "history" exist in relationship with each other. Experience is the sinewy, narrative connection between a person and their history; it is a view of history through a lived perspective. The difference between the two approaches may be teased out through the answers that are elicited from the questions, *What is your history?* and *What is your experience?* The former question brings out the "facts": Where a person was born and where they died; what awards they received and jobs they worked; and who they produced, be it books, children, or new ideas. Ask a person, *What is your experience?* and you are more likely to prompt answers that describe this history rather than itemize it. This question illuminates how people string together their "facts" into a narrative that is subjective, sensory, and highly personal.[3]

Narratives focused on experience might initially appear to be less substantive and more ephemeral than their factoid counterparts. But the strength of experiences lies in the stress test of comparison. Historical "facts" often parade as objective truth, while experiences are recognized as subjective truths. Because experiences are recognized as subjective and personalized from the start, they withstand the fault lines that undermine seemingly objective truths when new evidence surfaces. What can challenge the timeline of a historical event? A piece of documentation or a single eyewitness. Who can deny the experiences of a person who lived through the same event? No one, not even the older version of the same person.

SHARED VULNERABILITY

Eliciting an experience rather than a history suggests a relationship of trust between the questioner and the answerer—a relationship we hope to extend to visitors, as well. This is a challenging task, especially when visitors often engage with museums for a few short hours, at most. While trust may be built—and broken—in several ways, MSJE has taken the approach of shared vulnerability. Similar to the concept of shared authority, which emphasizes the importance of co-creating narratives, shared vulnerability seeks to build trust in a relationship through the commitment to crafting narratives of authenticity rather than narratives of idealization.[4]

Instead of being a museum exclusively composed of "Who's Who in Southern Jewish History," MSJE also exposes trauma and intolerance both experienced and perpetuated by Southern Jews. We position stories of Southern Jews elected as mayors alongside stories of those rejected by their neighbors in country clubs. Similarly, we highlight stories of Southern Jews who were active and outspoken in the civil rights movement alongside stories of those who were silent from fear of reprisals and even, in a select few cases, segregationists. Vulnerable storytelling is not embraced without risk, including the risk of presenting experiences to hostile individuals who might warp the narrative to fit antisemitic beliefs or agendas. Some stakeholders expressed concern at the length to which we discussed certain topics, namely slavery, fearing that opening the conversation could fuel antisemitic and false claims that Jews controlled the trade of enslaved individuals.[5] Through extensive conversations, we reached a consensus that approaching the hard points of history not only directly contradicts these antisemitic claims, but also builds credibility with our visitors and creates a space where we can discuss both failures and successes with candor. This act of vulnerability not only is responsible storytelling, but also an invitation to our visitors to embrace the same vulnerability when analyzing their own experiences.

STORYTELLING THROUGH DESIGN

Storytelling is at the bedrock of the Museum of the Southern Jewish Experience's exhibition design, from our layout and artifact labels to the built-in flexibility to update content regularly. Working with Gallagher & Associates, MSJE staff opted for an open floor plan organized by a series of archways, with introductory timelines to provide some chronological structure. The emphasis on literal overarching themes rather than strict chronology allows the time periods in each subsection to overlap each other.

In the first gallery, the three archways span roughly two hundred years, beginning with *Immigration to the American South.* This section includes immigration to American ports as well as migration to the interior of the American South, featuring large maps that trace movement within and beyond the boundaries of North America. The first section overlaps the chronology of the second section, *Navigating Southern Spaces*, which addresses constructed racial hierarchies and slavery from Colonial through antebellum times as well as the peddling and merchant network from the mid-1800s to early 1900s. The final section in Gallery 1, *Becoming Southern, Building Jewish Communities*, focuses on the establishment of social and religious institutions, as well as exploring cultural topics such as foodways. This section again overlaps with the second section, shifting the chronology slightly forward to focus on the 1870s to 1920s.

The second gallery departs the historical timeline and introduces Judaism's values, holidays, and life cycle events before leading to the third gallery, which again picks up the historical review in the early 1900s. The third gallery introduces the visitor to Southern Jewish debates concerning Zionism, or the

Figure 4.1. Archways demarcate major themes in the Museum of the Southern Jewish Experience, as pictured here in Gallery 1: From Immigrants to Southerners. Courtesy of the Museum of the Southern Jewish Experience.

establishment of a Jewish homeland, before entering a series of rooms with open floor plans examining Southern Jewish experiences during World War II and the Holocaust, the civil rights movement, the transformation of the rural American South, and popular culture, before ending in a review of Southern Jewish life today.

This emphasis on themes rather than chronology breaks down the tendency to bookend events and time periods, instead encouraging visitors to see interconnections across eras. In order for the open floor plan to maintain some element of structure, each archway theme is organized around a group of panels that provide context for both the era and the topic. All other elements explore the topic through a storytelling lens, using images, artifacts, quotes, and interactives.

Meaning Versus Value: Artifact Labels

Artifacts serve as one of our primary tools to introduce personal experiences in the museum. We opted for extended artifact labels over shorter identification labels so that the artifact serves as a platform for an experience, emphasizing the meanings people have given the object rather than viewing the object as intrinsically valuable.[6] While we do have objects on display that are of monetary value, anecdotally, individuals who have toured the museum in its opening weeks gravitated to seemingly nondescript artifacts, such as a pair of woolen socks. The extended label design allows significant space for the story of the artifact, so that we can provide Gerald Posner's recollection of how he and his US military unit gave dry socks to women and children caught in a combat zone during World War II. The visitors were drawn by the story of how the socks were unexpectedly returned by one of the now-grown children when Posner traveled to Belgium for the fiftieth anniversary of the Battle of the Bulge. By devoting significant space to describe stories like this that often transcend decades, the artifact labels are designed as anchors of meaning in the open floor plan.

Designed for Voices: Where Possible, Voices Must Lead

Perhaps one of the most imperative—and challenging—aspects of storytelling in an open floor plan is balancing context with individuals' voices. While the archways and subtext panels provide milestones to guide the visitors, we devote the majority of the space to individuals' stories. Apart from gallery titles, the largest fonts in the museum are used for quotes. This allows people's voices to lead, from African American students of Holocaust refugees who taught at HBCUs (Historically Black Colleges and Universities) to non-Jewish commentaries on the influx of Eastern European immigrants in the 1800s. We also incorporated quotes into several of the subtext panels, so that even the contextual spaces often are led by individual experiences.

Quotes were also a design strategy to confront narratives that previously have excluded underrepresented voices. In our section on civil rights and activism, our design intentionally featured quotes by women describing their own experiences and perspectives, including Kentucky activist Suzy Post, who noted that "it's a slur on my reputation that I was never able to get arrested."[7] While quotes are a necessary element of storytelling at the Museum of the Southern Jewish Experience, they nevertheless have their own complications. Whether they come from deceased or living sources, all quotes are inherently editorialized, and in reducing them to fit a word count or design, they become a narrative crafted by the curator. Where possible, in addition to gaining any necessary permissions from authors of secondary sources, we also located the person quoted and asked for their permission to include them in the museum. While the primary reason for this was to confirm permission to include their quote, we also were interested in whether they could direct us to another of their quotations—from a diary, a letter, or even an oral history record within the same time period—that they felt better described their experience.[8]

Rather than being directed to alternate quotes, these inquiries sometimes resulted in requests for alterations to the text, including by Holocaust survivor Murray Lynn, who added, "I would be happier if you would add a few words to give my quote more depth and meaning."[9] While his addition exceeded the prescribed word count, we included it. Naturally, we were unable to request permission for quotes when the authors were deceased, a challenge that I explore later in this chapter.

Flexibility for New Perspectives

A final key component of our design process focused on building in the flexibility to change content over time. On our gallery timelines, we installed dimensional milestones that are separate from the background mural, allowing us to replace key events without replacing the entire mural. This enables us to update the featured milestones as new research comes to light and public conversation shifts without being deterred by costly and time-consuming structural changes.

Another flexibility we built into the design was switching from physical flipbooks to digital flipbooks for our sections on merchant life, orphan care associations, and youth organizations. While the decision initially came as a response to limiting touch stations at the height of the COVID-19 pandemic, this shift also allows us the ability to expand our featured stories without the financial and logistical challenges involved in changing a physical text panel.

The intentionality of storytelling is around each corner of the museum. In retrospect, however, there are key areas where we need to grow, including providing additional "check-in" points for visitors to express their voices throughout the museum, and not just in the end experiences. Additionally, while we are in the process of developing audio tours, visitors who are not on a docent-led tour might miss some of the storytelling connections we interweave throughout the galleries. Overall, the model of storytelling helped us navigate challenging design decisions early in the process and ensures that the design of the museum reflects our investment in people's voices and the flexibility for ongoing conversation.

SELECTING THE STORIES

In addition to the museum's design, we also kept the concept of storytelling at the heart of our development of the narratives. As described in the previous section, the subtext panels provided broad themes by which the visitor could navigate diverse experiences. The stories we selected to explore these broad themes were of three categories: those that humanize the context by providing an experience; those that challenge the context by providing an alternate example; and those that diversify the context by providing conflicting perspectives.

For the first category, the digital and physical flipbooks located throughout the museum put names, faces, and experiences to the more abstract context introduced by the subtext panels. This also allows us to show the diversity of experiences that fall under the broad umbrella of our themes. In our flipbook exploring internal migration, we include six stories—that will be regularly rotated—from across the American South that show different paths into the interior of the region. The flipbook begins with an important acknowledgment of land seizure from Indigenous populations before highlighting the women and men who were among the first Jews in the rural American South. Rather than focus on institutional history or rosters of synagogues, the content focuses on individuals' experiences. This brief content often includes anecdotal stories such as that of Moses Weinberger, who purportedly peddled bananas to homesteaders as they set up their tents in Guthrie, Indian Territory, and Emma Ullman, who helped open the first known charity hospital in Birmingham, Alabama.

The second category of stories challenges the subtext panel's context, including well-worn tropes in Southern Jewish history like the peddler-to-store-owner success story. By presenting human stories that provide variations on a theme, our museum both introduces this trope to visitors who have no foundational knowledge of Southern Jewish peddling experiences and challenges the trope for those who are well-versed in this narrative. One example is that of Isaac Wolfe Bernheim. Bernheim's broad story follows the successful peddler narrative of a young Jewish man outfitted with a peddler's pack by a cousin or uncle who goes on, years later, to become a leader in his community. Arriving as an immigrant from Germany in 1867, Bernheim's story follows this trope at first glance, as he eventually establishes a successful distillery in Kentucky crafting I. W. Harper bourbon and becomes a prominent philanthropist. He was selected for the exhibition, however, partially because of the missteps along the way. Lore states that he only moved to Kentucky when his horse died, the final nail in the coffin of his failed peddling venture. In this variation, Bernheim succeeds in business despite his peddling, not because of it.

Finally, we selected stories that exhibited a range of perspectives on a single topic. This intentional approach was designed to break up monolithic narratives often assigned to underrepresented groups. By showing a range of conflicting voices, we exhibit the diversity of experience within Southern Jewish history and push back against an assumption that they thought, spoke, and acted with a single voice. One vital area in which this approach is used is in our section on Zionism, where we study the early perspectives on the movement to establish a Jewish homeland. Rather than iterate or condense individual perspectives, we exhibit five different news articles from both Jewish and non-Jewish presses. These excerpts range from the 1890s to 1930s and describe and quote southern Jews' wide range of opinions on the topic, from support to concern to outright rejection.

Representation and Storytelling

A challenge of curating a museum featuring an underrepresented community is resisting the pressure to make the museum a mausoleum of success stories, especially with ties to donors. In this case study, many of these challenges were sidestepped by the board, who recognized and supported the need to separate the curatorial mission from funding sources. This separation between curatorial and fundraising initiatives, along with the investment in vulnerable storytelling, was established and upheld through frequent and ongoing conversations between the executive board and museum staff.

While the museum traces more well-known histories, such as Louis Brandeis, the first Jewish justice on the US Supreme Court, our mission's focus on the breadth and diversity of the Southern Jewish experience drove us intentionally to seek out narratives of women, children, people of color, and low-wage earners. This approach took considerable intention and time, especially because much of MSJE's permanent collection is composed of objects that tell the stories of institutions and men who were prominent in their communities. Wherever we lacked artifacts, however, we included underrepresented demographics through images and narratives. In our section on Southern Jews and the American Revolution, we chose to highlight Abigail Minis's experience among numerous options, including political influencers and financiers of the war. In our section on foodways, we highlight the intimate but sometimes fraught relationships between African American cooks and Southern Jewish women, while in our subsection on "Becoming Southern, Building Jewish Communities," we highlight individual stories of orphans within the New Orleans Jewish Orphans' Home, quoting their experiences wherever possible. We also emphasize diversity in the Southern Jewish community today, including representation of Jews of Color, and end the museum's historical review with an image wall of events, individuals, and rituals that depict a range of backgrounds.

Finally, as previously explored, we included artifacts that initially might appear inconsequential. By interweaving storytelling with the artifacts, we highlight how the artifacts' power lies not in their material wealth or even rarity, but in the meaning ascribed to them by the families or communities that produced or used them. One object, a nondescript travel trunk from the early 1900s, becomes a moment to describe its owner's journey from Russia to America via the port of Galveston, Texas. Thanks to an oral history conducted by Lilian Kranitz toward the end of Shapiro's life, we included details from Rachmiel (Robert) Shapiro's harrowing journey as he secreted himself across borders to escape political oppression in Russia, eventually gaining passage to Texas.[10] As we build our audio tours, we hope to include selections from Shapiro's oral history, so that his voice ties the trunk to a wider context of immigration, politics, and identity.

The inclusion of these everyday objects in a museum prompts the visitor to reconsider the everyday objects in their family's possession. Rather than increasing the gap between visitor and displayed object, this emphasis on the stories as a measure of value brings a visitor closer to both the artifact on view as well as artifacts in their household. Cigarette cases, Shabbat candlesticks, travel trunks, and woolen socks displayed throughout the museum are positioned to spark points of recognition and connection between the individual and their own histories.

The Shortcomings of Storytelling

While the curatorial team selected content to reflect a range of experiences, there are nonetheless definite shortcomings in both the process of selection and in the portrayal of these stories. In terms of the process, I worked with a team of over thirty historical scholars who reviewed, edited, and critiqued the content, including offering suggestions to address blind spots in the museum content. Even with this wide range of historical input, as well as focus groups with key stakeholders and members of our target audiences, the opening days have revealed stories that would provide an added layer of nuance in our exploration of Southern Jewish history, ranging from Orthodox Jewish farmers' experiences in Tennessee to tense interactions with the Ku Klux Klan in rural Louisiana. While the flexibility built into our design and the artifact rotation will address some of these gaps, there will always be cracks in our storytelling where perspectives, experiences, and themes slip out of sight. Even though we attempt to provide a range of perspectives, we are still limited by space, the current field of research, and our own persistent blind spots. One way to combat this is to encourage the visitor to enter into the process of curation themselves, to model how many lives, names, and experiences are left on the cutting room floor. While we incorporate this nuance into our closing experience for visitors, addressed later in this chapter, it is perhaps too nuanced and introduced too late for visitors to embrace it fully.

A significant challenge of storytelling, especially given the encouragement of vulnerability we have embraced, is presenting deceased individuals' words and actions. Even though families and archives have provided consent to including these unwitting contributors' artifacts and images in our exhibitions, we do not have the opportunity to solicit the original individual's consent. This results in the exposure of sentiments, including those written in private diaries, that contribute significantly to the exploration of Southern Jewish experiences, but at the expense of permissions. This is especially challenging in the case of including underrepresented groups, including women and people of color, who had little to no opportunity for publication of their own words and experiences.

The curation of this museum has not unearthed a solution to this problem. Instead, it has brought the challenge to the forefront of our team's minds and renewed a commitment to positing this question to the public history field so that together we can discuss the responsible path forward. Like the stories presented in our museum, the opening of this institution is part of a continually unfolding narrative that prompts more questions—and opportunities for conversation—than answers.

STORYTELLING THROUGH TECHNOLOGY

Advancing technology provides an ever-expanding range of opportunities to incorporate storytelling into a museum. Working with Cortina Productions, we focused on how to utilize technology not only as a means of enhancing the storytelling experience for visitors, but also to bring the visitors into the storytelling process themselves.

Oral Histories: Experiences in Their Own Words

Oral histories achieve many of our goals of experience-storytelling. In our section on World War II and the Holocaust, we worked with several museums in the Southeast to compile a selection of Holocaust survivor narratives describing their experience after they immigrated to the United States, including the Museum of History and Holocaust Education; the Florida Holocaust Museum; the Dallas Holocaust and Human Rights Museum; and the Center for Holocaust, Genocide, and Human Rights Education of North Carolina. We limited our curatorial introduction of each interview in order for the speakers to introduce the themes. In doing so, the interviewees themselves illustrate the interconnectedness of seemingly disparate themes, including the challenges of finding jobs, encountering segregation, and navigating trauma. Norbert Friedman, who settled in Atlanta, describes the difficulties of leaving his doctoral program in Germany only to be told his status as an immigrant, non-Southerner, and Jew were "three strikes" against him, while Herbert Kohn, whose family escaped Germany following Kristallnacht in 1938, interweaves the obstacles of learning to farm in Demopolis, Alabama, with his memories of encountering segregation in schools.[11]

Video oral histories also provide nuances that are left out when employing text-only storytelling. The tone of voice, intonations, mannerisms, and facial expressions convey a world of information and also sense of connection between the speaker and the listener. Studies show that a significant percent of communication is nonverbal, and so, wherever possible, we provided opportunities for visitors to hear individuals describe their experiences not only in their own words, but also in their own voices.[12] Herbert Kohn's storytelling develops new levels of meaning when we see his hand gestures—including a wide sweep of his arms and a faint hint of a smile suggesting the surprising nature of his German Jewish mother raising chickens on a small farm in Alabama—and when we witness the studious pause between his description of the segregated high school and his relief to discover the school later was integrated, a description he ended with an emphatic "thank God."[13]

Pushing Back on the Mimetic: Contrary Perspectives

In addition to their emotional and often relatable material, oral histories also provide opportunities to display diversity in perspectives. In 1966, rabbinical student P. Allen Krause interviewed thirteen Reform rabbis in the American South about the civil rights movement. Assuring the rabbis he would embargo the conversations from the public for twenty-five years, Krause collected a corpus of remarkably candid responses from the rabbis, ranging from thoughts on segregation and concerns for safety to their congregants' often diverse views on the civil rights movement. While the resulting transcripts were eventually published posthumously in *To Stand Aside or Stand Alone: Southern Reform Rabbis and the Civil Rights Movement*, the audio had not yet been exhibited or incorporated into any known museum interactives prior to MSJE.[14]

Working with Cortina Productions and Allen's son, Stephen Krause, we developed an interactive oral history station where visitors could select questions and hear multiple rabbis' responses. The variance of these interviews disrupts the concept that Southern Jews spoke with one voice during the civil rights movement and provides space for the rabbis to phrase their perspectives in their own words.

State by State: Expanding Access to Stories

Storytelling is not only embodied in text, quotes, images, and oral histories, but also through the narratives that individuals wrap around objects and artifacts. While MSJE plans a high rotation of artifacts, both for preservation of the items on view as well as to incorporate additional perspectives, our limited physical footprint restricts us to displaying approximately 2 to 3 percent of our total artifact collection at any given time.

To open our collection to visitors, we developed an on-site interactive where people can explore unexhibited artifacts through a digital map of the American South. Visitors click on states, cities, and towns to view what artifacts are in our collection. In addition to the basic metadata of era, type, and accession information, we also include the stories shared by families and individuals who donated the item. This allows us to draw connections across eras, regions, and themes, and also to showcase items that might not be on display. One artifact, a fiftieth-anniversary booklet for Dante's Store in Dumas, Arkansas, is an excellent example of how an artifact may transcend topics and generations. The *State by State* interactive description begins with an expected summary of the booklet's business connection: Charles Dante, an immigrant from Poland, opened his first store in Dumas, Arkansas, in 1897 after accumulating enough savings from peddling and working in William Rosenzweig's mercantile company in nearby Pine Bluff. He opened a larger store, known as "The Globe Store," just three years later. After a 1925 fire destroyed The Globe, Dante rebuilt a larger establishment and named it "Dante's Department Store," which is featured on the cover of the anniversary booklet. Dante's son-in-law, Bernard

Tanenbaum, later joined the family business and opened the United Dollar Store with his son, Jerry, eventually growing the chain to approximately 250 locations across seven states.

The description does not finish with the "success story" narrative, however, but instead continues by highlighting themes that connect the Dante family to other topics and artifacts in the museum. The description notes that Charles Dante also worked to help family escape Nazi Europe in the 1930s. The documentation for this paper trail, where Dante wrote dozens of letters pleading for the US government to issue visas, is on display for the opening exhibitions. The description goes on to note that Harry Phillips, a nephew Dante successfully sponsored to immigrate to the United States, later married Ilse (Elsie) Hamburger, a Holocaust refugee from Germany who settled in McGehee, Arkansas. Hamburger's diary is also on view at the museum, with a photo of her on the boat from Germany to America in 1936.[15] Due to limited space on the artifact labels, we were unable to make these connections next to the physical artifacts, but it is described in detail for visitors who select artifacts from Dumas, Arkansas. The *State by State* interactive therefore provides the essential technology for visitors to read the connections between these seemingly disparate stories.

Tying It All Together: The Quilt Experience

Our final interactive in the museum encourages the visitor to engage in their own form of visual storytelling. We selected one artifact from our opening exhibition as a symbol of the intertwining histories presented throughout the museum. In 1885, the Jewish Ladies' Sewing Circle of Canton, Mississippi, came together to stitch a Victorian "crazy" quilt.[16] This quilt was likely raffled off in support of Canton's Temple B'nai Israel, a congregation that opened its doors in 1879. Each square was created by an individual quilter, with the asymmetrical lines and array of fabrics representing the trend of this type of quilt in the Victorian era. They are decorated with names and symbols of keys, beetles, flowers, and abstract designs that held meaning for the women who quilted them. They then pieced together those individual identities into a community quilt, threading together disparate patterns to create a cohesive whole. Step back, and the very inconsistencies of the fabrics, patterns, and symbols are what make the community quilt a reflection of their diverse experiences.

Working with Cortina Productions, our closing activity invites visitors to step into the role of storytelling and create their own identity quilt square. After providing a reminder of the historic quilt and a series of question prompts, visitors can choose from nearly fifty fabrics and dozens of patches to create their

Figure 4.2. ***The Community Quilt*** **interactive serves as the concluding experience at the Museum of the Southern Jewish Experience. Courtesy of the Museum of the Southern Jewish Experience. Photo by Frank Aymami.**

own quilt square. Our development team also overcame significant challenges to create software that enables people to "stitch" their own drawings and text, allowing for symbols and sayings that are not available in our pre-designed selection. After completing the quilt square, visitors then digitally stitch their square into the larger community quilt, composed of squares from friends, family, and strangers who visited the museum at the same time.

This interactive serves numerous purposes, including exposing the challenges and limits of storytelling. In facing the difficulty of condensing their identity to a quilt square, the visitor is prompted to examine how the stories and experiences throughout the museum are an equally limited view of expansive lives that defy simple narratives. Additionally, the quilt serves as a metaphor for the museum itself, as it also pulls together threads of disparate experiences, inviting visitors to examine both the individual and the landscape.

CONCLUSION

Opening a new museum provides a unique opportunity to consider not only what content to present, but also the way in which we present it. By focusing on storytelling, we invite visitors to engage with this history holistically, to consider what events individuals choose to remember and what artifacts they preserve on behalf of their family history.

While the opportunity to curate a brand-new museum is fairly rare, the act of curation is not. At the most simplistic level, curators bring together objects using themes and shared ideas, much like a folk artist strings together beads to make a necklace. And this is a craft we all share when we consider our own history: Who do we choose to represent us when we share our family history? What objects represent our past, and what stories do we thread between them? The Museum of the Southern Jewish Experience, in selecting storytelling as the framework for history, positions visitors in the role of listeners as well as storytellers themselves. The Museum of the Southern Jewish Experience is itself an artifact of the unfolding conversation, capturing conversations in a specific moment in time.

NOTES

1. While MSJE's scope includes the entire American South, the original collection heavily featured artifacts from Mississippi, Louisiana, and Arkansas due to their close proximity to Jacobs Camp. Several other museums and archives feature aspects of Jewish life in the American South, albeit with either a broader or more specific regional scope, including the William Breman Jewish Heritage Museum, the Jewish Heritage Collection at the College of Charleston, and the Houston Jewish History Archive at Rice University, all of which served as key content contributors and reviewers during the development of MSJE's opening exhibitions.

2. The dedication to inclusivity contributed significantly to the panel text used in the museum, where terms introduced for the first time are italicized and defined. The approach we used to define terms varied. Some were defined using context, as in the case of *Ashkenazi* and *Sephardic*, which refer to subcultural Jewish communities largely based on historical and cultural origins. Because these terms traditionally are applied based on region, with Ashkenazi Jews primarily coming from Europe and Sephardic (or *Sephardi*) Jews often tracing their roots to the Iberian Peninsula, North Africa, and regions of the Middle East, we introduced these terms alongside maps as well as text. We took a more direct approach for other terms, such as *antisemitism* (anti-Jewish sentiments and actions) and *Zionism* (dedication to building a Jewish homeland). Engaging a diverse set of readers was essential in this process, as people who did not identify as part of the Southern Jewish community alerted us to terms we did not initially consider necessary to define.

3. While we prioritize experiences throughout our storytelling narrative, both from the perspective of living and deceased witnesses, we were nevertheless committed to

fact-checking and indicated where subjective perspectives described an event, usually in the form of directly quoting the individual. Furthermore, as a museum focused on a people group whose membership has been discussed in realms that range from ethnic to religious to cultural inclusions and exclusions (and beyond), we were careful to present "Jewishness" through the lens of how individuals and communities ascribed or denied affiliation, both from within and outside the southern Jewish community.

4. For more on shared authority, see Michael H. Frisch, *A Shared Authority: Essays on the Craft and Meaning of Oral and Public History* (Albany: State University of New York Press, 1990). The concept of vulnerability is emerging as a popular topic in numerous fields, including social work; see Brené Brown, *Daring Greatly: How the Courage to Be Vulnerable Transforms the Way We Live, Love, Parent, and Lead* (New York: Avery, 2012).

5. We worked with several historians both to address Southern Jews involved in slavery as well as contradict the false claims that Jews controlled the trade of enslaved individuals, with the latter topic drawing on a range of scholarship, notably Eli Faber, *Jews, Slaves, and the Slave Trade: Setting the Record Straight* (New York: New York University Press, 1998). Some of the most informative conversations came from discussions from sites with public historians who were well-versed in discussing slavery, including from the Whitney Plantation in Wallace, Louisiana, which at the time of printing is the only museum in the state focused exclusively on sharing the stories of enslaved individuals.

6. For more on the interpretive approach to label writing, see Beverly Serrell, *Exhibit Labels: An Interpretive Approach* (second edition) (Lanham, MD: Rowman and Littlefield, 2015), https://rowman.com/ISBN/9781442249028/Exhibit-Labels-An-Interpretive-Approach-Second-Edition.

7. Mary Chellis Nelson, "Suzy Post: The Last Interview," *Louisville Magazine*, January 2019.

8. As discussed earlier in this chapter, descriptions of events usually change over time. We were careful to request quotations that were restricted to the time frame of the original proposed quote. In the following instance, Murray Lynn's original quote came from an interview conducted a few years prior to the museum opening, and so we were more open to alteration than if he had recommended editing a text he composed directly following the Holocaust.

9. Murray Lynn, email message to the author, July 2020. Lynn passed away in January 2021, and his wife, Sonia Lynn, provided additional approvals for this chapter in August 2021.

10. Rachmiel (Robert) Shapiro's granddaughter, Carla Klausner, donated the travel trunk and connected us with Rice University professor of history Paula Sanders, whose mother, Lilian Kranitz, interviewed Shapiro in 1974. Kranitz's own grandfather was a part of the same Galveston Movement that brought approximately ten thousand European Jews through the port of Galveston, Texas, between 1907 and 1914.

11. Norbert Freidman and Herbert Kohn's oral history interviews, among many others, are available to the public via the Museum of History and Holocaust Education's

online repository housed by the Kennesaw State University Archives, available at https://soar.kennesaw.edu/handle/11360/2173.

12. Albert Mehrabian, *Nonverbal Communication* (New Brunswick: Aldine Transaction, 1972).

13. Herbert Kohn Interview, Legacy Series Oral History Program, KSU/14/05/03/001, Museum of History and Holocaust Education, Kennesaw State University, December 11, 2013.

14. For a full transcript of the interviews, see P. Allen Krause, *To Stand Aside or Stand Alone: Southern Reform Rabbis and the Civil Rights Movement*, ed. Mark Bauman and Stephen Krause (Tuscaloosa: University of Alabama Press, 2016).

15. Much like the connections between Rachmiel Shapiro's travel trunk and oral history interview, the Dante family story continues a multigenerational tie. The donors of the diary, Rose Marie Phillips Wagman and Susan Phillips Good, are related to Jay Tanenbaum, MSJE board chair and great-grandson of Charles Dante.

16. For more on the complex histories and perspectives in the "crazy" quilt trend, see Jane Przybysz, "The Victorian Crazy Quilt as Comfort and Discomfort," *Quilt Journal* 3, no. 2 (1998).

5

UNEARTHING BURIED HISTORIES

Interpreting Individual and Collective History in Cemeteries

Marcy Breffle and Mary Margaret Fernandez

From object-filled galleries to mobile exhibits in Main Street storefronts, the diversity of places and spaces that define themselves as museums reflect an evolution within the field to embrace pluralism and inclusion in social and cultural spaces. But how do we recognize the cultural and historical value of spaces that are commonplace to the point of invisibility? Cemeteries are distinctive in the field of museums and historic sites. Gravestones and funerary art comprise their permanent collections, interpreters must dig (literally and figuratively) to uncover buried narratives, and public investment is required to keep both weeds and developers at bay. But like traditional museums and historic sites, cemeteries provide access points to social history and opportunities to learn and reflect. Cemeteries offer rich interpretive opportunities, exhibiting the tangible and intangible heritage of a community. The act of interpretation, dependent on individual and communal memory, can provide a critical avenue for the preservation and survival of cemeteries.

This chapter explores the realities, challenges, and opportunities of cemetery interpretation through the practice and daily considerations of the programming department at Oakland Cemetery in Atlanta, Georgia. Founded in 1850 by the city of Atlanta, Oakland Cemetery spans forty-eight acres of Victorian gardens and funerary art. Oakland Cemetery is the final resting place for more than seventy thousand people, affectionately referred to as "residents." The cemetery reflects the diverse historical development of Atlanta; noted Georgians are buried next to ordinary citizens, formerly enslaved individuals rest near their enslavers, and men and women transcend the social barriers of life to coexist in death.

Oakland Cemetery was founded with no perpetual care endowment in place and fell into neglect in the twentieth century. In 1976, a nonprofit group organized to save the cemetery. In partnership with the city of Atlanta, Historic Oakland Foundation (HOF) works to preserve, restore, enhance, and share Oakland Cemetery. Interpretation is critical to Oakland's survival. Interpretive programs and events bring in thousands of visitors every month, cultivating a public investment in the space that also provides the financial means for restoration and preservation.

The fulfillment of Historic Oakland Foundation's mission creates both opportunities and obstacles for programming staff. To present nuanced history, residents must be interpreted comprehensively and with the benefit of historical documentation and context. There should also be a priority to address the correction of historical erasures and absences and a commitment to sharing all aspects of an individual's story regardless of how they may negatively reflect upon the resident. But how do we navigate sharing narratives that might be viewed as controversial by living descendants, especially those in powerful stakeholder positions or who have deep personal connections to the site? The stories of newly buried individuals can provide context for contemporary events or recent history, but their loved ones' grief is still raw. How do we weigh our obligation to interpret for our visitors with the family's desire to grieve in peace? These challenges can lead to awkward situations and uncomfortable conversations, but more often they result in creative solutions and opportunities for learning.

Historic Oakland Foundation employs a variety of storytelling methods to share different facets of the cemetery's history. These include (but are not limited to) large-scale special events, guided tours, and self-guided activities for guests to complete on their own. From tour scripts to scavenger hunts, interpretation is crafted by trained staff members and public historians. A talented and dedicated group of volunteer docents, living history actors, and front-line ambassadors perform the interpretation.

Like blockbuster exhibitions, special events often serve as the first draw for a new visitor. Events are generally geared toward entertainment, though never at the expense of interpretive content. They often feature actors in first-person portrayals of cemetery residents, as is the case for Oakland's largest annual event, *Capturing the Spirit of Oakland*™.

Capturing the Spirit of Oakland™ character interpreters bring individuals to life and serve as a tangible link to the past. As those portrayals present history from the perspective of the resident in monologue format (and often feature an unreliable narrator), docent-led tours are more appropriate for sharing history that demands dialogue.

In the group tour setting, the docent serves as an interpreter and dialogue facilitator. They seek to tackle complex subject matter, including the site's segregated history and Confederate memorialization, which demands contextualization and conversation. Guided tours also can hone in on special interests, going into greater detail on one particular aspect of the site's history. Self-guided activities, such as scavenger hunts or cell phone tours, serve two audiences particularly well: repeat visitors who are looking for new ways to engage on their own and guests who are familiar with the site as a green space but have not yet participated in an interpretive program. Each interpretive approach has its own merits and shortcomings. But all allow for Historic Oakland Foundation staff and volunteers to share the unique site of Oakland Cemetery.

WHY CEMETERIES?

Cemeteries exist within a liminal space as historic sites. They are inherently transitional and yet they seldom change. Though they often contain some of the best evidence of a city's past—presenting a public show of tastes and styles, and more subdued displays of prejudice—they also exist as spaces of public mourning, imbued with a sacred nature that can both complicate and enrich the act of interpretation.

Given the unique constraints that cemetery interpretation can entail—the obligation to respect the concerns of living descendants, the limitations of what events, programs, or themes may or may not be appropriate within a cemetery setting—it is natural to ask why cemeteries are worth interpreting at all. What is their value as interpretive spaces when it may be less limiting or easier to tell history elsewhere?

On one level, cemeteries, particularly city cemeteries, contain a highly varied and often encyclopedic history of place. Those interred present a cross-section of a city's population, providing insight into gender, class, race, religious affiliation, and public health. Burial sites are mirrors that reflect the cultures, power structures, and priorities of both the individual and their community.

Visiting a cemetery can reveal deeper meaning and context about a place beyond a cursory examination of the markers and monuments that immortalize an individual in stone. Names and significant dates are a certainty, but so much more is communicated in the epitaphs, styles, proportions, materials, and placements of these markers. An individual's familial role, social position, religious belief, and socioeconomic class can be observed. If something was important enough to include on the limited surface of a gravestone, it was likely significant to that individual, their family, or their culture.

As outdoor galleries, cemeteries exhibit artistic styles and provide portraits of individuals expressing their character, status, and social connections through design. At Oakland Cemetery, a humble and hand-carved concrete headstone marks the final resting place of a community builder. A forest of Hebrew-inscribed gravestones in the Jewish sections reveals a close-knit community in life and death. Oakland's largest mausoleum, built by a financier and railroad tycoon, occupies the prime location on the cemetery's highest hill. Masonic symbols, Christian iconography, song lyrics, and etched portraits all reveal an element of the dead to share with the living.

Cemeteries also illuminate power structures and social inequalities within a community as they pertain to race and ethnicity. The erasure and the exclusion of Black, Indigenous, and People of Color (BIPOC) from the interpretive

Figure 5.1. Antoine Graves and Jasper Smith Mausoleums: Although vastly different in style, both mausoleums express the social significance and character of their owners through design, materials, and construction. A well-known eccentric, entrepreneur Jasper Newton Smith constructed his eclectic-style mausoleum more than a decade before his death in 1918. His statue faces Oakland's main entrance, which has earned him the moniker, "The Mayor of Oakland." Constructed in the early twentieth century for real estate broker Antoine Graves and his family, the Graves Mausoleum is the only stone home in the historic African American Burial Grounds. Although simple in design, the massive and expensive exterior blocks exhibit Graves's wealth. Courtesy of Historic Oakland Foundation.

narrative has long been a problem for historic buildings and sites. At many former plantation sites, outbuildings have been turned into welcome centers or gift shops. In both civic structures and houses, basements that once served as workspaces are often used to house HVAC systems. At historic theaters, "Black Only" entrances and bathrooms are often removed or converted. But in the United States, cemeteries uniquely preserve social injustices committed against BIPOC residents. The legal doctrine of "separate but equal" applied to schools, streetcars, *and* cemeteries alike, affecting predominantly Black Americans but in some regions Asian American, Indigenous, and Latine[1] communities as well. The constancy of the cemetery landscape preserves evidence of the racial segregation of burials, revealing how discrimination and prejudice carried over into death.

Oakland Cemetery's historically segregated African American Burial Grounds, home to over twelve thousand of the city's Black pioneers, also exhibits the inequality that came in the form of inferior facilities and services imposed upon Atlanta's Black population. Located on the northeast corner of the cemetery, the section's sloping burial grounds, the lowest-lying and most poorly draining area of the cemetery, has issues with erosion. Cemetery workers did not maintain the African American Burial Grounds to the same standards as the rest of the white-populated cemetery, which led to the deterioration of some of the section's hardscape. Even the most successful Black Atlantans could neither buy nor earn the right of equal treatment, in life or in death. In cemeteries where injustices have become a part of the physical landscape, it is crucial to have docents and other interpreters expose the history and provide opportunities to learn during guided tours and educational programs.

CHALLENGES IN CEMETERY INTERPRETATION

All interpreters and public historians face obstacles and opportunities unique to their particular historic site or museum. Cemeteries occupy the center of overlapping categories: hallowed ground, public green space, outdoor art gallery, and historic place. Cemeteries, like funerals, are for the living. As sacred burial grounds, they are spaces for grieving and reflection. As green spaces, cemeteries can be destinations for recreational activities from dog walking to first dates. As outdoor art galleries, cemeteries exhibit the stylistic movements of funerary and material culture and can serve as a backdrop for contemporary installations. And as historic sites, cemeteries are repositories for stories from the past. From accessibility to maintenance, cemetery staff must deal with challenges commonly found at historic sites. However, interpretive staff must also meet a multitude of challenges unique to cemeteries, including working with living stakeholders, overcoming social stigmas that may be associated with death and burials, and balancing the responsibility to present comprehensive narratives with ethical concerns over the right to privacy and grief. Moreover, whether visiting to grieve or to go on a tour, each visitor forms a personal connection with the site. These connections create a sense of ownership that varies in degree from stakeholder to stakeholder and creates a complex web of relationships for interpretive staff to navigate.

Living descendants are among the most significant stakeholders in a cemetery, with whom interpretive staff must work thoughtfully and intentionally. If cemetery agents sell burial lots, these individuals and families often hold deeds as property owners. The bones and remains of their ancestors are buried in these grounds, an act which sanctifies that space to a descendant. Living descendants are keepers of family anecdotes and stories that do not appear within the written record. These connections place descendants in positions of power with the ability to influence the interpretation, restoration, and operation of a cemetery, which may present opportunities or obstacles for staff seeking to tell their family member's story in an interpretive program.

In many cases descendants are often the galvanizing force behind the formation of nonprofits and "friends" groups that restore cemeteries. These individuals sit on the boards and governing bodies of cemeteries. It was through the hard work and dedication of many descendants that Historic Oakland Foundation came to exist in 1976. Through their continued support, Historic Oakland Foundation has been able to successfully serve as the caretaker for this important landmark.

To a different but still essential degree, non-descendants are also stakeholders. Whether attending programs or enjoying the space as a park, these visitors have a vested interest in the continued interpretation and upkeep of a cemetery. Their connection might be intangible, but it is highly personal. Non-descendent stakeholders ensure the longevity of a site, preserving and caring for its upkeep long after families have died out or moved away.

Interpretive staff must balance the responsibility of presenting collective, comprehensive history while recognizing that the choices made can impact both of these stakeholders differently and raise related ethical concerns. The following sections examine how best to navigate these webs of relationships in the creation of a range of interpretive programs at historic Oakland Cemetery and present examples of possible best practices for cemetery interpretation.

Interpretive First Steps

There are a few practical questions that must be asked before selecting a cemetery resident to interpret. How long has it been since their passing? Could the interpretation of a resident invade the privacy of or harm their living descendants? Is the resident considered a public figure or a private individual?

Generally speaking, HOF maintains a twenty-five-year buffer between the internment of a resident and when they are considered "free" to interpret. Cemeteries are places for families to grieve, and both space and time should be given for that act. Families might also object to any interpretation of their loved one, positive or negative, regardless of content. HOF staff will always try to adhere to the wishes of active descendants when it comes to complete anonymity. But a resident's status as a public figure or private individual will impact how much input a family has in any interpretation.

HOF loosely defines a public figure by the following standards:

- Their story is currently public knowledge, either in the local community and/or on the national stage.
- The individual shared their views widely in public forums during their life; for example, politicians or celebrities.
- The individual had a significant impact or contribution beyond the scope of their immediate community that was widely acknowledged during or after their life.

HOF considers politicians, business leaders, celebrities, sports figures, and artists as public figures. Their stories, contributions, failures, and successes are often well-documented in media, and in the case of public figures, we often include them in an interpretive program even if they passed away within the twenty-five-year waiting period.

Disagreements with Living Stakeholders

As with other historic sites, for cemeteries to present comprehensive and equitable history, residents must be interpreted objectively and free from sentimentality, nostalgia, and family folklore. This might lead to disagreements or conflicts with families for whom the cemetery and their loved-one's gravesite is a sacred space of mourning. The actions taken by an interpreter to provide nuanced content can create conflict with descendants, especially if the descendant feels that it paints their ancestor in a negative light. Interpretive guidelines should include clarifying language, correctives to attempts to romanticize history, and provide context without excusing behavior.

Descendants may find it difficult to acknowledge or accept a particular element of an ancestor's story for many possible reasons, including embarrassment, concern for contemporary judgment, feelings of loyalty to family, love for the recently deceased, not wanting to disrespect or speak ill of the dead, dislike of the narrative, genuine ignorance of the full story, or feeling the need to defend their family's legacy

HOF has found that the most direct way to address the potential for concern on the part of a descendant is always communication and transparency. As public historians committed to equity, we owe those who have been marginalized the naming of wrong practices in our past and the naming of individuals who perpetuated them. As a cemetery and the final resting place of family, we owe descendants the opportunity to learn about their ancestors' stories, process their history, and have a reasonable say in how their ancestors are portrayed within the site itself. This process may not fully apply to every resident—particularly those with no known descendants or particularly public figures—but it is critical to keep in mind for the site.

When talking to descendants:

- Come ready to learn as well as to teach.
- Prepare your research in advance.
- Open lines of communication before, and not after, public interpretation.
- Operate from a place of empathy and seek to build trust.
- Have clear and accessible citations for any elements of a story that might be rejected by descendants.
- Explain why the information is important in nonjudgmental language.

When faced with a situation where a descendant objects to the telling of some aspect of a resident's story, it might be that the only way to both respect the stakeholder's wishes and to practice ethical public history is to choose a different resident for your interpretive program whose story you can tell without compromising your interpretive and ethical standards. Cemeteries are inherently different from other historical sites. Because Oakland functions as a site of personal legacy and mourning, relatives of the deceased do have the right to have more input than they might at, for instance, a battleground or a historic house museum. The goal of sharing a cemetery's history is not to "out" bad actors, but rather to provide a venue for examining a place's past in an honest and equitable manner. At the same time, respecting the relationship someone might have with the final resting place of their loved one should never mean uncritically perpetuating the idealized and incomplete image of an individual. Oftentimes, with the exception of public figures, whose stories are generally free to tell fully, an individual resident's story primarily serves as a means to discuss the era in which they lived, historical events they witnessed, or the nature of their profession or social status. This objective can usually be met with a different resident's story. There are seventy thousand individuals buried at Oakland Cemetery, and seventy thousand different perspectives to share.

While this approach may seem limiting at first, having to shift to a different narrative when faced with this dynamic can provide the opportunity to tell a story from an underrepresented perspective: The inhumanity of slavery can be much more meaningfully conveyed by an individual who was enslaved compared to an enslaver; the story of how a city grew to become a major hub can be told just as well by the laborer who built the roadways and witnessed the growth, compared to the businessman who funded the projects. This approach can also reframe history in a more dynamic way and allow a site's interpretation to fill out the gaps in the narrative of how history is traditionally shared.

The history at a cemetery is personal, and so must be the process of educating and reeducating the public (descendants and otherwise) on the more complete and equitable ways of reshaping a community's historic narratives to meet contemporary best practices.

DESCENDANT DILEMMA: AN OAKLAND CEMETERY CASE STUDY

One of the residents featured in a recent *Capturing the Spirit of Oakland*™ tour was a local Atlanta landowner and transportation magnate in the mid-nineteenth century. Although prominent in his time, this individual does not meet the aforementioned criteria for being categorized as a public figure. The resident was heavily involved with a large railroad company that enslaved hundreds of Black men in the construction of the rail lines around Atlanta. Additionally, the resident owned a midsize plantation in northwest Georgia and enslaved more than a dozen people. The inclusion of this information in the resident's biography was essential to both the narrative and to meet the ethical standards of interpretation on-site. As the interpretation of the resident included a discussion of his contributions to the growth of Atlanta, it was important to emphasize that, first, others were carrying out the physical work to make these accomplishments possible, and second, the resident would not have achieved the same level of success had they not had the advantage of stolen labor.

Thrilled to share an aspect of his family's history, a descendant of this resident encouraged the portrayal. But while attending the tour, the descendant discovered that the event handbill, which features brief biographies of each highlighted resident, named his ancestor as a slaveholder. After the event, the descendant reached out, upset, and insisted that he had never heard of his ancestor's enslavement of human beings, challenging the narrative HOF presented to the public. The descendant's family had long prided themselves on the idea that their forefather was a self-made man, and the history of his slaveholding had been lost in family lore.

In response, HOF staff provided the descendant with the historic documentation and evidence of the resident's slaveholding activity. Staff walked the descendant through the information and helped the descendant process the new information in a way that brought him into understanding the importance of sharing the history.

While the staff was ultimately able to bring the descendant to a better understanding of his ancestor's past, the situation ultimately could have been avoided with the act of preemptively reaching out to the family and making sure that they understood the history before it was shared publicly. Unfortunately, the family was put into the position of being caught off-guard, affecting their relationship to the cemetery, which is a site in which they have the right to feel comfortable as the final resting place of their loved ones.

This example also raised the question of whose story was not being told on-site. The narrative of the enslaver certainly cannot capture the experiences of those he or she enslaved. If the goal of sharing this particular resident's story was to look at what helped create modern-day Atlanta, it would be more appropriate to share the stories of the enslaved workers whose labor literally paved the way for the growth of the city. In the following year's *Capturing the Spirit of Oakland*™ tour, HOF staff chose to share one such story, detailing the life of Guilford Ezzard, a formerly enslaved man who lived and worked in the city, and who survived to see Emancipation.

OPPORTUNITIES IN CEMETERY INTERPRETATION

While interpreting a cemetery and its residents can be challenging, the unique nature of the site affords opportunities to present comprehensive and equitable history through creative mediums. Historic Oakland Foundation staff are correcting past interpretive failures, combatting historical erasures, facilitating local conversations about national dialogues, and embracing the awareness of death in our society.

Course-Correcting Interpretation

For decades, HOF staff and volunteer-interpreters romanticized cemetery residents and their narratives to adhere to the "Speak no ill of the dead" aphorism. The belief that the dead cannot defend themselves penetrated tour scripts and brochures, creating stilted interpretations that lacked nuance. Uncomfortable topics were dismissed and problematic histories were swept aside with the explanation, "He was just a man of his time."

The phrase "he was a man of his time" is frequently employed as a way to dismiss, minimize, or willfully ignore the analysis of a person's autonomous actions, relegating choices made by an individual simply to being the natural product of his (or her) society's course. While it is true that individuals were influenced by the eras in which they lived, the assertion that one is a person of their time erases the stories of those whose views ran counter to the hegemonies. Additionally, it defines an era by the views of the powerful, erasing the experiences of those marginalized by prevailing social or political orders.

As HOF staff has grown in size, professional training, and experience, trained public historians in the programming department are working to correct past interpretive shortcomings, and continuing education for volunteers and staff will continue to be vital. The human element of interpretive programming cannot be dismissed and must be invested in to ensure historically accurate and nuanced interpretation takes place on-site. A trained and educated ambassador, whether staff or volunteer, will acknowledge that individuals are responsible for their actions, historical events do not take place in a vacuum, and no historical event is inevitable. Embracing people-first language, contextualization, nuanced definitions, and varied perspectives are other principal guidelines for interpretation. Moreover, internal dialogues and honest conversations are also critical to crafting outward-facing programs and interpretation. Staff must investigate their own biases to present history as objectively as possible. Just like Oakland residents, we must hold ourselves accountable.

Combatting Erasure

It is not enough to correct past interpretive mistakes. Cemetery interpreters must also be active agents in preventing the erasure of historical narratives and sites. This is most evident in historic Black burial grounds, sites that have faced extraordinary levels of erasure and desecration. Those that have been preserved are critically important physical spaces that preserve Black narratives where the written record has failed or where the willful destruction of the Black-built environment has taken place.

The written historic record before 1870 (the year of the first federal census following Emancipation and the first to record many formerly enslaved men and women by name) often excludes, obscures, and erases the stories of Black individuals. Enslaved men and women had a limited ability to keep written records. Documents about the enslaved experience are typically written by outsiders and do not accurately reflect the perspectives of those within the system of chattel slavery. Often, public historians must rely on storytelling, songs, and other oral lineal methods to discover the narratives, relationships, experiences, and dreams of enslaved men and women.

Figure 5.2. Capturing the Spirit of Oakland Storytelling: Oakland tours and events, most notably the *Capturing the Spirit of Oakland*™ tours, embrace and continue the tradition of oral storytelling. In this photo, Jason C. Louder and Deborah Strahorn portray Oakland residents Dr. James Reynold Porter and Henrietta Curtis Porter. Dr. Porter was a prominent medical professional in the state of Georgia, and Henrietta Porter organized several significant women's organizations, some of which are still extant today. Courtesy of the Historic Oakland Foundation.

Cemeteries, especially those with burials dating earlier than the twentieth century, can be some of the few surviving physical spaces that preserve historic Black narratives. These narratives include the individuals at rest below the earth and those who shaped the burial landscapes with their labor. For formerly enslaved people, burial plots were frequently the first and only land over which they held ownership. Grave markers serve as a physical record of an individual. Their name, birth date, death date, familial connections, faith, and other facets of their identity were not inked onto a page but carved into stone. Concrete markers at Oakland Cemetery and other cemeteries in the region display the celebrated tradition of Black-owned funeral homes and mortuary businesses in Atlanta. Born from segregation, the practice grew into a culturally and economically significant part of the city's living story. There is an intimacy in the way in which a burial lot can preserve a family's aesthetic preferences and economic situation through design and landscaping. Even the lack of a gravestone speaks to cultural traditions and individual choices. Out of both preference and necessity, common African American burial practices included using trees, shrubs, wooden markers, or the personal possessions of the dead to mark their resting place.

There are ways to explore other histories of the site beyond the numbers reflected in burial records. By approaching the materiality of the site, we can access stories of laborers and craftspeople that aren't otherwise captured by the identities of our residents. One significant example of this can be found in Oakland's extensive network of brick pathways, which give insight into the stories of those who were enslaved at brickyards through Georgia's convict leasing system.

The landscape of a cemetery and the physical presence of graves and markers assert the presence of marginalized communities in a place and time emphatically and irrefutably. Black cemeteries that have survived neglect and destruction are persistent reminders of their community's own perseverance and the radical act of intentional community building in the face of violence, separation, and discrimination.

SERVING A MORE DIVERSE COMMUNITY

Historic cemeteries are temporal, capturing a snapshot of a community and its citizens during a certain time and place. But as communities evolve through population growth and immigration, the demographics of current populations will often vary from the demographics of historical burials. This trend is most evident when comparing the racial makeup of Oakland burials with Atlanta population statistics. Oakland Cemetery was the final destination for most Atlanta citizens during the Victorian period and remained popular until the mid-twentieth century. Oakland's peak in burials predates the waves of global immigration that make Atlanta the rich multicultural urban area it is today. Like the municipal population during the nineteenth and early twentieth centuries, the majority of Oakland residents would have identified as either white or Black. Although Oakland remains an active site for burials today, the racial and ethnic makeup of its residents has not caught up with the rich diversity of Atlanta's multicultural population.

When faced with balancing the needs of a diverse audience with the realities of less diverse narrative sources, efforts must be made to serve the present while sharing the past. Historic Oakland Foundation employs several strategies to meet both of these equally vital goals. These strategies include developing reciprocal partnerships with inclusive collaborators and serving as a platform for diverse voices in special events and programs.

Death is, of course, a universal experience, and the ways in which varying cultures approach death and dying is a common theme explored in cemetery education programming. Anchoring interpretation in a theme that transcends the individual creates opportunities to connect audiences and source material. In past years, Historic Oakland Foundation welcomed staff from the Mexican Consulate in Atlanta to share the history and traditions of *Día de los Muertos* during Oakland festivals and homeschool programs. During Juneteenth events, Gullah storytellers led participants in creating a drumbeat to welcome a soul home. A Chinese American artist explored death and shared funerary practices and the concept of the unknown in an installation named after the Cantonese words for *death* and *four* during the *Arts at Oakland* special event in 2021.

In these instances, Oakland interpreters and staff members stepped aside to promote voices of cultural authority. The act of "passing the mic" requires an understanding of privilege and cultural ownership. By inviting a wide range of artists and storytellers to activate the site and tap into the universal themes that can be found within its landscape, staff seek to forge connections and expand representation.

The work in this area is not, and will not ever be, complete. As Atlanta continues to grow and change, Oakland's interpretation must change and adapt to the community. Staff is working to increase the representation of the site's Indigenous history through land acknowledgments, programming, and encouraging direct support of Indigenous-serving organizations. Future plans include producing printed materials in a variety of languages and recruiting staff and volunteers who are able to provide multilingual tours. With these ongoing efforts, Historic Oakland Foundation staff hope to live our mission to share Oakland Cemetery in as inclusive and welcoming a way as possible.

LOCAL CONVERSATION, NATIONAL DIALOGUE

Cemeteries provide local and individual perspectives on complex events, trends, and national narratives. Dialogue and debate are important for civil discourse as the United States continues to wrestle with its history and its history's meaning, determining which values should be uplifted or de-emphasized.

Oakland Cemetery is the final resting place of more than seven thousand Confederate soldiers and the site of two Confederate monuments. Located in the central areas of the cemetery, the sixty-five-foot-tall Confederate Obelisk (1874) and the *Lion of Atlanta* sculpture (1894) were commissioned by the Atlanta Ladies Memorial Association to "preserve and foster the memory of our Confederate dead." The Confederate Obelisk does not delineate the location of any internment and is therefore exclusively a monument and not a grave marker. Though the *Lion of Atlanta* was installed to mark the graves of unknown Confederate dead, both the timing of its installation and the themes found in its design mean that it also exists as a monument to the Confederacy itself. From its installation, the Obelisk was a gathering place for Confederate Memorial Day celebrations in Atlanta, as was the *Lion of Atlanta*. The lived use of the monuments further shifted the primary function of the monuments towards serving as representations of Lost Cause Ideology, which ignores slavery as the main cause of the Civil War and commemorates a racial hierarchy where African Americans were subservient to whites. The Lost Cause remained a powerful influence in the South for generations and is still embedded in public discourse about the Civil War.

The meanings of all historical monuments, including Confederate monuments, reflect current times and are not static or frozen in the moment of their erection. In recent years, there has been several instances of vandalism of the Confederate monuments at Oakland Cemetery. This vandalism is part of the accrued history of the objects. The very act of vandalism is a statement in the conversation surrounding the meaning and future of Confederate monuments, asserting support over their removal.

Our public interpretation of the *Lion of Atlanta*, Confederate Obelisk, and Confederate burials includes docent-led tours, interpretive panels, and digital interpretation. Beyond the history of these monuments, this interpretation includes a discussion of the relationship between memorialization and public memory, the shifting intentions of monument-building, and how our understanding of history changes over time.[2]

EMBRACING DEATH

Public historians and museum professionals have diverse goals and objectives for the experiences of their guests, including to learn, explore, discover, create, reflect, empathize, and understand. The action verb may change, but the end goal is always ultimately engagement. Cemeteries and other memorial spaces also encourage the contemplation of death's inevitability.

Every aspect of a cemetery serves as a memento mori, an artistic or symbolic reminder of death. Ornate gravestones remind visitors that, one day, they too will pass on from the earthly realm. Strategically placed benches in thoughtfully landscaped gardens encourage quiet reflection and open up space for grief. Even the statues in the cemetery are designed with messages of mortality. Uplifted eyes speak to hope for eternal life while downcast eyes symbolize contemplation of one's mortality.

While most Oakland tours and events focus on interpreting the lives of residents, HOF staff is learning to embrace death- and grief-related programs. Examples include a death-themed tour ("Fifty Ways to Die"), author talks on Victorian mourning traditions, and hosting group gatherings where strangers gather to drink tea, eat cake, and discuss death. These "Death Cafes" allow participants to increase their awareness of death in an accessible and confidential space. Held throughout the nation, these meetings have one objective—to help "people make the most of their (finite) lives."

In even the darkest of times, there are opportunities to create moments of fellowship and embrace grief. During the coronavirus pandemic in 2020, HOF had to cancel or reconfigure almost all of its programs and events, including an annual Juneteenth celebration. Unable to hold structured special events, HOF released virtual tours, storytelling videos, and musical performances during a digital Juneteenth celebration. But in the wake of the police killings of George Floyd and numerous Black Americans in early 2020, staff recognized that there was a communal need to not only celebrate Black history and narratives but also to grieve and reflect on our national trauma.

On the evening before Juneteenth, on June 18, 2020, HOF invited the public to walk Oakland's grounds for an hour of communal reflection and remembrance. Visitors were provided with maps of the cemetery featuring sites of African American history and open spaces for quiet reflection. HOF commissioned a prayer from local writer Amina McIntyre titled "A Litany for Liberation," which was also shared with visitors. Unlike other contemporary events, there were no speeches or songs. Visitors were simply encouraged to find a quiet spot to sit, reflect, and find space to reckon with their traumas, whether recent or ancestral. This act of collective grieving made the following day's Juneteenth celebrations all the more poignant.

LAST WORDS

There are many reasons why it is worthwhile to interpret cemeteries, but beyond their historical value, the interpretation of these sites may also be critical for their very survival. Interpretation, and the use of a range of diverse interpretive techniques, reminds the public of the contemporary value of cemeteries. They serve as reminders of the past, but they also have value as public green spaces, as places of respite, *and* as places of education. The nature of these unique sites, however, requires intentionality and care as interpreters navigate a realm of issues and divergent stakeholders that make this work both potentially challenging but equally as rewarding and impactful. The interpretation of a historic cemetery can ultimately cultivate the kind of public investment that provides the financial means for restoration and preservation, making cemeteries thriving places alive with the past rather than becoming unutilized, dead space in a community.

NOTES

1. Latine is used in place of Latinx in this chapter as it is both gender neutral and compatible with Spanish grammar. This word choice allows the term to be more inclusive and accessible to monolingual Spanish-speaking communities.

2. In August 2021, the Atlanta City Council unanimously voted to approve the removal of the *Lion of Atlanta* statue from Oakland Cemetery as "necessary and appropriate for the preservation, protection, and interpretation of the monument." The *Lion* was removed on Wednesday, August 18, 2021, under the direction of the Mayor's Office of Cultural Affairs. This chapter was written prior to the statue's removal.

6

INTERCONNECTION

How Personal Stories Are Expanding the Public Narrative

Miriam Bader

I have always been fascinated by the place between "yours" and "ours" and the distance from "me" to "we." This space bridges individuals to people and places outside of themselves. Within this space of interconnection, people are empowered to define their identity and to recognize the ways they are similar to and different from each other. This exchange has the capacity to build critically needed equity, empathy, and cultural humility. As Elif. M. Gokcigdem articulates in *Designing for Empathy: Perspectives on the Museum Experience*, "In order to navigate the rough difficult time of divisiveness, injustice, and inequality, oneness—the essential interconnectedness of all being, could just be the filter which we may need to reevaluate our existence as parts of a greater whole."

This chapter examines two projects centered on interconnection through storytelling: *Your Story, Our Story* at the Tenement Museum, where I was the director of education, and Do-It-Yourself Tookits at JDC Entwine, where I am currently the director of design and organizational development. Both projects break down the physical walls of museums and classrooms and the traditional roles of staff and participants. They ask big questions about identity: What does it mean to be an American? What does it mean to be a Jew? And they use story as a means to explore the complexity, multiplicity of responses, and intersectionality of race, class, gender, and other individual characteristics which overlap to transform individual experience in the world. These projects illustrate the power of equity and of cultural humility, a self-reflective approach that recognizes one's inability to ever fully comprehend someone else's experience, to transform storytelling and gathering and to create space for interconnection and new stories to emerge.

THE THEORY

Before delving into the details and lessons from the projects, let's understand the theory that underpinned their development.

The theory: Interconnection emerges when equity and cultural humility are activated and results in an expanded idea of possibility.

Interconnection relates to the connections that can be made between people, ideas, and places, both past and present. It relates to our capacity to build multiple connections across sameness and difference. Interconnection can be visualized as the space inside a Venn diagram—where the two exterior circles are labeled "their story" and "my story" and the overlapping interior circle is "our story." In this dynamic space exchange happens, and ideas and understandings about ourselves in relation to others are linked.

Emergence relates to the surfacing of new possibilities and the fact that one cannot truly anticipate them. It recognizes and celebrates one's inherent inability to plan for anything other than surprise. In the book *Emergent Strategy: Shaping Change, Changing Worlds*, activist adrienne maree brown explains, "Emergence is our inheritance as a part of this universe; it is how we change."[1] This dynamic understanding of continuous evolution welcomes a disruption to existing narratives, making room for a multitude of alternatives.

Equity recognizes that every individual is unique and worthy of contributing and shaping the story. It encompasses the goal to move from recognized past exclusion and underrepresentation of some, along with overrepresentation of others, to achieving genuine inclusion. As equity is not where historical choices have led us, we must deliberately apply time, resources, and consideration to achieve this goal. A commitment to equity emphasizes the humanity of storytelling, challenging the notion that some people's stories are more worthy than others and the certainty of a dominant cultural narrative. It acknowledges the people traditionally left out and celebrates a space large enough for everyone to use their voice and contribute. In this way, storytelling and gathering with a commitment to equity redistributes power, decentralizing it from the institution by inviting and empowering people to use their voices to take an active role in shaping the narrative.

Cultural humility acknowledges one's inability to know the full story. The term and concept were developed by doctors Melanie Tervalon and Jann Murray-Garcia in order to address health disparities and institutional inequities in medicine and is now used across industries.[2] Unlike cultural competency, which assumes that learning is finite and masterable, cultural humility recognizes the ongoing nature of this work. While one can never fully understand someone else, they can bring curiosity and a commitment to critical self-reflection and ongoing learning to each interaction. It is about humbly recognizing that there are things one doesn't know and is likely never going to understand about a culture that is not their own and having this knowledge guide one's thinking, behavior, and actions. This practice encourages us to realize our power, privileges, and prejudices, to be willing to acknowledge we don't have all the answers, and to embrace the complexity and nuance of human dynamics.

Expanded possibilities emerge when the values of equity and cultural humility intersect. By inviting people to speak for themselves and generously listening with the knowledge that one can never fully understand another's individual experience, a co-constructed space is actively created where people are inspired to imagine what can be. In this infinite space, perception can be shifted and one can see things differently. Ideas, people, and the world can be different than we expect.

THE THEORY IN PRACTICE

Your Story, Our Story, the Tenement Museum

The Tenement Museum shaped my approach to education and connection making. Early in my career as their education intern, I was in awe of the museum's ability to challenge existing conventions. The museum itself—based in two tenement buildings located in Manhattan's Lower East Side—stands in contrast to fancy museum architecture housing expensive collections. Founded in 1988 by Ruth Abram and Anita Jacobson, the buildings are a testament to the lives of ordinary people who once called the building home and their ability to shape America and American identity. The richness of the collection lies in its layers of wallpaper and everyday objects, and in the stories they bring to life of the people who once used them to work, take care of each other, and build a life. Tours led by educators take visitors inside re-created family apartments, immersing them in the lived experience of residents and facilitating connections between those stories and their own.

Launched in 2014, *Your Story, Our Story* (YSOS) is a museum initiative where users submit a picture of an object that is key to their own family's immigration and migration experiences or cultural identity and tell its story through a website. These user-generated stories become part of a larger collection of stories about identity and a source of interconnection between the storytellers and readers, who can access them through the site's dynamic search and tagging systems, bringing them forth in endless combinations. In 2020, the site's creators reflected, "We were building a website but it wasn't really about the website. It was about connecting. The website just made everything possible."[3]

Embedded in YSOS's structure is a commitment to equity and cultural humility. Core to the project is the museum's acknowledgment that its story-gathering practices and collection are incomplete and reliant on people outside of itself. The project is also an invitation to others to participate. At its heart, the project is human-centered, and this human touchpoint has been critical to making people feel comfortable co-constructing the space together and shaping new understanding and possibilities around what it means to be an immigrant, migrant, and human. Part of this work included building intentional partnerships with schools and other museums and iteratively building processes that remove barriers to participation.

What has emerged from the project are new ways of thinking about identity and belonging. The site has the capacity to hold infinite stories, and these sto-

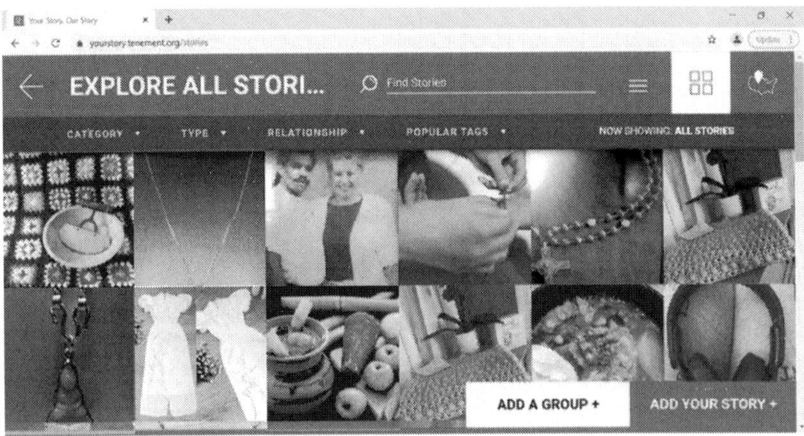

Figure 6.1. Your Story, Our Story website. Screenshot courtesy of Miriam Bader.

ries can be explored in multiple ways, resulting in new patterns, connections, and narratives awaiting emergence. This inherent interconnection is powerfully described by site users:

> Growing up in America, I felt like I was never seen as like an American, then like going back to my country, I was seen like a foreigner. So I wasn't able to fit in, in either place. I felt like I was alone in that, but reading these, I saw so many people who were like, "Oh yeah, my family came from another country and now I'm here." So that was definitely an eye-opening moment because I felt some type of solidarity. Even though I didn't know these people, I knew exactly how they felt.[4]

> When we shared with classmates, we could hear different backgrounds and objects. When you learn about somebody's background and when you listen you feel better, like "oh wow I share a similar story." It's also my opportunity to tell about West Africa and Ghana and the tribes and dialects and cultures and beliefs. Many Americans just think of Africa as one country.[5]

> We all have our own story but there is just something human about seeing some of the personal stories. And it was, I don't know, not so much relief, but it was a sense of a mutual understanding. We are broader. We share unspeakable things. We are interwoven.[6]

These comments demonstrate the site's ability to reflect underrepresented stories and highlight the transformational quality of storytelling and gathering to generate empathy, challenge assumptions, and build knowledge about ourselves and others. They also describe the multiple possibilities for interconnection that emerge—from an individual, familial, class, and larger universal lens. The connections were always there; however, without YSOS, there were fewer opportunities to unearth them.

Do-It-Yourself Toolkits, JDC Entwine

My experience at the Tenement Museum inspired me to explore alternate paths to generate discovery, interconnection, and civic engagement. I have come to see the world as a museum—flowing with possibilities for immersive learning, and I went on to work at Entwine, a part of the American Jewish Joint Distribution Committee (JDC), the global Jewish humanitarian organization. This gave me the opportunity to continue to experiment with co-constructed experience design using new formats and to bring an inquiry-based learning approach to the design of overseas travel experiences and pop-up exhibitions. While on the surface, a museum and a humanitarian organization may seem unrelated, my work in both institutions echoes each other, seeking to create entry points for interconnection in service of a social good.

For more than one hundred years, JDC has been strengthening Jews, Jewish communities, and others in need in seventy countries around the world. Entwine was founded in 2008 to connect young Jewish adults to the global Jewish world and to each other. Its vision includes developing a generation of young Jews who lead a life of action with global Jewish responsibility at its core. Central to this work is representing, celebrating, and elevating the diversity of the global Jewish community and educating our participants about its richness.

Do-It-Yourself (DIY) toolkits were created to make it easy for community members to engage others in their personal networks in conversations surrounding identity, responsibility, and impact. Accordingly, each toolkit helps organize and facilitate a group event where someone can bring people together for story sharing and connection making, whether through a film night or a service event, or over a shabbat or holiday dinner. We give users content and how-to materials to make it easier to engage with Jewish values and explore Jewish identity with others in their homes.

The toolkits were designed with a you-do-you approach, giving users agency to choose what parts resonated with them. Each includes conversation starters

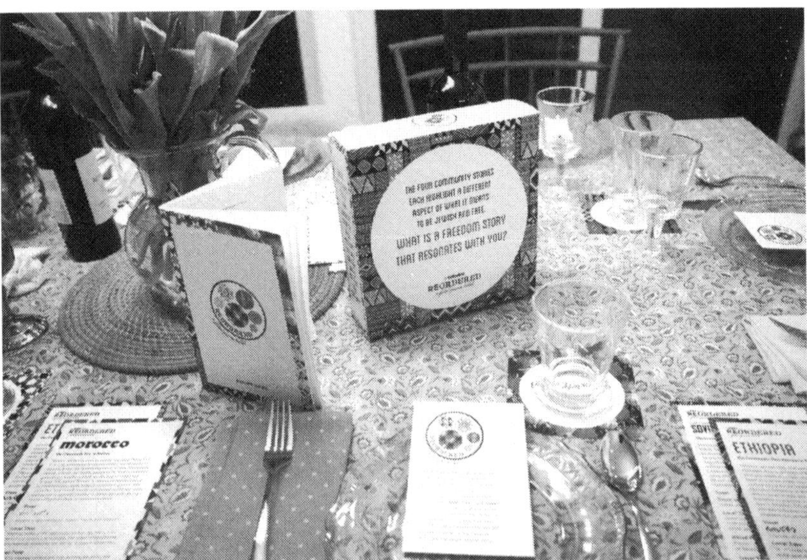

Figure 6.2. ReOrdered Global Passover Toolkit components. Courtesy of Entwine.

to break the ice and start the storytelling, creating spaces for sharing and listening that acknowledges the unique perspectives each individual brings. They also feature a range of individual stories from across the global Jewish community highlighting the lack of a singular dominant Jewish narrative and emphasizing the existence and celebration of many different stories. As one user noted, "The kit was a door opener to deepest questions about Jewish diversity, Jewish education, and Jewish identity that went for hours and hours."

Central to the toolkits is the idea that conversations about Jewish identity and values are ongoing and benefit from diverse voices. Entwine asks DIY toolkit users to express their leadership by inviting people to share their stories and be a part of building a new Jewish narrative reflective of its expansiveness and inherent multiethnic, multiracial, multiheritage, multicultural, pluralistic, and ever-evolving state. In this way, toolkits support users in becoming confident and competent hosts who can hold space for complex conversations about identity and belonging, as these users of the ReOrdered Global Passover Toolkit describe:

> This was the first time my non-Jewish, atheist partner celebrated Passover, and the toolkit enabled us to take a non-denominational, secular and humanist approach to a holiday that is very important to me. It was a great opening for discussion.
>
> The ReOrdered Toolkit made my first experience hosting a Passover Seder as an adult unique and engaging for my guests. The toolkit exposed us to new stories and pushed our conversation to relate the traditional Passover Exodus to modern-day Jews.

This ability to support users in connecting global stories to their individual lived experience and making ancient stories relevant and relatable is a key feature of the toolkit's content and structure.

PRACTICAL APPLICATIONS

These projects provide lessons for storytelling and gathering designed with equity and cultural humility. Six guiding principles emerged that can be used by practitioners to support this objective:

Break free of your building. Homes—the places people live—are the most accessible spaces for storytelling. They are natural and organic and filled with tables for people to sit around and objects to inspire them. Exploring identity and interconnectedness is inherently vulnerable and can be fraught. People are generally more comfortable in the spaces they inhabit, and this setting is a powerful generator and holder of stories.

Make it human. Both projects center human relationships and see people as producers of stories. Therefore, the stories shared are tied to human emotion and memory and unfold people's perceptions of themselves in relation to other individuals and the human experience. The Tenement Museum prides itself on the in-person human touchpoints central to its process. While the YSOS project could theoretically be automated in more ways, it was least successful when it was automated. Museums who left it alone in a gallery kiosk or digitally solicited participation generated very few stories, while partnerships and programs that brought people together for the story process yielded far greater results.[7] Entwine's DIY toolkits are similarly designed with the understanding that hosted events that bring people together are key. Personal invitations and relationship-building are at the heart of storytelling and enrich it.

Embrace not knowing. These projects humbly proclaim that we don't know the full story and that the stories in our existing collections are missing voices and perspectives. They invite others to coauthor a new narrative, one inclusive of their story. It can be worrying to not know the results, but it is through our embrace of "not knowing" answers that cultural humility is uplifted and centered, creating the foundation necessary for interconnection and new possibilities to emerge.

Plan to iterate. These projects have evolved over the years and continue to evolve through user input. From their inception, iteration was part of the design, and users brought new awareness and creativity to the way the projects were understood. Interestingly, while both projects have always sought to elevate marginalized stories, each took on a larger social justice lens over time. Today, both organizations celebrate their ability to diversify the story and to challenge dominant narratives about who and what an American or a Jew looks like.

Champion agency. A you-do-you approach recognizes that there is no single way to engage with storytelling and gathering and that situations and needs change over time. Users choose where their attention goes. Both YSOS and the toolkits give users agency to do what works for them, to pick the parts that resonate, and to be as vulnerable as they are comfortable. This nonlinear approach centers flexibility and fluidity throughout the process, creating more possibilities than staff could have imagined.

Small is good. In *Emergent Strategy*, brown explains this principle, noting that "small is all (the large is the reflection of the small)."[8] This insight recognizes that small story events—one classroom using YSOS; one dinner featuring a toolkit—is worthy. While both projects are designed to scale infinitely, they honor the intimate interaction and its power to produce interconnectedness and possibilities. They also recognize that "What we practice at the small scale sets the patterns for the whole system."[9]

CONCLUSION

Both YSOS and DIY toolkits challenge traditional practices of museums and cultural organizations. They embrace people where they are—in their homes—and invite them into shaping the story. Throughout history, organizational story-gathering and how those stories are presented and interpreted has traditionally been enacted by white people and often reinforces dominant cultural narratives and transactional practices. Similarly, in the majority of Jewish institutions, it has been the narrative of and by Ashkenazi Jews (those Jews who hail from Western, Central, and Eastern Europe) that has influenced the Jewish narrative. These projects acknowledge this reality and seek to create new opportunities to tell a different story about American and Jewish identity, respectively. They center equity and cultural humility within the process, inviting people to share their stories. What emerges is interconnection and new possibilities for understanding ourselves and the world around us.

NOTES

1. adrienne maree brown, *Emergent Strategy: Shaping Change, Changing Worlds* (Chico, CA: AK Press, 2017), 3.
2. Melanie Tervalon and Jann Murray-Garcia, "Cultural Humility Versus Cultural Competence: A Critical Distinction in Defining Physician Training Outcomes in Multicultural Education," *Journal of Healthcare for the Poor and Underserved* 9, no 2 (1998): 117.
3. HG&Co., *Your Story, Our Story Final Summative Evaluation Report*, 2020, x.
4. HG&Co., *Your Story, Our Story Final Summative Evaluation Report*, 2020, 16.
5. HG&Co., *Your Story, Our Story Final Summative Evaluation Report*, 2020, 18.
6. HG&Co., *Your Story, Our Story Final Summative Evaluation Report*, 2020, 17.
7. HG&Co., *Your Story, Our Story Final Summative Evaluation Report*, 2020, 26.
8. adrienne maree brown, *Emergent Strategy: Shaping Change, Changing Worlds* (Chico, CA: AK Press, 2017), 41.
9. adrienne maree brown, *Emergent Strategy: Shaping Change, Changing Worlds* (Chico, CA: AK Press, 2017), 53.

7

MOBILIZING PERSONAL NARRATIVE

Storytelling at Holocaust Museums

Adina Langer

STORYTELLING FOR RELEVANCE

Holocaust museums play a central role in moral education around the world.[1] Our visitors have come to expect encounters with stories that challenge them to test and expand their moral imagination. They come to learn about the extremes of humankind's capacity for inhumanity as well as humankind's potential for moral courage. By engaging with the history of the Holocaust and the experiences of people who went through it, visitors are challenged to ask themselves questions: What might I do? When, and why, might I act? Would I believe that things would simply get better? Why don't more people stand up to injustice?

People expect to be moved by their experience of a Holocaust museum. Many hope that they will be moved to moral action, redoubling their efforts to combat hatred and stand up for those who are targeted or scapegoated in contemporary spaces. Holocaust museums have come to rely on personal narratives to provide visitors with that moving experience. Museums gather and tell stories of survival and stories of loss. They share stories of rescue and stories of resistance. They provide examples of people who acted as perpetrators and examples of those who stood aside as others were acted upon.

The nature of storytelling in Holocaust museums has, by necessity, changed over time.[2] For years, people could rely on the opportunity to meet a survivor and hear stories directly from the source. The museum was there to provide historical context, a venue for the encounter, and a safe space for the narrator to share their story with minimal risk of re-traumatization.[3] Yet, as the survivor community ages and speakers reach the end of their natural lifespans, opportunities for direct encounters are quickly disappearing. Holocaust museums must shift their role accordingly. At the same time, we know that the desire to hear these stories must not be taken for granted, even as we approach the stewardship of these stories with care. Our audiences might not have any direct connection to the Holocaust, so part of our role is to make the history relevant to them.

As the curator of a Holocaust museum based at a regional university in the American Southeast, I am driven by the challenge to help my audiences find relevance. And I am not alone.[4] Rooted in a shared legacy, Holocaust museums have developed a toolkit to mobilize the stories at the heart of our missions, seeking to promote their relevance in the future while maintaining the personal stories entrusted to our care.

Origins of Personal Stories in Holocaust Museums

The first decades after the end of World War II were a time for Holocaust survivors to rebuild their lives. Some, like Otto Frank, father of the now-famous diarist Anne Frank, returned to the welcoming arms of those who had attempted to hide him and his family. Frank later helped to establish the Anne Frank House at the site where he and his family had hid in Amsterdam, creating the first site-based educational organization rooted in a single family story.[5]

Many other survivors had no place to return to. Instead, they navigated a pathway from Displaced Persons camps in Europe to resettlement as refugees. More than 140,000 survivors settled in the new state of Israel between 1948 and 1951. The United States took in 96,000 survivors as a result of the Displaced Persons Act of 1948.[6] These survivors carried their stories with them along with the imperative for future public historical interpretations of the Holocaust.

When survivors first began to emigrate to the United States, many were counseled by family members and friends alike to "forget the past" and, instead, focus on building a new life among people who knew little of their history.[7] "When we came to the United States," survivor Norbert Friedman explained in 2013, "you try to tell your experiences. And people either wouldn't listen, and if they listened, they didn't understand what you were talking about. So the survivors' community clammed up, stopped talking about it. We went inwards."[8] Survivor Tosia Schneider put it this way: "I went to Peekskill, New York, and my cousin was very kind, very nice person but one thing she told me, is forget about the past and start a new life as though that was possible. So I never talked about it, people didn't ask and I didn't tell."[9] Even if forgiveness was out of the question, the prevailing wisdom, as described by the majority of survivors I've met personally,[10] suggested that the best way to start a new life was to move on from the horrors of the Holocaust, or at least to avoid talking about them.

Yet, some were moved to speak about their experiences at the request of their children in the 1960s and 1970s. In a recollection that is supported by today's literature in trauma psychology,[11] Friedman remembered the tremendous relief that he felt when he first spoke about his experiences in his Long Island synagogue in the 1970s. Twenty years later, Holocaust survivors felt the pull of their grandchildren's generation's need for education and the correlating need to preserve their firsthand testimony. Institutions such as the US Holocaust Memorial Museum and the Museum of Jewish Heritage were born from this awareness. Survivors partnered with museum professionals to create some of the first institutions dedicated more to telling stories than to collecting and preserving the elite material culture of the past.[12]

As a part of their preservation missions, these museums and other projects spearheaded by Holocaust survivors and their archivist allies began recording tremendous amounts of testimony. Informed by psychoanalytic theory and memory studies, oral historians codified guidelines for interviews with members of the Holocaust survivor community that aimed to respect their past experiences and avoid re-traumatizing them, while recognizing the importance of preserving their stories for posterity. The guidelines published by the Shoah Foundation provide a good example.[13] Even in the 1990s, there was a sense of urgency among history professionals and survivor communities.[14] Adults who had come through the Holocaust in their forties were in their nineties already. Their children would be approaching the end of their natural lifespans by 2020. The partnerships between survivors and history professionals to create repositories of testimony left a legacy for the future.

The need to connect with personal stories to gain entry into a larger historical narrative (sometimes called historical empathy[15]) varies with distance from the historical event. The first articles by public historians advocating strongly for the inclusion of survivor testimony videos in museum exhibits began to appear in the early 2000s.[16] By the turn of the twenty-first century, there were many hours of available testimony. At the same time, Holocaust education was emerging as a field with a distinctive pedagogy.[17] Live witness testimony was seen as the gold standard for fostering student empathy and encouraging action to prevent future atrocities. What, then, should museums devoted to Holocaust education do when faced with a shrinking set of storytellers available to give firsthand testimony?

Two Case Studies

In this chapter, I focus on two organizations that I know well: the Museum of History and Holocaust Education (MHHE) at Kennesaw State University in Georgia, where I am the curator, and the Center for Holocaust, Human Rights, and Genocide Education (Chhange) at Brookdale Community College in New Jersey, where members of my childhood synagogue community volunteer.

Chhange was founded in 1979 when professors Seymour Siegler, Ed.D., and Jack Needle organized a series of "Lunch and Learn" events at Brookdale Community College with local Holocaust survivors. Chhange's mission is to educate about the Holocaust, genocide, and human rights and to work to eliminate racism, antisemitism, and all forms of prejudice.[18] Over the organization's forty-plus years, educators at Chhange have repeatedly demonstrated the power of the human story of genocide to be the most effective tool to advance both parts of its mission: education and reduction of prejudice and the impact of hate towards others.

The MHHE came about when Kennesaw State University (KSU) agreed to host the traveling exhibit *Anne Frank in the World* (as well as house the Georgia Commission on the Holocaust) in 2003, in part to address a perceived culture of intolerance on campus that was manifesting publicly through a series of lawsuits alleging antisemitic and racial discrimination in faculty hiring. KSU cemented its commitment to the new MHHE by hiring Dr. Catherine Lewis as a full-time member of the history faculty, whose responsibilities included serving as MHHE's director. The MHHE embraced a mission to "present public events, exhibits, and educational resources focused on World War II and the Holocaust in an effort to promote education and dialogue about the past and its significance today."[19]

Both organizations evolved to become permanent museums after their missions had taken root on their respective campuses. Chhange moved into a permanent space in 2012 and opened its first permanent exhibition, *Journeys Beyond Genocide: The Human Experience*, in 2017. The MHHE established a permanent exhibit, *Parallel Journeys: The Holocaust Through the Eyes of Teens*, in 2006 after *Anne Frank in the World* and the Georgia Commission on the Holocaust moved to a new home in Sandy Springs, Georgia. Over the next fifteen years, the MHHE would turn its attention to establishing an oral history program to preserve community stories. To mobilize its mission through its region, it also launched more than eighteen traveling exhibits of its own.

FACING THE FUTURE

In a dwindling environment of living storytellers, choice underscores the curatorial prerogative in the use of personal stories in museum exhibits. The curator must choose wisely, with an ear toward accuracy, a respect for the storyteller's intentions, and an awareness of the place of the individual part within the wholeness of the visitor's narrative experience and engagement with free-choice learning. In this environment marked by a long legacy and an uncertain future, Chhange and MHHE employ different techniques to mobilize personal narratives to extend the mission of their respective museums.

For Chhange, the seeds for connection and continuity were planted in 2000 when the organization hired Dale Daniels, a former volunteer, to be its first executive director, a role geared toward envisioning the future of the institution. Although Daniels was drawn to volunteering with the organization as a result of witnessing a Holocaust survivor speak to her son's sixth-grade class, she began her administration by discussing what to do when the survivors were no longer able to speak to students. At first, they published a book of survivors sharing five hundred-word summaries of their Holocaust experiences, but they quickly realized that these summaries left out the parts of their lives most salient to forging connections with young people: the normalcy before and the resilience/rebuilding afterward.

Under Daniels's leadership, Chhange launched its signature "Suitcase Project." Survivors in their network were asked to create scrapbooks that included images and objects representative of their life stories. Schools could request these suitcases through which they would learn about everyday people whose lives were disrupted by the circumstances of the Holocaust.

Looking to the future, Chhange embraced comparative genocide education.[20] They began by tapping into the deep roots of their local Armenian community, whose members appreciated the opportunity to house their family archives permanently, and to give voice to the story of a genocide that was not officially recognized by the United States until 2019. Chhange also reached out to local survivors of the Rwandan Genocide of 1994 through a network associated with the college. In the programs and permanent exhibit that resulted from these efforts, Chhange committed to an approach that emphasized the humanity of the survivors, giving equal weight to the "before," the "during," and the "after," as well as centering multiple forms of resistance.[21]

As they expanded their mission to include the Armenian and Rwandan genocides, they worked with Armenian families and Rwandan survivors to create suitcases about their experiences as well.[22] The Armenian storytelling took place almost a hundred years after the events of the genocide, but the local families embraced their roles as memory keepers. Both Daniels and Sara Brown, Chhange's current executive director, believe that more "next generation" family members will embrace this role of memory keeper for the Holocaust as well as other historical moments of traumatic disruption. Coupled with curated products, like the suitcase project and image- and artifact-rich exhibits, these memory keepers can continue to provide the kind of resonant storytelling that had been the hallmark of testimony-based Holocaust education throughout the last quarter of the twentieth century and first decades of the twenty-first.

Having taken on leadership of Chhange after working as a post-doc with the USC Shoah Foundation: The Institute for Visual History and Education on its famous survivor hologram project, Dimensions in Testimony, Brown embraces all forms of continuation of the encounter method of storytelling in Holocaust museums.[23] She noted in an interview that although she was skeptical at first, she witnessed the ways in which visitors interacting with the survivor holograms produced by the Shoah Foundation exhibited concern for their feelings. Even the simulation of human interaction elicited empathy from those who sought the survivors' conversation.[24] At the same time, Brown is excited by the flexibility that Chhange has already exhibited in its first-person storytelling around genocide. The organization's experience with the Armenian families demonstrates a willingness to embrace descendant representation in humanistic storytelling around traumatic events as well as a comparative approach to genocide. The comparative approach is key in that it demonstrates that just as personal narratives reveal each person's unique humanity (and thus help others make connections across distance and difference), each genocide is different and yet exhibits similar warning signs and stages of violence (including classification, dehumanization, polarization, extermination, and denial).[25] Humans learn through comparison and analogy, just as they learn through connections with others across the most mundane vectors of life.

Chhange's comparative genocide studies approach permeates both their new museum exhibit as well as middle school curricula exemplified by their Building Bridges program.[26] The program is a yearlong interdisciplinary approach to "establish a safe environment for students/individuals to examine difficult topics related to prejudice, bias and discrimination, reexamine moral dilemmas and challenge their own thinking." Tools developed by Chhange through their personal stories approach include the survivor suitcase project, close and critical reading of diaries and poetry of adolescent Holocaust/genocide victims, and repeated exposure to positive role models (survivors, rescuers, resisters, human rights activists). As of the writing of this chapter, Chhange is in the midst of a large-scale evaluation of this project, but preliminary findings show intensive participation at in-classroom sessions and Chhange exhibits and events throughout the middle school experience leads to increased knowledge, as well as positive changes in how students perceive their own responsibility to address injustice.[27]

To address the challenges of maintaining its relevance in the third decade of the twenty-first century, the MHHE has focused its efforts on creating resonant experiences for its local and regional community and extending its impact beyond the walls of the museum. Early in its development, the MHHE adopted the tagline "meet history face-to-face" and committed to making personal narrative a central part of its programming. Educational activities, such as its "Moral Passports" program, centered on direct encounters with personal stories where visitors were challenged to assess how individuals might play multiple roles (perpetrator, rescuer, victim, bystander) at different times during their historical journeys.[28] In 2015, the MHHE broadened its mission to embrace the experiences of World War II veterans, home front workers, and Holocaust survivors who eventually came to call Georgia their home by adding a second permanent exhibit, *Georgia Journeys: Legacies of World War II*. The juxtaposition of these World War II stories helped to contextualize the Holocaust for local visitors. In 2017, the museum opened a permanent exhibit about the Georgia home front, *Georgia Goes to War*. This local approach was intended to help visitors resonate with the history of the Holocaust and World War II and the generational change represented by these pivotal events of the twentieth century. It was also driven by the museum's commitment to its primary audience of kindergarten through college students with an emphasis on fifth and eighth grade when World War II, the Holocaust, and Georgia history appeared in the Georgia Standards of Excellence for social studies.[29] While the new on-site exhibits focused on Georgia, the museum's slate of traveling exhibits were free to explore a variety of topics that radiated outward from the museum's World War II and Holocaust core. These themes included immigration, antisemitism, civil rights, intra- and inter-group relationships, and the role of different generational actors in the process of commemoration and storytelling.

Although the MHHE has been a museum for almost twice as long as Chhange, it has long measured its impact beyond its walls as even more significant than what is rooted in on-site visitation (even before the pandemic). In the 2018–2019 school year, the MHHE served over 64,000 K–12 students both on-site and off-site, and its traveling exhibits served over 74,800 people, with 18,200 in schools and 56,690 in other locations. In addition, tens of thousands more were served through digital programming.[30] To get a better sense for the impact of their traveling exhibits program, the MHHE launched an evaluative survey in 2020 to venues that have hosted multiple traveling exhibits over the past decade. Included in the survey were questions specific to the role of personal narratives in traveling history exhibits.

The results of the survey are telling. The twenty responses to the survey as of the writing of this chapter represent a mix of the museum's clients for traveling exhibits: schools, public libraries, community centers, retirement homes/assisted living facilities, and religious institutions. The ages of the audiences served varied from children to older adults, with clusters in the ten- to fifteen-year-old range and fifty-five-plus. All of the institutions surveyed counted English as a primary language, but a few also included Spanish, Korean, and Japanese. Across institutions, about a third of patrons required some form of accessibility assistance, including mobility aids, hearing assistance, or vision assistance, and about a quarter benefited from special cognitive or sensory environments. For institutions that requested the same exhibits more than once, the top reasons given were that they aligned with curriculum standards and that they were enjoyable or engaging, especially for students.[31]

The MHHE found that traveling exhibits were most effective when paired with programs and activities. Although those who were able to access live guest speakers ("real Rosies" or Holocaust survivors, for example) found those to be exceptionally effective when paired with the traveling exhibits; positive feedback was also given for pairings with film/media presentations, virtual docent tours, and transformation of usually mundane spaces to create unique environments for teaching ("Night at the Museum," for example). The use of gallery guides, teacher's guides, translated materials, and online exhibits were also rated highly in conjunction with visitor experience.

Behaviorally, traveling exhibits seem especially well-suited to prompting conversation among visitors as well as repeat visitation within the time the exhibit is present at a particular venue. Students often benefit from prescribed activities, while adult groups seem more comfortable with spontaneous and prolonged conversations.

It's in the assessment of the impact of the traveling exhibits that institutional representatives emphasize their power to help forge connections between the past and the present as well as the effect of personal narratives on visitor experience. A sample of answers to the question, "What do you remember most from the traveling exhibits that you've hosted at your institution?" include: "The excitement from my students and their inquiry throughout the exhibit"; "The response from those who interacted with it. They took their time and also made sure to come and share their thoughts on it and how impactful it was"; "The discussions that students had about past versus current racial tensions in the U.S."; "Photos have been very impressive. Also, first-person accounts have been impactful"; "Stories of people."

Asked to pick which exhibits they felt were most impactful, respondents included a wide variety of traveling exhibits on topics ranging from the Holocaust to Japanese internment. These exhibits combine rich images and primary source documents with brief contextual information. Many also feature quotations from personal narratives. When asked: "Why do you feel these exhibits have been most impactful?" their answers ranged from anecdotes on student response, such as "The students who paid attention seemed impacted," to comments on the novelty and specificity of the content: "Students learned about real-life accounts of people who lived through the Holocaust"; "They provide information that most do not know on the history that we have in our country related to these topics"; "It shows how genocide and war impacts populations, most specifically certain ethnic groups"; "Unique stories."

The last cluster of questions in the traveling exhibits survey hinged on the relative importance of characteristics of the content. These characteristics included: is historically accurate, includes personal stories, includes unique or surprising information, meets educational standards, includes a variety of primary sources, narrative is easy to understand, includes statistics or info-graphics, includes maps, and includes timelines. Respondents could choose from Essential, Very Important, Important, Somewhat Important, and Not Important for each characteristic. In the "essential" category, the top three characteristics were: is historically accurate, narrative is easy to understand, and includes personal stories. The category "very important" was more evenly distributed across: includes unknown or surprising information, includes a variety of primary sources, includes maps, and includes timelines. Most respondents also felt that the meeting of educational standards was, at least, important, as well as the inclusion of statistics or info-graphics.

Respondents were also invited to respond freehand to the prompt, "What ways do you find most interesting to learn about the past?" Although responses varied across delivery methods, more than half of respondents included a reference to "personal stories" in their response.

On the specific topic of personal stories in historical exhibits, the majority of respondents had interacted with one of the MHHE's exhibits that included personal stories and also another historical exhibit that included personal stories. Respondents also indicated a two-thirds preference for personal stories related to a historical topic or theme over broad historical information in exhibits.

When asked how they felt when they encountered a personal story in a historical exhibit, most respondents used terminology related to connection, emotion, and meaning. Responses included: "more connected to the historical event"; "Proud (when the information is accurate) and relieved that the information is being told/forwarded"; "Makes it more real and meaningful"; "More connected"; "It makes the history come alive and more real"; "Depending on the story—sad, empathetic, joy, hopeful"; "It allows me to use empathy. It makes me reflective over my life and think about how I would have responded"; "Very emotional"; "It makes me feel more connected to the community that I serve"; "Connected to the past"; "Connected."

At the end of the survey, respondents were asked one more important question: "Why do you think it's important for people to learn about history?" Although this question did not specifically ask about the Holocaust, many of the answers related to perceived negative events in the past: "To learn both the positive and negative actions of the past"; "So we know who we are as a people and understand the historical lessons as to not repeat the violence, wars, and injustice that continues to happen"; "So we don't repeat it"; "It's vital to learn about history to learn from others' experiences and not to make the same mistakes"; "Because it sparks conversation"; "To hopefully not repeat the mistakes of the past"; "If we don't learn about it we are destined to repeat it"; "It's important because we need to recognize similar events as it occurs during our own time"; "If we do not know where we have come from, we will repeat mistakes of the past"; "Helps them feel connected to each other."

Taken together, the survey responses affirm the MHHE's approach to traveling exhibits, including their increased inclusion of personal narratives. These exhibits are helping the MHHE meet their goals of providing relevant historical experiences to visitors that help them make connections between the past and the present. At the same time, these responses raise some important questions for the ongoing work of Holocaust museums.

AVOIDING THE MISTAKES OF THE PAST?

From the earliest days of the European memorials and national museums to the proliferation of smaller educational institutions, Holocaust museums have been predicated, at least in part, on the very ideas articulated by these representatives of institutions who hosted the MHHE's traveling exhibits: learning about history (of the Holocaust) is essential so that we can avoid repeating the mistakes of the past. And yet, genocides around the world and the ever-present seeds of intolerance belie the "inoculation" effect implied by this educational cliché. Why then do we cling to it so? Perhaps the key lies in the commonality between these case studies: the power of personal stories. Visitors crave the connection of personal stories juxtaposed with historical narratives because we learn through encounter and re-encounter. We are social creatures. If it has done anything, the COVID-19 pandemic has underscored the human need for connection. The staying power of personal stories in Holocaust museums is thus illuminated. We return to this history to reconnect with it, to find ways of sharing across generations. We relate to the stories of the people of the past, and we fit the stories of our lives within the context of the past's impact on our world today. We teach our children through sharing stories—our own and those we know—and we do it for emotional reasons as well as moral reasons. It is not a process of inoculation. Instead, it is more like nourishment. Personal stories in Holocaust museums nourish the moral imperative.[32] They encourage visitors to be more than passive consumers of stories and to act, instead, as witnesses. They fortify us in our role as educators for the present and ambassadors for the people of the past. That is not a passing role; it is the role of a lifetime.

NOTES

1. For a comprehensive review of literature related to teaching and learning about the Holocaust, see: Monique Eckmann, Doyle Stevick, Jolanta Ambrosewicz-Jacobs, and International Holocaust Remembrance Alliance, eds., *Research in Teaching and Learning about the Holocaust: A Dialogue beyond Borders*, IHRA Series, vol. 3 (Berlin: Metropol, 2017).

2. For more on the evolution of the public history of the Holocaust, see Adina Langer, "Holocaust History—The Inclusive Historian's Handbook," November 4, 2019, https://inclusivehistorian.com/holocaust-history/.

3. For a discussion of potential scenarios for re-traumatization and its associated effects, see: "Supporting Survivors of Trauma: How to Avoid Re-Traumatization,"

accessed October 7, 2021, https://www.onlinemswprograms.com/resources/social-issues/how-to-be-mindful-re-traumatization/.

4. It is important to note that these institutions are among dozens of Holocaust education centers based at colleges and universities. Although many exist, few have created full-scale museums. For a list of more than 370 Holocaust organizations around the world, see the Association for Holocaust Organizations, "Membership," accessed July 21, 2021, https://www.ahoinfo.org/membership.

5. For an in-depth look at the history of the Anne Frank House and the impact of Anne Frank's story, see Gillian Walnes Perry, *The Legacy of Anne Frank* (Yorkshire: Pen and Sword History, 2018).

6. My Jewish Learning, "Jewish Refugees during and after the Holocaust," accessed June 25, 2021, https://www.myjewishlearning.com/article/jewish-refugees-during-and-after-the-holocaust/.

7. Erika Bourguignon, "Bringing the Past into the Present: Family Narratives of Holocaust, Exile, and Diaspora: Memory in an Amnesic World: Holocaust, Exile, and the Return of the Suppressed," *Anthropological Quarterly* 78, no. 1 (2005): 63–88.

8. Norbert Friedman Interview, 2013-11-11, Legacy Series Oral History Program, 2013, KSU/14/05/03/001, Museum of History and Holocaust Education, Kennesaw State University.

9. Tosia Schneider Interview, 2014-07-08, Legacy Series Oral History Program, 2013-, KSU/14/05/03/001, Museum of History and Holocaust Education, Kennesaw State University.

10. Hasia Diner offers a notable counter-narrative to the common story of American reticence to engage with the Holocaust in the postwar years. Hasia R. Diner, *We Remember with Reverence and Love: American Jews and the Myth of Silence after the Holocaust, 1945–1962* (first edition) (New York: New York University Press, 2009).

11. Judith L. Herman, *Trauma and Recovery: The Aftermath of Violence—from Domestic Abuse to Political Terror* (1R edition) (New York: Basic Books, 2015).

12. Michael Berenbaum, *The World Must Know: The History of the Holocaust as Told in the United States Holocaust Memorial Museum* (revised edition) (Baltimore, MD: Johns Hopkins University Press, 2006).

13. USC Shoah Foundation, "Collecting Testimonies," accessed December 14, 2020, https://sfi.usc.edu/collecting.

14. This sense of urgency is well-summarized in: Michael Rothberg and Jared Stark, "After the Witness: A Report from the Twentieth Anniversary Conference of the Fortunoff Video Archive for Holocaust Testimonies at Yale," *History and Memory* 15, no. 1 (2003): 85–96, https://doi.org/10.2979/his.2003.15.1.85.

15. Historical empathy is a concept gaining traction in history education theory. For a recent case study on the effectiveness of its use in a middle school classroom, see: Jason L. Endacott and Christina Pelekanos, "Slaves, Women, and War! Engaging Middle School Students in Historical Empathy for Enduring Understanding," *The Social Studies*, no. 106 (2015): 1–7.

16. Steve Humphries, "Unseen Stories: Video History in Museums," *Oral History* 31, no. 2 (2003): 75–84.

17. David H. Lindquist, "Avoiding Inappropriate Pedagogy in Middle School Teaching of the Holocaust," *Middle School Journal* 39, no. 1 (2007): 24–31; David H. Lindquist, "Meeting a Moral Imperative: A Rationale for Teaching the Holocaust," *The Clearing House* 84, no. 1 (2011): 26–30; Jenna Berger, "Review Essay: Teaching History, Teaching Tolerance—Holocaust Education in Houston," *The Public Historian* 25, no. 4 (2003): 125–31, https://doi.org/10.1525/tph.2003.25.4.125.

18. "Mission Statement and History Chhange: The Center for Holocaust, Human Rights & Genocide Education," accessed June 24, 2021, https://www.chhange.org/about/history-of-chhange.

19. "Mission: Museum of History and Holocaust Education," accessed August 17, 2021, https://historymuseum.kennesaw.edu/about/mission.php.

20. The term genocide was first coined by Polish Jewish refugee Raphael Lempkin in the 1944 book *Axis Rule in Occupied Europe*, in which he described the Nazi policies to destroy entire national and ethnic groups, including Europe's Jews. In 1948, the United Nations approved the Convention on the Prevention and Punishment of Genocide. During the latter part of the twentieth century, historians, museum professionals, and others discussed and debated the relationship between the Holocaust and other genocides around the world and the ways in which these events should be taught together or separately. For perspective on the origins of and debates about comparative genocide education, see Alan S Rosenbaum, *Is the Holocaust Unique? Perspectives on Comparative Genocide* (third edition) (Boulder, CO: Routledge, 2009), https://search.ebscohost.com/login.aspx?direct=true&AuthType=ip,shib&db=nlebk&AN=253635&site=eds-live&scope=site.

21. Dale Daniels, Discussion of the Evolution of Chhange with Its First Executive Director, interview by Adina Langer, Zoom, June 9, 2021.

22. Dale Daniels, Discussion of the Evolution of Chhange with Its First Executive Director, Interview by Adina Langer, Zoom, June 9, 2021.

23. "Artificial Intelligence Project Lets Holocaust Survivors Share Their Stories Forever," accessed June 25, 2021, https://www.cbsnews.com/news/artificial-intelligence-holocaust-remembrance-60-minutes-2020-04-03/.

24. Sara Brown, Discussion with Chhange Executive Director on the Future of Storytelling in Holocaust Museums, Interview by Adina Langer, Zoom, June 9, 2021.

25. "10 Stages of Genocide," accessed June 25, 2021, http://genocidewatch.net/genocide-2/8-stages-of-genocide/.

26. "Building Bridges Chhange: The Center for Holocaust, Human Rights & Genocide Education," accessed June 24, 2021, https://www.chhange.org/programs/educators/building-bridges.

27. Dale Daniels, Discussion of the Evolution of Chhange with Its First Executive Director, Interview by Adina Langer, Zoom, June 9, 2021.

28. For more on "Moral Passports," see the Teacher's Guide for *Parallel Journeys* on this page: "Teacher's Guides—Museum of History and Holocaust Education," accessed October 7, 2021, https://historymuseum.kennesaw.edu/education/digital-education/teachers-guides.php.

29. "Social Studies Georgia Standards of Excellence (GSE)," accessed July 21, 2021, https://www.georgiastandards.org/georgia-standards/pages/social-studies.aspx.

30. Catherine Lewis, "Museums, Archives, and Rare Books 2018–2019 Overview," Kennesaw State University, October 14, 2019.

31. Adina Langer, "Report | Qualtrics Experience Management: Assessing the Content and Quality of Traveling Historical Exhibits," accessed June 25, 2021, https://kennesaw.co1.qualtrics.com/results/?surveyId=SV_832A2KWOd9x7OOp#/surveys/SV_832A2KWOd9x7OOp/containers/6036c635c2b5f6000ffb63a1/pages/Page_9004ff9d-5705-43f0-9e83-df25faa14eaf.

32. For a masterful exploration of the moral imperative in *Vergangenheitsaufarbeitung*, the German term for "working off the past," see Susan Neiman, *Learning from the Germans: Race and the Memory of Evil* (New York: Farrar, Straus and Giroux, 2019).

8

REFLECTIONS ON PRACTICING *SANKOFA* IN MUSEUMS AND THEATERS

Deitrah J. Taylor

According to the National Council on Public History, the purpose of public history is to help visitors "[apply] history to real-world issues." Public historians hold many job titles; however, all make historical interpretation pertinent and useful to the public.[1] History is often thought to be merely the study of past events; yet, it is active and increasingly hotly debated in the public sphere. Akan people (Ghana) call this process *Sankofa*—the literal translation of the word and the symbol is "it is not taboo to fetch what is at risk of being left behind."[2] There are two images of this concept, one a bird and the other a heart (see figure 8.1). The bird represents the present. The bird's feet face forward and it looks back to retrieve the past. The bird was carrying the past with it, but not acknowledging the past. The bird acknowledges the past, moves through the present, and creates a new future. The heart image features symmetrical spirals turned inward at the center and ornate feet at the base. Museums and theater use *Sankofa* to provide memorable experiences and deeper understanding of the past for visitors. When done accurately, this work can dispel damaging historical mythologies and provide new perspectives on the past. History both explains how we arrived at the present moment and has an active role in

Figure 8.1. **This gold weight in the form of a bird from the Akan kingdoms of southern Ghana is a visual representation of the principle of *Sankofa* (retrieve, go back and fetch), originating from the Akan, Twi, and Fante languages of Ghana. Sankofa translates to it is not taboo to fetch what you have left behind. Courtesy of the Brooklyn Museum.**

shaping where society goes in the future. As a public historian and dramaturg, my approach to the work of *Sankofa* was shaped by my experiences at historic house museums and with museum theater.

Historical house museums and grounds are artifacts that contain artifacts. Museum professionals interpret and provide care for the house and grounds as an artifact along with the collection as the whole historic site. Curators document the changes not only to the built environment but the grounds as well in order to tell the entire story of how people lived and labored on a site. Thus, as artifacts of the built environment, historical house museums are unique in that they attempt to immerse visitors in time. Visitors are exposed to original historical environments, original artifacts when possible, or period examples of objects used by historical figures, which helps visitors understand and perhaps relate to how people lived in the past. Curators use primary source documents and other sources to accurately represent people and events in the past, reaching present audiences and illuminating their understanding of the past. Public historians work in multiple mediums using similar methods to tell historically accurate stories and engage audiences with the past. Colonial Williamsburg (Virginia) is a well-known pioneer in first-person interpretation. The largest living history museum in the United States of America offers authenticity through research and solid facts.[3] Williamsburg's interpretation has changed since its creation in 1926, reflecting current inclusive historiography found in academic and public history practices. As a result, first-person interpretation includes stories of Native Americans, skilled enslaved craftspeople and artisans. Monticello, the Virginia home of Thomas Jefferson, has first-person interpretation programs centering on James Hemmings, a carpenter and joiner who built Jefferson's furniture at multiple Jefferson properties.[4]

Historical theater inside museums as well as historically themed productions are also an important component of public history and how the public remembers history. Theatrical productions bring history to life and help audiences make meaning of the past. Some museums have playwrights and dramaturgs on staff helping to bring exhibits to life. Addae Moon, formerly of the Atlanta History Center, notes that museum theater is in its infancy in America but is common throughout the rest of the world. Moon wrote *Four Days of Fury*, a play that connected museum visitors with the Atlanta Race Riot of 1906, which was an immersive theatrical experience.[5] The International Museum Theatre Alliance states their mission as using theater to "cultivate emotional connection, provoke action and add public value to the museum experience."[6] Emotional connections are key to creating memory. Visitors will remember stories, the place where the story was told, and the impact of the story. Dramaturgy is a discipline within the theater world that has many meanings and applications, as does public history. As defined by the Literary Managers and Dramaturgs of the Americas, "Dramaturgs contextualize the world of a play; establish connections among the text, actors, and audience; offer opportunities for playwrights; generate projects and programs; and create conversations about plays in their communities."[7] Dramaturgs come from a variety of disciplines to create live art. At museums and historical sites, providing living history experiences or museum theater, dramaturgs do public history as part of their work. Public historians can also commit acts of dramaturgy when they work as historical consultants with directors, designers, production teams, and actors making a historically accurate artistic vision a reality in live theater productions for theater companies. Theater in museums helps audiences process, engage, and remember history. The emphasis on historical accuracy and immersion in the historical environment for visitors is the same in museums and theatrical productions. *Hamilton* and *Ain't Too Proud to Beg* are two popular Broadway theatrical productions that have received much critical analysis on historical accuracy and artistic message to contemporary audiences. Since history is not merely about the past, but present events and how we understand them, historical interpretation in museums, theaters, film, and even monuments have been increasingly hot topics in the public. Experiences at historic house museums shaped my career as a public historian and my approach to dramaturgy.

Milledgeville, Georgia, served as the antebellum capital of the state from 1804 to 1868. At the Old Governor's Mansion (1838–1868), visitors can step back in time to the 1850s. The Old Governor's Mansion completed restoration in 2005. The interpretation of the house includes original and period pieces dating from the time the building was used by the state of Georgia as the governor's residence. Visitors can learn the way the wealthy and politically powerful families lived in the home as every effort is made to hide the present technology throughout the home. Modern touches are explained and dated for visitors, such as the Otis elevator used for visitor accessibility added during the use of the building by Georgia State College for Women's presidents. Offices where computers reside are not included on tours. The education building used to orient visitors sits on the foundation of one of the outbuildings and is the last exposure, aside from those who use the elevator, to anything from the present. HVAC systems are discretely hidden from view but can be spotted by sharp-eyed visitors looking up at the egg and dart molding original to the building. Immersion in the physical environment of 1850 helps visitors understand the complex issues of class, race, gender, and politics that dominated society while the governors and their families used the mansion. The dedication to accurately reflecting place and time and immersing visitors in that environment is a different approach to museums with galleries. Galleries display artifacts and information but not in the context of the original environment, therefore visitors to historic house museums that are fully interpreted can experience the time period more vividly than the gallery experience. House museum educators allow visitors to understand time and place, providing context and connections to daily human experiences.

Living history days at the mansion took place in the fall, in the winter with Christmas candlelight tours, and in the spring as a part of a spring concert and Civil War commemoration. On those special tour dates, docents gave tours in costume and immersion in the historical environment was more complete. Visitor observations and questions extended beyond furnishings and political ideology to focus on how people lived and moved through the spaces. Visitors noted how objects were used (questions about spittoons and chamber pots), the enslaved people responsible for creating the objects, and the relationship between the enslaved and free people who worked at the mansion. Gender was also expressed through clothing during the period the mansion was in government use. Gender roles in the southern United States of America were reinforced by clothing. Clothing also expressed socioeconomic status, as did homes and transportation. Living history days at the Old Governor's Mansion required interpreters to accurately reflect these concepts through clothing which further immersed visitors in the place and time. The docents' gendered clothing affected the way they moved through the space. Visitors would also be able to notice the designated racial and gender spaces inherent in the design of the building more easily than when docents were dressed in collared shirts. Docents were also photographed by visitors and instructed to remove any modern accoutrements from view.

Although I could appreciate the benefit of the living history experiences to the public, I was also keenly aware of the challenges in conducting living history as one who identifies as African American and Black. Black interpreters confront visitor stereotypes and at times hostile questions concerning slavery and the Civil War and the Black community at present.[8] Black people participating in living history face these challenges in order to tell the stories of the enslaved and create social change.[9] The Old Governor's Mansion was the seat of political power when my Georgia enslaved relatives were in bondage. I felt I had an obligation to tell their stories accurately and represent them in some way. I knew I did not want my dignity to be compromised in the process. Representation can assist visitors in making visible the lives of enslaved people and free Black people and is also emotionally and spiritually taxing for interpreters. Breaks between tours for these interpreters should be considered as part of good practice. My research led me to Lavinia Robinson Flagg, a free Black woman married to Reverend Wilkes Flagg, a paid employee at the mansion for many administrations. Reverend Flagg worked as a maître'd for special events and founded Flagg Chapel Baptist Church, which still is an active church in Milledgeville, Georgia. Mrs. Flagg was known to visit the First Ladies of Georgia and work odd jobs for them. The free Black population in Georgia was small during the time that Milledgeville was the capital of Georgia. My dress was created from the collection at the Atlanta History Center, which sold the pattern in their gift shop. The dress reflected what would have been worn by middle-class women, Black or white, during the era. Images of free Black women came from a collection of photographs of Black women in Atlanta. I created the "Labor Behind the Veil" tour, centering Black American life at the mansion. These tours were of interest to many visitors, who asked thoughtful questions and allowed me to highlight the skilled work done by enslaved and free Black people on the property. Immersion of visitors in the time period, whether on living history days or regular tours, is a key to creating a world and a concept useful for the practice of dramaturgy.

Dramaturgs are researchers for theatrical productions, and they can come from many disciplines. As a public historian doing cultural and collaborative work in a higher education setting, practicing dramaturgy was perfect for growing and expanding my scholarship. Production dramaturgs help build the world of the play. Research is present in every aspect from set design, props, costumes, and makeup to character development. Having expertise on the production can save time for the director, actors, and designers as they rely on the dramaturg to find information quickly and make it accessible to the production. Knowing how to locate a variety of audio and visual primary sources for the entire production team helps immerse the team in the world. Dramaturgs curate the theatrical production with directors giving the final informed approval of what audiences experience. When the production opens to the public, the actors, set, and sounds create understanding and empathy for audiences. The actors use historical events as tools engaging their memory banks and emotions to relate to the character and the time period, fulfilling Freeman Tilden's "Principles of Interpretation."[10] Actors use these emotions to create empathy for their characters and the sectors of society the characters represent, and to convey that to audiences. Spectators respond to the work of the actors intellectually, and emotionally in what Aristotle identified as catharsis. Ancient Africans practiced what the Greeks called theater as part of daily spiritual, communal, and personal practices. The ancient Greeks first made contact with the African continent through Kemet, which they translated to Egypt.[11] Scholars credit Kemet with the birth of theater as pageantry, and religious performances took place there with no special venue. These performances scholars call Egyptian mystery plays. Some of them focused on the death of Osiris and his path to eternal life.[12] In West Africa, the Yoruba tradition of the Egungun masquerades were critical to honor the ancestors in a community. In the Yoruba community, the Egungun is the materialization of ancestors in the community visiting for celebrations, and remembrance.[13] The masks and regalia worn by these dancers is sacred and an example of the central role of theater in Ancient Africa. The dynamic of the actor playing a part onstage resulting in audience response mirrors the African diasporic tradition of call and response in music, dance, and other artforms. Call and response creates community among all participants and becomes a crucial part of the shared experiences between artists and audience. As a public historian and dramaturg, my research starts the call and response/catharsis process resulting in the activation and transmission of *Sankofa*.[14] The past provides reason for the present and a pathway for the future for audiences and artists alike. Working with actors, the focus is making distant historical time periods meaningful so that the lines are conveyed with emotion for the audience—history as empathy. During my dramaturgy sessions, I guide casts as they process and apply historical events to themselves and the world of the play. Actors respond emotionally as they take in new historical information and apply it to the world of the play and the current sociopolitical climate. I worked with theatrical companies within and outside the academy that choose plays in their seasons to respond to social ills such as gentrification and displacement (Kenny Leon's True Colors Theatre Company's production of Dominique Morrisseau's *Skeleton Crew* 2019) and traumatic events including the deaths of unarmed Black people.[15] Actors had to contend with plays set in the past that spoke to current traumas in the Black community. The purpose of the actors' process is to understand the links between past and present traumas and then accurately convey them to audiences in hopes of raising awareness and sparking social change. When I meet with a director, production team, and/or playwright, I always ask what impact they would like the piece to have on an audience. This is also a key question for me when I work in museum spaces. Connection and social change seem to be at the heart of the answer every time.

As a public historian working in the world of theater, my dramaturgy informs other aspects of the production other than the director, cast, and audience. Dramaturgs help the production team curate the public presentation of the theatrical work. Dramaturgs assist in setting a time frame for props, music, set design, makeup, and costumes. The creators imagine and build the world of the play based on historical research and assistance of the dramaturg. As the world is curated to keep the audience in this world, members of the production team ask the dramaturg questions. In turn, they provide further resources to bring the world of the play to life for the actors and audience members. The dramaturg is not merely a source of information but a guide for the production team as they construct the world of the play. Dramaturgy for me is an act of curation and public history. I curated sets for a play and a musical at Georgia College: Dominique Morrisseau's *Detroit '67* (another story of the Great Migration) directed by Dr. Amy Pinney, and Regina Taylor's *Crowns* (a story of migrating from North to South) codirected by Dr. Amy Pinney and Valeka J. Holt. Both of these productions had set design elements and production team resources to support the director's overall vision and provide a thought partner for historical accuracy experimentation and imagination. These were key elements learned from years working at a historic house museum giving visitors a clear experience of place and time.

Morriesseau's *Detroit '67* dramaturgical process was a challenge as it is set during the 1967 Detroit rebellion, which had many layers and was slowly unpacked for the cast and production team six hours weekly during the rehearsal process. We explored the celebrity, music, and meaning of Motown and the political messages activists interpreted in songs such as "Dancing in the Street." Fashion, hair, and makeup were also discussed as Detroit was influential for American fashion and had great influence on the Black community as the home of Motown Records, the most successful Black music company to date. Bunny was the most fashion-forward character in the play, and her looks were built by student designer Haley Grannon, who received first place in costume design at the Kennedy Center America College Theatre Festival for her work on *Detriot '67*. Haley Grannon notes, "[Dramaturgy work] gave me more insight. What Deitrah presented to us gave me more images of what people wore, and connected the characters to their environments. The historical research helped me create the characters."[16]

Deep historical research helped Haley become confident in her design choices for Bunny and the rest of the characters on stage. The political causes and responses to the uprising were unpacked over three dramaturgical sessions, including an opportunity for the cast and crew to talk to Mr. Douglass R. Carter, a participant and survivor of the rebellion. Mr. Carter also came to the final production of *Detroit '67* and stated, "It was like seeing my life on stage. I felt transported back to my college days in Detroit. I knew women with long eyelashes like Bunny and I witnessed the police arrest people."

Costumes designed with historical accuracy, imagination, and meaning, tell a lot about a person—their economic class, aspirations, status as conformist or non-conformist, and their membership in a certain generation. The accuracy in re-creating these important cultural artifacts is critical for actors, audiences, and witnesses to the historic events alike. Historically accurate costumes help actors embody their character when they are fitted and rehearse in costume affecting movement differently than at rehearsals without these tools. Costumes provide another connection to place, time, and character that actors use to convey meaning to audiences. The importance of costumes and their application for living history performers, actors, and audiences was also something that connected back to my work at historic house museums as yet another example of how *Sankofa* works in my life.

Just as docents at historic house museums serve as guides for visitors, dramaturgs serve as guides for cast, production teams, and audiences so learning occurs at all levels of production just as education is the outcome in museum spaces. Dramaturgs curate the world of the play on sets, collaborating with the director and scenic design team in making sure period items and/replicas are used to immerse audiences in place and time of all skills learned working in a historic house museum. At times, set design also calls for artwork to be displayed as part of a home or a religious or business setting usually described by the playwright. Dramaturgs often consult art museums and art collections with the goal of providing accuracy for sets. In my practice, I center museum collections as resources for research on works of art. The plays *Detroit '67*, *Crowns*, and *Stick Fly* provide examples of using artwork within the world of the play.

In *Detroit '67*, Dominique Morrisseau describes five pieces of art that are in the garage of the Poindexter family. Pictures of Malcolm X, Joe Louis, and Muhammad Ali and paintings done by the main characters and their father as they were growing up, including a fist (inspired by Detroit's own Joe Louis), a little Black girl, and a velvet painting. These pieces were put together by the cast and Beate Czogolla. There was a small library of books dating to 1967, a functioning 8-track player and 45 record-player. Audiences would know that this space is a place that the family and their guests can express themselves freely while also serving as a place for empowerment in a world that does not value blackness. It is also a place of memory as the Poindexter siblings come to remember their father and his life lessons.

The basement of *Detroit '67* is central to the issues of race and economic uplift at the center of the Detroit Rebellion. Lank and Chelle Poindexter are siblings running an unlicensed bar, or blind pig, from their basement. The funds secure college tuition for Chelle's son Julius and ensure the Poindexters always have a place to stay in a city experiencing white flight and the threat of gentrification. The dream the Poindexters have is of a thriving Black community in Detroit, home of the racial barrier breaking Motown, called the "sound of young America," a slogan credited to publicist Al Abrams.[17] The basement in *Detroit '67* is as much a part of the storytelling as the costumes, the actors, and the plot. As the dramaturg, my job was to help the set designers tell the story through the temporary built environment creating shared experiences for the actors and audience members. The location of Chelle and Lank's basement is in the heart of the 12th Street and Clairmount intersection where the rebellion takes place. They have witnessed the neighborhood change over the years, experiencing returning Vietnam veterans, white flight, and more police presence and harassment. Chelle and Lank open the basement to facilitate their own dreams and provide their community with a place to enjoy life for a while. The decor reflects empowerment, aspirations, and self-expression.

Georgia College's production of *Stick Fly*, written by Lydia Diamond, was another set through which artwork helped to tell the story. *Stick Fly* is a work that centers the unravelling of the affluent LeVay family as long-held secrets are revealed and partners are brought home for the first time. As a dramaturg, I looked again at works by Romare Bearden and contemporary artwork that could represent an affluent vacation home in Martha's Vineyard. *I Wanna Be Where You Are*, contemporary work by DL Warfield, decorated the living room of the LeVay home.[18] The play's themes focus on race and wealth in the LeVay family and the problems related to both. The play connects to the life experiences of Michael Jackson, who as Scarecrow in *The Wiz* noted that success and fame is an illusion, something that could easily be an epitaph for his life. Wealth, racism, and secrets carried by the LeVay family and Taylor, a young Black biology student and fiancé of the main character, describe the impact of isolation and secrets in America. There are things the LeVays will not talk about but their environment speaks volumes.

Another curated set was Georgia College's production of Regina Taylor's *Crowns*. This play is based on Craig Marberry and Michael Cunningham's book *Crowns: Portraits of Black Women in Church Hats* and centers African survival and South Carolina Gullah-Geechee culture. The main characters are a grandmother (Mother Shaw) and her recently relocated Brooklyn, New York, granddaughter (Yolanda), who is sent south to heal from the tragic murder of her brother. This work represents the Great Migration and the phenomenon of the reverse migration of Black Americans to the Southern United States from 1970 to the present, highlighting the continuity of Black American culture. Regina Taylor writes each character as an *Orisha*, Yoruba religious deities, honored in many parts of the African diaspora. Recently, the *Orisha* have entered American popular culture through such works as Beyonce's *Lemonade* visual album (2016) and Marvel's *The Black Panther* (2018). Each *Orisha* has a signature color and a parallel narrative (human and divine narrative) that helps heal Yolanda. Each lady is also part of a group of hat queens led by Yolanda's grandmother. The hats are active historical artifacts connecting each woman to her ancestral line, African and Christian spiritual practices that have helped the women face racism, sexism, and economic strife. Through focusing on the practice of wearing church hats, *Crowns* celebrates Black women and the divine connections they have to their ancestors. Taylor writes a play that puts *Sankofa* into action, and this was the production approach in all aspects of *Crowns*. Audiences needed to experience *Sankofa* in the design of the building, the church hats, the music, dances, and language the actors were using to convey this story.

Crowns set pieces were inspired by the stained-glass art tradition in black churches, particularly the Richard Allen window (circa 1890),[19] the windows of 16th Street Baptist Church in Birmingham,[20] and the contemporary artwork of Kehinde Wiley, who depicted contemporary Black Madonna and child windows.[21] Director Valeka J. Holt was most excited about Kehinde Wiley's work as she stated it best matched her vision of what the stained-glass window of the church should look like. Scenic designer Isaac Ramsey took my research for the windows and the research on Gullah Geechee praise houses and created a contemporary window of a powerful Black woman with an African crown giving side-eye to all who enter the church.

Churches are places for self-expression, healing, organization, and social change in the Black community. Churches such as 16th Street Baptist in Montgomery, Alabama, Ebenezer Baptist Church in Atlanta, Georgia, and Mother Emmanuel AME in Charleston, South Carolina, are just a few historically Black churches that have played a civic and spiritual role in the community.[22] The design of the church in this production of *Crowns* represented the sacredness of this space particularly for Black women and girls. Our production also provided several visual circles as part of the set design, including the church hats, the *Sankofa* bird symbol spray-painted on the bricks of the church, and the blocking (positions) of the actors as they completed an adaptation of a Gullah-Geechee ring shout allowing the audience to make a physical and spiritual connection to the *Sankofa* messages in the show. The connections between the generations of characters is also another circular connection as the hat queens passed their stories to Yolanda for her and the audience to carry into the future.

Theater, like museum work, relies on visitors experiencing time using as many of the five senses as possible. Touch is often missing in these experiences in order to provide a safe environment for people and objects. The sounds audiences/visitors hear are just as important as what can be seen. Music and sound set time period, convey social and political mood, and can be written or created for the piece or in pre/post-show soundtrack. *Detroit '67* is set in the home of Motown and *Crowns* is a musical (sometimes described as a play with music) set in a Black church: music is critical to tell both stories completely. As a dramaturg, I assisted the casts and production team in interpreting the songs as well as researching the African traditions used in both genres, namely rhythms and call and response. African music traditions use call and response to create community, communicate messages, and pass songs from one generation to another. In Black American music, call and response appears in both sacred and secular songs. The music of *Crowns* used spirituals and Gospel music featuring heavy call and response. The choreographer also used call and response in the dances created for the piece, which is also seen in performances by dancers such as the Nicholas Brothers.[23] The director of Georgia College's production of *Detriot '67*, Dr. Amy Pinney, and sound designer Clay Garland decided to use original music by Black artists that had more famous covers by white artists, including "Tainted Love" and "Louis Louis" as a result of dramaturgical work. Dr. Pinney wanted to tell the story of segregation and exploitation in the music industry juxtaposed with the Motown music called for by playwright Dominique Morrisseau. Both the casts of *Crowns* and *Detroit '67* created musical playlists inspired by the history of the play and their characters to keep them energized before performances.

Dramaturgs who are public historians are detail-oriented world builders. They use many skills, including research, observation, interpretation, and empathy-building, in order to give history meaning. Public historians who wish to practice dramaturgy should look for opportunities to absorb and critique theatrical endeavors at museums, historic sites, theaters, and film viewings. Study historic house museum interpretations to learn more about building worlds, original and period collection pieces, and what makes visitors at particular sites curious. As you study and observe various museum settings, focus on favorite objects and stories that piqued your interest. Living history interpretations at museums and historic sites provide insights and observations for approaches to interpretation. Note what draws visitors at these sites. Look for moments of *Sankofa*: What connections to everyday life were made? How might that compare to current daily tasks? Note approaches living historians take to interpreting their role and making connections for visitors. Does the experience at the site change how you viewed place, time, race, class, and gender? Historical theater performances in museums and theaters should be analyzed for accuracy. Attend talk-backs and ask questions of actors and production teams. Look for what was included and what if anything was missing. Museums give orientations in a variety of methods. Theaters give audiences orientations in playbills; look for the statements from production team members. If you are in a museum, was your orientation effective? Did it make you curious? Watch historically inspired film and television and practice interpreting the historical art forms encountered in these spaces. Get involved in living history days at museums and historical sites and theatrical productions. Use every opportunity to practice historical interpretation and collaborate with others.

Theater in museums is still in its infancy; however, theatrical practices are powerful and inspirational tools for public historians and visitors alike. The practice creates shared experiences for audiences and colleagues whether as interpreters, actors, dramaturgs, public historians, visitors, or audience members. Impact is achieved when all participants connect the past to the present and engage in the work of memory and imagination. Positive social change can happen when people take time to remember and reflect on the past and the way it continues to shape the present and inform the future.

NOTES

1. National Council on Public History, "What Is Public History," accessed July 1, 2021, https://ncph.org/what-is-public-history/about-the-field/.

2. The Carter G. Woodson Center, "The Power of Sankofa: Know History," accessed July 1, 2021, https://www.berea.edu/cgwc/the-power-of-sankofa/.

3. Freeman Tilden, *Interpreting Our Heritage*, edited by R. Bruce Craig (Chapel Hill: University of North Carolina Press, 2007), 27.

4. Annette Gordon Reed, *On Juneteenth* (United Kingdom: Liveright, 2021), 71.

5. Atlanta History Center, "When You Work at a Museum," accessed July 1, 2021, https://www.atlantahistorycenter.com/blog/when-you-work-at-a-museum/.

6. International Museum Theatre Alliance, accessed July 1, 2021, http://www.imtal-us.org/.

7. Literary Managers and Dramaturgs of the Americas (LMDA), "The Role of the Dramaturg," accessed July 1, 2021, https://lmda.org/dramaturgy.

8. James Oliver Horton and Lois E. Horton, eds., *Slavery and Public History: The Tough Stuff of American Memory* (New York: New Press, 2006), 49–53.

9. Azie Mira Dungey, *Ask a Slave: The Web Series*, 2013, http://www.askaslave.com/. Comedy web series based on Dungey's experiences as a Black first-person interpreter, museum educator, and actress. Dungey is a native of the DMV area (Washington, D.C., Maryland, Virginia), which is filled with great regional theaters and museums. Dungey portrays Lizzie Mae, a fictional enslaved person on Mount Vernon.

10. Freeman Tilden, *Interpreting Our Heritage*, edited by R. Bruce Craig (Chapel Hill: University of North Carolina Press, 2007), 34–35.

11. Joshua Mark, "Ancient Egypt," *World History Encyclopedia*, accessed November 1, 2021, https://www.worldhistory.org/egypt/.

12. University of Massachusetts Boston, "The Ancient Egyptian Theatre," accessed November 1, 2021, https://www.faculty.umb.edu/gary_zabel/Courses/Phil%20281b/Philosophy%20of%20Magic/Arcana/Neoplatonism/theatre.htm.

13. National Museum of African Art, "Egungun Masquerade Dance Constume: Ekuu Egungun," accessed July 1, 2021, https://africa.si.edu/exhibits/resonance/44.html.

14. The Carter G. Woodson Center, "The Power of Sankofa: Know History," accessed July 1, 2021, https://www.berea.edu/cgwc/the-power-of-sankofa/.

15. Trayvon Martin, Michael Brown, Freddie Gray, Sandra Bland, Atatiana Jefferson, Renisha Mcbride, Tony McDade, Ahmaud Arbery, Rayshard Brooks, George Floyd, Breonna Taylor, and Briana Hamilton.

16. Georgia College, "Student Places First in National Costume Design Contest for 60s Inspired Garb," *Georgia College Arts and Sciences Newsletter*, Spring 2018, page 21, https://www.gcsu.edu/sites/files/page-assets/node-2046/attachments/spring_2018.pdf.

17. Daniel Kreps, "Al Abrams, Motown Records Pioneer, Dead at 74," *Rolling Stone*, accessed July 1, 2021, https://www.rollingstone.com/music/music-news/al-abrams-motown-records-pioneer-dead-at-74-161907/.

18. DL Warfield, "I Wanna Be Where You Are," accessed July 1, 2021, https://dlwarfield.com/.

19. U.S. History.org, "Mother Bethel AME Church," accessed July 1, 2021, https://www.ushistory.org/tour/mother-bethel5.htm.

20. National Museum of African American History and Culture, "Ten Shards," accessed July 1, 2021, https://nmaahc.si.edu/object/nmaahc_2010.71.1.1-.10, and *Birmingham Times*, "The Iconic Wales Window inside 16th Street Baptist Church," accessed July 1, 2021, https://www.birminghamtimes.com/2018/10/the-iconic-wales-window-inside-16th-street-baptist-church/.

21. Kehinde Wiley, "Stained Glass," accessed July 1, 2021, https://kehindewiley.com/works/stained-glass/. See also Brooklyn Museum, "Kehinde Wiley: A New Republic," accessed July 1, 2021, https://www.brooklynmuseum.org/opencollection/exhibitions/3312; and see also Kehinde Wiley, "Madonna and Child," https://www.alamy.com/stock-photo-stained-glass-window-entitled-madonna-and-child-2016-by-african-american-131522630.html.

Stained-glass window entitled *Sancta Maria, Mater Dei* (2016) by African American contemporary painter Kehinde Wiley displayed at his exhibition in the Petit Palais in Paris, France. The exhibition ran until January 15, 2017.

22. Jeffrey Brown and Leah Nagy, "Henry Louis Gates Jr. on His New Series 'The Black Church,'" accessed July 1, 2021, https://www.pbs.org/newshour/show/henry-louis-gates-jr-on-his-new-series-the-black-church.

23. Nicholas Brothers' performances can be found here: https://www.youtube.com/watch?v=zBb9hTyLjfM and https://www.loc.gov/item/jots.200019641.

9

STORYTELLING IN SCIENCE MUSEUMS

Rebecca Melsheimer and Jose Santamaria

Whether stated or not in the mission statement, the objective of a science museum should be to increase and enhance science literacy. For the visitor, it all boils down to learning and accepting the facts. What the facts can't do, however, is help people recall the concepts or make them care or act. Storytelling helps address these difficulties. As facts wrapped in emotions, stories have been used to share knowledge and to make meaning since the earliest days of humankind.[1] While emotions may seem at odds with facts, they are necessary for understanding.

The value of storytelling to science communication and education in the museum world is in contextualizing objects and information to explain the world around us. Ultimately, we are attempting to build connections between the person and the natural world and to generate excitement about the science.[2] Neuroscience research has shown that vivid language and rich narrative activate multiple regions in the brain, increasing engagement and recall of facts.[3] This holds true regardless of the listener's or reader's level of knowledge or basic interest in a particular topic.[4] So, how can all this be applied in a science museum, especially when relying on text rather than direct communication?

While no longer a display of objects that were properly classified but without interpretation, as in museums of old,[5] today's science museums still largely rely on the objects in their collections.[6] At Tellus Science Museum, a good exhibit moves beyond display and simple identification of objects and engages the visitor by integrating the object with its story in the reader panel. Although stories are naturally incorporated in our public programming and workshops, we still must provide the same opportunities of understanding for those unable to participate in these additional activities. For us, the reader panels and graphics are the key way we spark the visitors' interest in learning more once they leave while providing the context for interpretation.

Science museums, with their preponderance of interesting objects, have it both easy and hard. It's easy to wow visitors—young or old—with large dinosaurs, sparkly crystals, aircraft, rockets, engines, and even unknown contraptions that spark the imagination. The hard part is conveying to visitors the significance of an object and why they should care about it. Doing this in two hundred words or less, that's the challenge of storytelling in science museums.

KEEP IT TO THE POINT

Even though we want to tell a story to encourage engagement, we still need to present the correct information to our visitors of all ages without overwhelming them. Our guiding principle here at Tellus for our reader panels is "*less is more*," to quote architect Mies van der Rohe. While it may seem that *less* is *less* in this situation—how can something complex be simplified without losing important information—our experience is that *more* will not be read. Then the challenge begins in determining how much information is enough and how to deliver it in an impactful manner. While it is tempting to bring in too much background material, keep in mind how much a visitor can digest in a museum setting. The visitor may tune out because of information overload, and there are so many interesting things to see and experience in a museum that visitors may be easily distracted or limited on time.

Forcing yourself to limit wordiness encourages you to focus on what you really want the visitor to know when they walk away. In this case, every word counts in providing meaning and understanding for the object. Also remember that people are more likely to retain ideas, not facts.

Another consideration is the judicious use of graphics. These may be more effective than words in conveying stories and the meaning of the objects in front of the visitor. For example, a paleontology exhibition should introduce the vastness of geologic time. But how? Instead of words, how about a timeline? Better yet, a yardstick, 46 inches long, with each inch representing 100 million years. The length totals 4.6 billion years, the currently accepted age of Earth (give or take about 50 million years).[7] Add illustrations at the proper intervals, a few descriptive phrases, and the visitor can see the story of life on our planet at a glance, as shown in figure 9.1.

REMEMBER THAT SCIENCE IS DONE BY PEOPLE

Humanizing the endeavor is an important aspect of storytelling in science. In many of our exhibits, we weave people into the interpretation of scientific objects. For example, the story of the geologist who discovered the only known footprint of a *Tyrannosaurus rex*, the story of the Civil War veteran who founded one of the first electric car companies in 1897, and the story of the Wright Brothers and their methodical efforts to achieve the first manned and controlled powered flight in 1903 show the people behind scientific and technological advancements.

Including the narratives of scientific discovery itself is important to help visitors understand that the people who work in science are not emotionless robots who work in perfect precision. Scientists are motivated by their curiosity about the world around them. The focus on how scientists achieve their work also provides a natural storytelling framework while demonstrating that science is ever-changing.[8] In the museum, we can present the changing science while contextualizing how science is done. In fact, one of our most impressive objects in the museum provided us an opportunity to apply this concept.

A sauropod skeleton holds pride of place in Tellus's Macke Great Hall, and it immediately attracts "oohs" and "aahs" from children as they walk toward other galleries. When the museum opened, it was exhibited as an *Apatosaurus*. However, new research in 2015 determined that it should be classified as a *Brontosaurus*,[9] resurrecting a name that had been discredited for decades but that mainstream media popularized to generations of young dinosaur enthusiasts.[10] In the updated panel, we presented the story of why *Brontosaurus* was once, then it was not, and is now again, giving both a memorable story to the saga and a perspective on how science is revised as new data become available.

We have also taken this human-centered approach to storytelling in our temporary exhibitions. In the spring of 2020, Tellus opened a temporary exhibition of some of the highest-quality mineral specimens ever shown at the museum. They were on loan from a couple who had been collecting minerals for only

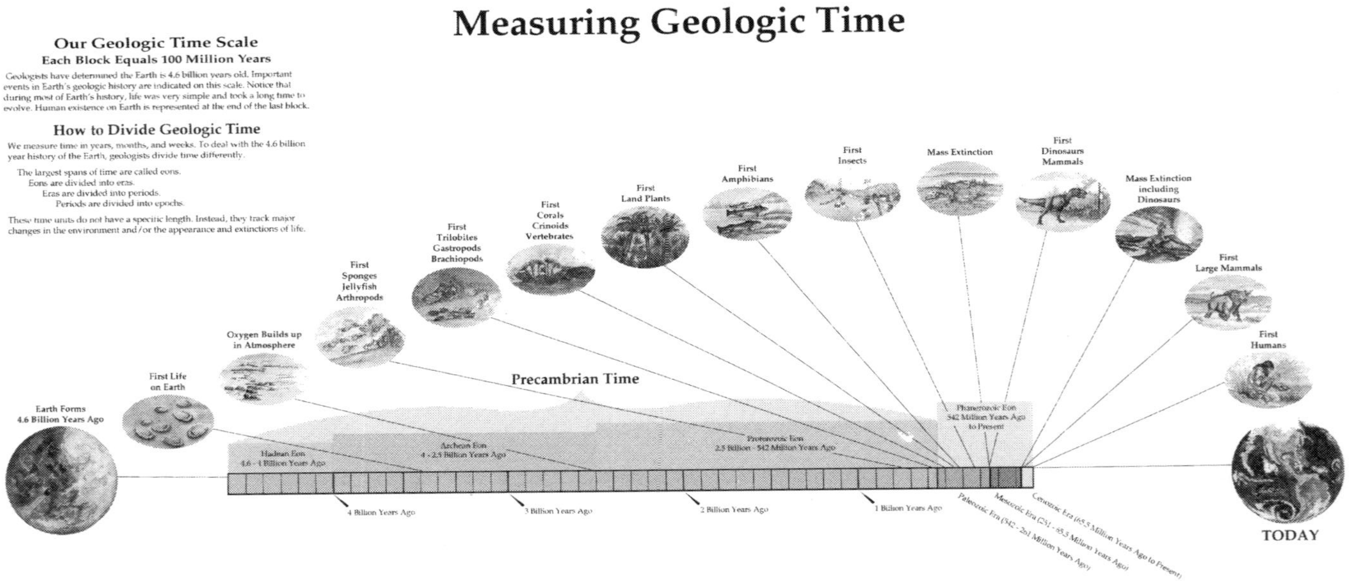

Measuring Geologic Time
Our Geologic Time Scale
Each Block Equals 100 Million Years
Geologists have determined the Earth is 4.6 billion years old. Important events in Earth's geologic history are indicated on this scale. Notice that during most of Earth's history, life was very simple and took a long time to evolve. Human existence on Earth is represented at the end of the last block.
How to Divide Geologic Time
We measure time in years, months, and weeks. To deal with the 4.6 billion year history of the Earth, geologists divide time differently.
The largest spans of time are called eons.
Eons are divided into eras.
Eras are divided into periods.
Periods are divided into epochs.
These time units do not have a specific length. Instead, they track major changes in the environment and/or the appearance and extinctions of life.
Earth Forms 4.6 Billion Years Ago
First Life on Earth
Oxygen Builds up in Atmosphere
First Sponges Jellyfish Arthropods
First Trilobites Gastropods Brachiopods
First Corals Crinoids Vertebrates
First Land Plants
First Amphibians
First Insects
Mass Extinction
First Dinosaurs Mammals
Mass Extinction including Dinosaurs
First Large Mammals
First Humans
TODAY
Precambrian Time
Hadean Eon 4.6 - 4 Billion Years Ago
Archean Eon 4 - 2.5 Billion Years Ago
Proterozoic Eon 2.5 Billion - 542 Million Years Ago
Phanerozoic Eon 542 Million Years Ago to Present
4 Billion Years Ago
3 Billion Years Ago
2 Billion Years Ago
1 Billion Years Ago
Paleozoic Era (542 - 251 Million Years Ago)
Mesozoic Era (251 - 65.5 Million Years Ago)
Cenozoic Era (65.5 Million Years Ago to Present)

Figure 9.1. The geologic time scale as it appears in the Fossil Gallery. Courtesy of the Tellus Science Museum.

fourteen years. As we got to know them, their story became as fascinating as the minerals and became the framework for the exhibit.

It was a story of how they became mineral collectors, how they love to share their passion, and how important education is to them. The narrative followed some of their early acquisitions, their individual tastes and preferences, and even their sense of humor in collecting. The basic principles of mineralogy and mineral collecting were included within this framework, making the "sciencey" part of the exhibit approachable. Emphasizing the connections between the visitors and the couple featured in the exhibit elicited an emotional response from our guests. This encouraged visitors to look into mineralogy and collecting once they left the museum, supporting both our educational goals and those of the lenders. To direct further learning, the text within the exhibit provided places to look for additional information and ways to participate in mineral collecting within the local community. Because of this exhibit, several families pursued their children's interest in minerals and collecting by interacting with Tellus staff, who provided a handout with information they could take home.

MAKE IT LOCAL AND PERSONAL

There is a perception that science is something done far away by people who are locked apart from daily life in an ivory tower. Many people haven't met an actual scientist, and they don't see science and its processes as a part of their everyday experiences.[11] Bringing science and scientific discoveries into the community is a way for scientists to encourage interest and create personal connections.

A good example of community interest and personal connections is our temporary exhibit on the dimension (building) stone industry in Georgia. Interweaving the history of the area with advancements in quarrying technology provided context for how influential and important marble from Tate and granite from both Stone Mountain and Elberton were throughout the United States. The exhibit offered differing perspectives on both the micro and macro scales. Another advantage to this approach in particular is that it helped the museum forge relationships with community members, industry representatives, archivists, and historical society members who provided stories and objects to enrich the fabric of the exhibit.

In using these personal stories within an exhibit, we also must not forget that an equally important part of storytelling is beyond what we "tell" the visitors. Despite science being viewed as something out of reach and divided from daily life, part of what "other" people do, it plays an integral part in how we interact with our environment and with each other. One only has to look at the changes wrought by the smartphone to see how much. For our temporary exhibit about the technology found in your smartphone, we encouraged staff and visitors to share their personal experiences with their families or other visitors.

An introductory graphic of a word cloud was created by asking staff and volunteers what they used the smartphone for. The more often a use was cited, the larger the text for that use. This generated a more accurate representation of what smartphones might mean to our visitors than just listing the many possible uses of them. In fact, we were surprised that making phone calls wasn't the most common. The most cited uses were for directions and as a camera. Using this as a base, the exhibit drew links between the technologies of yesteryear to that of today while still providing an opportunity for visitors to share their own experiences with using "old" phones, gaming systems, or even record players.[12] Moreover, a few of the cases did not have object labels, prompting discussion among visitors about what that object might be or what it was used for. Through sharing their stories, visitors were creating their own meaning and contextualizing the place technology holds in society, while being guided by the overarching theme we developed within the exhibit.

For our *Periodic Table* exhibit, rather than going into detail about chemistry as the building blocks of what we can see and touch (and some that we can't), the museum took a different approach. A physical periodic table was created with most elements displayed and represented by something they are used for. While it may not seem like an "interactive" exhibit, we have documented that it has higher engagement for our visitors than some of those that are specifically designed to be interactive.[13] The visually engaging presentation of information provides parents the opportunity to interact with their children about the elements by relating it to daily life, even when they may not have extensive background knowledge of the topic themselves.

CHECK FOR UNDERSTANDING

A word of caution should be considered here. Regardless of how well we think the text is written, how understandable the graphics seem, and how well-laid the ancillary elements of an exhibit are, it is important for an exhibition to be understood by the audience. Who is best equipped to help determine this? Not the curator, nor the exhibit designer, nor the executive director. No, it's the average Joes and Janes on our staff.

The input from these staff members who are totally unfamiliar with the subject is absolutely crucial for us. As the number of words in a reader panel shrinks, the content still remains complex. It is easy to assume we are successfully conveying a clearly understood story. What is easy to miss is what is actually being said. So many things can slip by "we who know so much" that seem obvious once they are pointed out by our "Joes and Janes." More important—if they do not understand it, the general public will not either.

A good illustration of this is in our attempts to describe the importance of the meteorite that crashed into the town of Barwell in Leicester, England, in 1965 that was on display in one of our temporary exhibits. It completely changed scientists' ideas of how meteoroids and asteroids formed. Despite it seeming self-explanatory to us in writing the text that this discovery was very important, it took several rounds of review and edits from staff before we could be sure that the average visitor would understand why and how. In this case, we started with this:

> The Barwell meteorite changed the way scientists thought about how meteoroids formed. Locked within its chondrite structure is melted material. At the time, scientists thought that any melting only occurred after the early material coalesced to form stony meteorites. The melted material within the unmelted material showed a complicated process of meteoroid and asteroid formation, opening new avenues for research.

And ended up with this:

> The Barwell meteorite had an impact on not just the town, but on science itself. Before Barwell, scientists thought that the formation of a meteoroid was simple: after an asteroid formed, it was broken apart into smaller fragments. The Barwell meteorite was different. Locked within its structure were fragments of another asteroid. Called "pebbles," these showed that pieces of broken asteroids could be cemented together with space debris into new meteoroids early in the formation of the Solar System.

The final version is a bit longer, yes, but it doesn't assume that people already know what a chondrite is, how scientists thought meteoroids and asteroids formed, or what they think now. Without staff feedback, we would have missed out on another opportunity to educate our visitors.

PUTTING IT ALL TOGETHER

We have used each of these techniques—limiting text, humanizing the process, and creating local connections—to provide different entry points into the same scientific topic. Using multiple approaches gives us a better opportunity to spark curiosity and learning and reach different types of audiences.

As a demonstration of this, consider our presentation of meteorites throughout the museum. Meteorites have much to tell us as they are valuable sources of information about the early Solar System. However, the science of meteorites can be dense and hard to understand, and meteorites may seem unimportant to the average visitor.

Starting with the Cartersville meteorite—a rock from space that hit a house just a few miles from the museum—is a good way to build an emotional connection. The story?

> On March 9, 2010, this meteorite hit a house seven miles from the museum. It went through the roof, deflected off a joist, crashed through the ceiling, bounced off a door, and landed on the carpet.

There was no need to begin with the history of the Solar System. In telling the story of the meteorite, the active verbs almost make you feel a part of the action as it flew through the house. This draws in the visitor and encourages them to explore the other exhibits within the gallery that focus on the science of meteorites. Additionally, the personal connection helps people understand the relevance of studying meteorites, since you never know when one might hit close to home.

Further in the gallery are more meteorites from Georgia and beyond with more information about their science. Keeping the text short and to the point provides enough context for what the Cartersville meteorite is while not overwhelming the visitors with too much detail. For example:

> A meteorite is a rock from space. Most originate from the Asteroid Belt, a swarm of rocky bodies orbiting the sun between Mars and Jupiter. When large, they are called *asteroids*; when small, *meteoroids*. When one gets knocked off course and collides with Earth's atmosphere, friction causes a streak of light called a *meteor*. If it survives and lands, it is called a *meteorite*.

In sixty-four words, we described a subject about which volumes are written.

A larger temporary exhibit focused on other meteorites that had hit things. These stories are inherently dramatic: Rocks travelling from millions of miles away come hurtling to Earth, occasionally hitting objects, animals, and (rarely!) even people. Within this exhibit, the stories were presented as front-page "news" with catchy headlines. Woven within the structure of each of these stories was information about the science of meteorites and how that information is gained. Instead of dense explanations, we broke up the scientific facts with more engaging narrative, making the information easily accessible and less intimidating.

WHAT WE REALLY WANT YOU TO KNOW

In keeping with our own guidelines, what do we really want you to take away from this chapter (and can we do it in two hundred words or less)?

Storytelling should be an important part of science education and communication, and there is no place better to practice this than in a museum. We have the privilege of sharing with the general public the knowledge and objects from the earliest days of Earth to today and the responsibility to ensure that they come away with a good understanding of how all this came to be. This can be accomplished by focusing on the object, using clear and concise wording and graphics, checking for understanding, and weaving in the human and personal into the story. Storytelling allows us to build upon the sense of wonder created by these objects (a beautiful mineral or a massive dinosaur) to form an emotional connection between the visitor and science. Ultimately, we want to inspire them to continue learning even after they leave the museum.

NOTES

1. David A. Kirby, *Lab Coats in Hollywood: Science, Scientists, and Cinema* (Cambridge, MA: MIT Press, 2015), 97–103.
2. Stephanie J. Green, Kirsten Grorud-Colvert, and Heather Mannix, "Uniting Science and Stories: Perspectives on the Value of Storytelling for Communicating Science," *Facets* 3 (2018): 164–73, doi.org/10.1139/facets-2016-0079.
3. Sara J. ElShafie, "Making Science Meaningful for Broad Audiences through Stories," *Integrative and Comparative Biology* 58, no. 6 (2018): 1213–23, doi.org/10.1093/icb/icy103.
4. Arthur C. Graesser, Brent Olde, and Bianca Klettke, "How Does the Mind Construct and Represent Stories?" in *Narrative Impact: Social Cognitive Foundations*, ed. Melanie C. Green, Jeffrey J. Strange, and Timothy C. Brock (Mahwah, NJ: L. Erlebaum Associates, 2002), 229–62.

5. Bernard Schiele, "Science Museums and Science Centres," in *Handbook of Public Communication of Science and Technology*, ed. Massimiano Bucchi and Brian Trench (New York: Routledge, 2008), 27–39.

6. This is in contrast to science centers, which often focus on interactive experiences and have few collection objects. For further discussion, see: Edward P. Alexander, Mary Alexander, and Juilee Decker, *Museums in Motion: An Introduction to the History and Functions of Museums* (third edition) (Lanham, MD: Rowman and Littlefield, 2017), 23–27.

7. For further discussion of how the age of the Earth is determined, see: G. Brent Dalrymple, "The Age of the Earth in the Twentieth Century: A Problem (Mostly) Solved," in *The Age of the Earth: From 4004 BC to AD 2002*, ed. C. L. E. Lewis and S. J. Knell (London: Geological Society of London, 2001), 205–21.

8. Randy Olson, *Houston, We Have a Narrative: Why Science Needs Story* (Chicago, IL: University of Chicago Press, 2015), 33–52.

9. Emmanuel Tschopp, Octavio Mateus, and Roger B. J. Benson, "A Specimen-Level Phylogenetic Analysis and Taxonomic Revision of Diplodocidae (Dinosauria, Sauropodia)," *PeerJ* 3 (2015): e857, doi.org/10.7717/peerj.857.

10. For a general discussion of the earlier shift from *Brontosaurus* to *Apatosaurus*, see: Brian Switek, *My Beloved Brontosaurus: On the Road with Old Bones, New Science, and Our Favorite Dinosaurs* (New York: Farrar, Straus and Giroux, 2013).

11. Sarah L. Sheffield et al., "Perceptions of Scientists Held by U.S. Students Can Be Broadened Through Inclusive Classroom Interventions," *Communications Earth & Environment* 2:83 (2021), doi.org/10.1038/s43247-021-00156-0.

12. Particularly popular was the working rotary phone in the exhibit. Parents and grandparents needed to show children how to make a call using the finger wheel, creating an opportunity for intergenerational communication.

13. Camille Pace, email message, July 17, 2013.

10

MUSEUMS IN YOUR POCKET

Digital Storytelling Strategies in Cultural Institutions

Lois E. Carlisle

The world is in your pocket. One Wikipedia rabbit hole can tell us more about recorded human history than one museum could possibly place in an exhibition hall. With a growing shift toward distance learning and digital storytelling brought about by the ongoing COVID-19 pandemic, it is more important than ever for museums to allocate substantial time and resources to expand their digital presence.

Two 2019 studies by the American Alliance of Museums' Center for the Future of Museums and Impacts concluded that Americans trust museums more than they trust federal agencies, nongovernmental organizations, and news outlets.[1] This is likely because the general public believes that museums present raw data—not interpreted material.[2] As with all narratives being presented in museum spaces, the words of an exhibition are seen as gospel truth. Even if this public trust may be based on a false sense among museumgoers that museum content lacks interpretation, museums have a unique opportunity to create trusted digital spaces for communal learning and growth. By creating dynamic digital spaces and implementing one-to-one storytelling strategies, museums can successfully foster the same audience trust online as they do in their physical spaces.

My work as content coordinator and digital storytelling strategist on the Marketing and Brand Experience team at Atlanta History Center gave me insight into the need for serious, meaningful investment of organizational time and resources into the creation and maintenance of digital spaces. Atlanta History Center began as a small, archival-focused historical society in 1926. Since then, it has grown to encompass thirty-three acres of curated gardens, including four historic houses and a working farm stocked with heritage breed animals. The History Center's programming is varied and ranges in everything from author talks, birdwatching walks, children's story time, and late-night events for young (and young-at-heart) professionals. Within the Atlanta History Museum itself are a range of signature exhibitions that tell the many stories of Atlanta and her citizens. The History Center's mission—to connect people, history, and culture—is stewarded by a commitment to serving members of our community wherever they are, including the internet. Finding ways to successfully market our programs to their vastly different target audiences proved to be a significant challenge to which our small team rose by embracing a wholistic digital marketing strategy.

CANDY, VITAMINS, AND PAINKILLERS: DIGITAL STRATEGY IN A PRE-COVID WORLD

In 2018, Atlanta History Center began to shift away from traditional forms of marketing (print ads, billboards, bench and bus wraps) and toward digital content marketing. Content marketing, unlike traditional marketing, positions a business as a source of knowledge. The goal of our Marketing and Brand Experience Department (comprising a director of design, a director of social media and marketing, marketing coordinator, and graphic designer) was to craft an institutional reputation for being a trusted source for all things Atlanta—from OutKast to the '96 Olympics and all of the weird and wonderful things in between. For the purposes of this case study, traditional marketing can be defined as frontloading logistical information to customers; content marketing uses storytelling to position an institution as a source of accessible, invaluable knowledge.

Based on consumer research conducted by students at the Goizueta Business School at Emory University at the behest of our Marketing Department, Atlanta History Center determined a need to grow our marketing team. Research showed that the two target audiences we wanted to reach—young, "busy bee" families and millennials—engaged primarily with similar local cultural institutions digitally, specifically on social media. Our existing traditional marketing strategy wasn't reaching these audiences "where they lived," so to speak. Instead, we relied on newspapers, magazines, and other regional tourism-focused publications to promote our general offerings. In order to foster a greater sense of being *Atlanta's* history center, the decision was made to pivot entirely away from print and physical advertising, opting instead to meet busy-bee families and millennials in the digital world.[3]

I was hired as the History Center's first full-time marketing coordinator in 2019. Mine was an entirely new role, responsible for creation and maintenance of a compelling social media and blog presence. Marketing with storytelling drives new traffic and is like a cross between journalism and advertising for the services of the institution. This is a unique opportunity for museums, because what they're "selling" is the opportunity for deep learning and meaningful connections.

In order to get the most mileage out of our social media accounts, we modeled our content strategy after an adapted version of Kevin Fong's Candy, Vitamins, and Painkillers Model.[4] In Fong's original model, each of the three correspond to different business types. For our purposes, each individual social media post could be qualified as a Candy, a Vitamin, or a Painkiller.

- Posts that make us smile with distraction, relief, and recognition are *Candy*
- Posts that try to educate holistically in order to promote institutional values are *Vitamins*
- Posts that disrupt popular thought, innovate, or ask uncomfortable questions are *Painkillers*

As it is with their culinary counterparts, no person can survive on one category alone. Too much candy rots your teeth; too many painkillers make audiences numb to your mission. To avoid burnout, our team dwelled primarily in the realm of Candy and Vitamins, doling out Painkillers sparingly. We did this for two reasons: the first was that too many potentially uncomfortable or controversial posts can cause audiences to ignore your posts—sites like Instagram and Twitter are designed for microblogging. Monolithic text in an Instagram caption can turn readers off. Second, we needed to build trust while growing our audience. One of our department's directives was not to alienate an existing audience, but also not to pull punches related to difficult history. To that end, our Candy and Vitamins acted as thematic bread crumbs, leading readers down the path toward an eventual Painkiller.

Here's an example: We wanted to promote the opening of our *Women's Suffrage* exhibition. A traditional marketing approach on social media might look something like this:

> *Traditional Marketing*: [Paired with an image of the gallery space, empty of people]
>
> Atlanta History Center invites you to explore our newest exhibition, *Any Great Change: The Centennial of the 19th Amendment*, on the third floor of Swan House. Opening March 18.

Marketing without storytelling is hollow and relies on preexisting relationships with visitors. Where is Swan House? What can I expect from an exhibition? Why should I go to your exhibition when I can go see a screening of *Suffragette* at a local theater?

Driven by curiosity and storytelling, our content marketing posts looked like this:

> *Candy*: [Paired with an image of a *Votes for Women* sash hung around the shoulders of a beautifully dressed mannequin] Drop a [ballot box emoji] in the comments if you're a registered voter.
>
> *Vitamin*: [Accompanied by a graphic of a poster from the exhibition reading "A Woman Living Here Has Registered to Vote!"] Raise your hand if you're registered to vote. [Raised-hand emoji] What does it mean to be an active citizen? *Votes for Women*, for one thing. Our new exhibit, *Any Great Change*, explores that question through the lens of women's suffrage. Tell us how you participate in your local government!
>
> *Painkiller*: [Accompanied by an image of suffragist Mary Heart Tyrell] [Ballot box emoji] On this day in 1919, Congress approved the women's suffrage amendment by joint resolution, granting women the right to vote.
>
> [Ballot box emoji] While monumental, the passage of the 19th Amendment did not mean all women could cast ballots. White women were the primary beneficiaries as most African American women still could not vote, nor could Native American or Chinese women. Jim Crow laws created barriers in southern states for African American women, and Native American and Chinese women were not granted citizenship until 1924 and 1945, respectively.

[Ballot box emoji] Learn more about how women gained the right to vote and the ways they have used political power over the last century by checking out our exhibition, *Any Great Change: The Centennial of the 19th Amendment.* Link in our bio!

By utilizing a 40 percent Candy, 50 percent Vitamin, 10 percent Painkiller ratio, we were able to build trust with our audience and get them to engage with difficult topics. During the first year of this strategy's implementation, we saw total engagements increase (likes, comments, re-shares, etc.) across all platforms (Twitter, Instagram, and Facebook) by just under 60 percent. Toward the end of the first year, our readership demographics trended towards the 25–34 and 35–44 age ranges (whereas before it stood solidly in the 55–64 range).[5] It was highly encouraging evidence that our digital content marketing strategy was effective.

As we worked to build out our social media presence, we also homed in on the marketing identity of Atlanta History Center's blog. Our early blog posts were Candy-adjacent and SEO-friendly (meaning they could be crawled easily by a search engine)—"5 Things to Know about the Battle of Atlanta Cyclorama," "Atlanta's Best History Tours," "Historic Southern Holiday Traditions." As our audience grew, so did our stories. Each blog post aligned with the Candy-Vitamin-Painkiller model and could easily be linked to any of our social media posts. Being able to drive individual users from your social pages back to your own website is a crucial part in the conversion of a potential visitor to patron.

INDIVIDUAL STORIES AND COVID-19

Our marketing team (now comprised of a full-time vice president of marketing and brand experience, project manager, content coordinator, designer, and freelance copyeditor) was in the process of further growing our virtual footprint when the COVID-19 pandemic hit. With our thirty-three-acre campus shuttered in the interest of public safety, our team (from our home offices, kitchen counters, and childhood bedrooms) began to reimagine our digital strategy. After a year of building ourselves as a trusted source of historical data, we needed to find a way to both educate and entertain visitors—at a distance.

Across the globe, museums were offering virtual reality walkthroughs of their galleries. From my two-bedroom apartment, I could wander the halls of the Louvre while the world stood still outside. But after a few weeks, the novelty of just pacing the virtual halls of premier cultural institutions began to fade. If simply seeing the sights wasn't enough, what was?

Our team began to construct what our ideal "pocket museums" would look like. If we were to each pull out our phones and arrive at the digital front doors of Atlanta History Center, what would we want to see? What did our guests want to see? So, we asked them. On social, via email newsletter, and young professional networks: How can we be of use to you?

What our Atlanta wanted was a museum that responded in real time. People were curious to know about the history of epidemics in the Unites States, why the CDC (which is headquartered in Atlanta) was founded, and how leaders from across our city's history made brave and often difficult choices in the face of extreme adversity. Those were the stories we told. Our story on the 1918 flu epidemic's impact on Atlanta was picked up and shared by the local news station, as well as popular magazine *The Bitter Southerner*.[6] It also appeared on the local news in a segment which directed Atlantans back to our museum's digitized archives for socially distant exploration. It became the most-viewed story we'd ever shared.

In the early days of the pandemic, it became clear that our website lacked the capabilities needed to tell the stories our institution wanted to tell. At best, we were a digital bulletin board: able to provide hyperlinked lists to resources, oral histories, and our live sheep cam. People weren't interested in visiting our site because they didn't see their own experiences represented therein.

To that end, the Marketing and Brand Experience team at Atlanta History Center—in partnership with If/Then Studio—redesigned the center's website to more accurately reflect the diverse offerings and community services the institution offers. We divided the site into two parts: *Visit* and *Virtual*. Visitors to our homepage can toggle between one or the other in order to see the most relevant information to them.

> *Visit* comprised what you might expect to see on a traditional museum website: frontloading information for purchasing tickets, navigating campus, public health protocols, and renewing memberships. It clearly delineated our on-site offerings (including group tours, programs and events, rental opportunities, and more).
>
> *Virtual* was where the site came to life. A bespoke digital platform allowed us to both expand upon on-site exhibitions with attritional material and to launch novel online-only exhibitions.

The more guests clicked through the *Visit* portion of the site, the more they would be pushed toward *Virtual*. If they wanted to learn more about the programs and events offerings on the *Visit* side of the website, we offered links to long-form stories, digital exhibitions, and virtual programming at the bottom of each page. The notion was to create an endless "curiosity loop" of interrelated content that fed into visitors' interests and kept them on the site for as long as possible.

Respondents to our original question, How can we be of use to you? also expressed a desire to share their stories and objects with the museum so that their pandemic stories could be shared with future generations. The active collection of contemporary stories in order to capture history as it happens is an invaluable tool in the arsenal of storytelling. Often to museum guests, the distance between events of the past—History with a capital H—and current events is immeasurable. By prioritizing the collection of contemporary stories, objects, images, and other mission-aligned resources, museums can begin to foster a healthy relationship between the shared histories of their constituencies. By offering guests a direct connection to museums, we help to alleviate the stereotype of stuffy, academic spaces. When museums work to pair historic objects, stories, and themes with current events, they have the power to bridge an otherwise impassable gap for the public. Humanizing history by holding it against the backdrop of contemporary events is the most powerful tool a museum can wield to foster empathy because it allows guests to see themselves as part of a larger timeline that began before they were born and will extend far into the future.

The project: Operating under our CEO's favorite axiom of "what is common shall become uncommon," Atlanta History Center set out to capture all elements of life in Atlanta during the COVID-19 pandemic. The Atlanta Corona Collective (ACC), which began following the nationwide shutdown in March 2020, seeks to use only personal narrative to tell the story of all elements of life during the COVID-19 pandemic. ACC brings community members' narratives to the fore so that they can see how their everyday choices make history.

The toolkit: To effectively capture, archive, and interpret community stories, the Marketing and Brand Experience team created a three-pronged digital framework: create a bespoke digital exhibitions platform, generate compelling long-form content, and tell individuals' stories on social media. All three of these initiatives pushed viewers back to our site.

In order to explore individual stories, we launched a long-form storytelling platform (which replaced our existing blog) on which we could unpack complex historical ideas and connect them to current events. This platform, called Stories, gave us the space to take individual stories submitted to us from the ACC initiative and explore them in a historical context.

Following the murders of George Floyd and Rayshard Brooks,[7] Atlanta Corona Collective began receiving stories from protesters who put their lives on the line—in more ways than one—to march for equality during the global pandemic. Atlanta History Center received hundreds of images, stories, and recordings of protesters, including a video of protesters marching in front of the Margaret Mitchell House, a historic house museum owned and operated by the History Center in Midtown Atlanta. Because the institution was already primed and ready to collect rapidly the stories of COVID-era life in Atlanta, it was a straightforward process to pivot and begin bringing in stories related to Black Lives Matter protests. The Collections Department independently commissioned photographers to capture the experience of Atlantans as they went about their daily lives during this difficult period—standing in line to vote, attending Black Lives Matter protests, and attending socially distanced events. Because of the nimbleness of our collections team, our marketing team could seamlessly incorporate contemporary images into digital storytelling initiatives.

Our Stories platform provided space for material that was thematically linked to current events and current digital/physical offerings. On the heels of the 1918 influenza story, we published a history of the CDC and its relationship to Atlanta, which allowed us to explore tensions between local and federal public health officials. It also allowed us to place Atlanta in the larger timeline of public health initiatives in the United States. Following the announcement of the two runoff elections for both of Georgia's senate seats, we were able to share stories of local student protests in 2020 in the context of the Atlanta Student Movement of the 1960s. Being able to have a digital space where we could display long-form text, audio recordings of protest songs, and beautiful full-screen images alongside pull quotes made for another impactful story. Through both of these stories, and the ongoing social media push back to the website, the Marketing and Brand Experience team continued to drive people back to Atlanta Corona Collective with each story, creating an infinite loop of learning.

Our partners at IfThen designed a custom digital exhibitions platform which allowed the website to become a central venue for Atlanta History Center to collect, create, organize, and immersively display its content. The platform allowed the organization to communicate a broader understanding of our shared and complex history and foundationally serve as a public resource while supplementing and expanding on-site activities with rich digital content that adds perspective and evokes curiosity.[8]

After the initial construction costs, the bespoke exhibitions platform allowed us to create new exhibitions at little expense. Online exhibitions don't require the same production budget as physical exhibitions; panels and wall labels don't need to be printed, display cases don't need to be used, and objects can be photographed and returned to storage, limiting their exposure to potentially harmful long-term display. A digital exhibition also has the benefit of being available twenty-four hours a day, without needing to be monitored or attended by staff.

Museums don't need a major budget to do this. Platforms like Google Arts & Culture provide free ways for institutions (no matter their size) to digitize exhibitions and share collections highlights online.[9]

The Atlanta Corona Collective was able to flourish on this new site. The Marketing and Brand Experience team established a webform and forged a partnership with the popular personal narrative organization StoryCorps, whose Atlanta headquarters are at Atlanta History Center.[10] The online submission form's design intentionally captured not just the collections data necessary for processing an item, but the personal, first-person story that went alongside it. If Atlantans wanted to submit a story without an artifact, image, or recording to accompany it, they could. In its early days, the initiative captured stories about socially distant ninetieth birthday parties, running kindergartens from kitchen tables, and essential workers.

The partnership with StoryCorps also allowed Atlanta History Center to capture meaningful, substantive conversations between family members, community leaders, and even the museum's own staff. To do this, a hashtag in the new StoryCorps Connect app was launched and shared a common questionnaire for participants to use in order to ensure consistency across interviews. Facilitated conversations by StoryCorps allowed for a level of comfort to be attained that may not have been possible for a professional oral historian to reach if attempting to document the COVID-19 pandemic's impact on the lives of Atlantans in 2020 and 2021.

MUSEUMS DO DIGITAL DIFFERENTLY

As institutions, museums and historical societies have the unique capability to bring together objects, authentic stories, dialogue, experience, and reflection—both in person and online. As a species, humans are hardwired to connect with one another. Empathy is a shared human value.[11] Museums can generate transformative experiences through the cultivation of historical thinking, overcoming ethnocentric narratives, promoting multiple perspectives, and fostering empathy.[12]

By tapping into the power of first-person storytelling in digital spaces, museums can inspire empathy by connecting with visitors' personal experiences and inspire action influenced by those experiences. In the words of Emlyn Koster, "Sometimes a place that relives distressing stories can also convey great joy when remarkable perseverance and courage triumphs over seemingly insurmountable adversity. Empathy, after all, exists across a wide spectrum of deeply absorbed feelings."[13] Autobiographical, first-person accounts don't just include stories *about* individuals, but stories *told by the individuals themselves*. While each historical figure is distinct—just as every museum guest is distinct—cross-generational shared human experiences create connectedness and enhance empathy: We have, all of us, experienced fear, joy, wonder, and loss in some form or another.

As we continue to collect stories of the pandemic and its impact on Atlanta's many communities, We do so with the knowledge that we are not preserving objects, but memories for future generations to study. At the time of writing, Atlanta Corona Collective remains an ongoing project. The goal is for future generations to have personal connections to those of us who experienced firsthand the COVID-19 pandemic in Atlanta. This is what we're doing today, actively and intentionally, to allow future generations to have those engaging experiences that build connection and empathy, and to allow them to understand—on a granular and emotional level—history as we make it.

In order to better interpret history as it happens and maintain their status as vital community resources, museums must learn to implement comprehensive digital storytelling strategies. By empowering staff and drawing on deep wells of knowledge and experience both across departments and within communities, this can be done effectively and sustainably.

NOTES

1. IMPACTS Experience, National Awareness, Attitudes, and Usage Study.
2. John Dichtl, president and CEO of the American Association of State and Local History (AASLH), speaks further about this public (mis)conception in his article *Most Trust Museums as Sources of Historical Information* on the AASLH blog.
3. Marketing for events spaces offered by the museum remained in bridal magazines, however. The target audience for weddings at Atlanta History Center is different from that of the museum itself.
4. Michelle Bower, "Is Your Brand a Painkiller, Vitamin, or Candy?" Dalziel and Pow, https://www.dalziel-pow.com/news/is-your-brand-a-painkiller-vitamin-or-candy.
5. These numbers reflect only our owned marketing. We also had a small budget to boost posts on Facebook and Instagram. The Meta for Business platform provides such specific audience tags that it was possible for us to tailor ad campaigns that reached very specific audiences for very little money. A \$50–\$100 ad aimed at the right segments on

Facebook and Instagram is an invaluable tool for institutions that don't have unlimited marketing budgets.

6. "Atlanta History Center Shares Similarities between 1918 Spanish Flu and COVID-19," WSB-TV, People2People, https://www.wsbtv.com/community/people-2-people/atlanta-history-center-shares-similarities-between-1918-spanish-flu-covid-19/LOLHGCWKHZJGF7M2W3NPALENWY/?fbclid=IwAR3cOzIyzIdf9KcUWP_mb3gGJgGh_L6oozwSWW7GSxoWnfLu-zTuopWt7uU.

7. Police officers murdered George Floyd on May 25, 2020, in Minneapolis, Minnesota. His killing sparked nationwide attention for the Black Lives Matter movement, as well as police brutality and criminal justice reform. On June 12, 2020, police officers shot and killed Rayshard Brooks in a parking lot in Atlanta after he was found sleeping in his car. Officers shot and killed Brooks as he fled the parking lot. His murder became one of the driving forces behind Atlanta's Black Lives Matter movement.

8. IfThen, "Case Study|Atlanta History Reimagined," https://www.ifthen.com/case-study/atlanta-history-center.

9. The downside to using a platform like Google Arts & Culture is that, in order to view your content, guests will have to navigate away from your site. The desire to increase native traffic to our website and increased audience retention led us to create a platform of our own on the Atlanta History Center site.

10. StoryCorps' mission is to preserve and share humanity's stories in order to build connections between people and create a more just and compassionate world. Modeled after the Works Progress Administration interviews of the 1930s, StoryCorps facilitates and collects informal interviews between members of the general public. The peer-to-peer style of interviewing typically makes for open, honest conversation through often deeply personal stories.

11. Dina Bailey, "Finding Inspiration Inside: Engaging Empathy to Empower Everyone," in *Fostering Empathy in Museums*, ed. Elif M. Gokcigdem (Lanham, MD: Rowman and Littlefield, 2016.

12. Charis Psaltis, Mario Carretero, and Sabina Čehajić-Clancy, "Preface," in *History Education and Conflict Transformation*, ed. Charis Psaltis, Mario Carretero, and Sabina Čehajić-Clancy (London: Palgrave Macmillan, 2017); Rezarta Bilali and Rima Mahmoud, "Confronting History and Reconciliation: A Review of Civil Society's Approaches to Transforming Conflict Narratives," in *History Education and Conflict Transformation*, ed. Charis Psaltis, Mario Carretero, and Sabina Čehajić-Clancy (London: Palgrave Macmillan, 2017).

13. Emlyn Koster, "Forward," in *Fostering Empathy Through Museums*, ed. Elif M. Gokcigdem (Lanham, MD: Rowman and Littlefield, 2016).

II

STORYTELLING IN THE COMMUNITY

WORKING ON STORYTELLING

A Pioneering Initiative in a Changing Context for the Moroccan Museum Culture

Samir El Azhar

It is universally acknowledged that museums preserve cultural heritage. They are depositories of history's treasures, an essential symbol of the richness and dynamism of a culture. Nevertheless, museum practices vary from one country to another depending on historical, economic, and cultural circumstances specific to each country. This chapter, on the one hand, seeks to explore the changing museum culture in Morocco, and, on the other hand, envisages investigating the extent to which the practice of storytelling has been embraced by some Moroccan museums. To my knowledge, the only two museums that have adopted this approach are the Ben M'sik Community Museum (BMCM), a case study in this chapter, and the Museum of Moroccan Judaism in Casablanca, which has launched a radio program, "Nass El Mellah" (People of the Mellah), that interviews Moroccan Jews from different backgrounds about their experience of being Jewish in Morocco.

HISTORICAL BACKGROUND

Morocco is located in the northwest corner of Africa. Just about eight miles from Europe across the Mediterranean, Morocco shares its international borders with Spain (north), Algeria (east) and Mauritania (south). This privileged strategic location has fostered for centuries a blend of cultures. Amazigh (Berber), Jewish, Arab, African, and European influences are all part of the country's mosaic patrimony. The former official website of the Ministry of Tourism in Morocco advertised the attractiveness of the Moroccan museums: "Inhabited since prehistoric times, with a culture that goes back thirty centuries, at the crossroads of Roman, Berber [Amazigh] and Arab civilizations, Morocco is rich in museums overflowing with treasures."[1] It seems interesting to consider to what extent this virtual representation of Moroccan museums corresponded to reality.

Most of Moroccan museums were created under the colonial French administration (1912–1956) and were founded then by the Indigenous Arts Service with the aim of promoting the artisanal sector and maintaining the local artistic traditions. They looked more or less like an Ali Baba cave that included artifacts without any museological purpose.

Museums under the Authority of the Ministry of Culture

Since the independence of the country from the French Protectorate in 1956, Moroccan museums were first managed by the Ministry of Culture. The Ministry of Culture proved to be insufficient and inadequate for the task of stewardship of Morocco's museums. As a government body, the Ministry of Culture was in charge of many cultural and artistic activities; to name only a few, tangible and intangible cultural heritage, theater, cinema, visual arts, books, and so on. Thus, according to its administrative organizational chart, museums fell under the responsibility of the Department of Cultural Heritage. Ironically, the Ministry of Culture did not have enough financial resources to meet the needs and expectations of these creative and cultural activities.

During this period, Moroccan museums failed to reflect the richness and diversity of Moroccan culture and to make Moroccans appreciate and visit these cultural institutions. To put it differently, they failed to enhance Moroccan identity and to attract new audiences that would be proud of their history and cultural heritage. Several logistical, financial, managerial, and cognitive factors made these museums deserted buildings forsaken by Moroccans. Ten years of conversations with Moroccan museum professionals allowed Katarzyna Pieprzak to make the following statement:

> I argue [. . .] the museum in Morocco was never founded as a public institution [. . .] It functioned as a conservatory for artisanal practices valorized by colonial administrators and a depository for objects collected through a Protectorate discourse on dying local culture and modernizing reform.[2]

The National Foundation of Museums

The year 2011 was a turning point in the history of Moroccan museums, initiating a new phase of administrative governance. A new body, named the National Foundation of Museums (NFM), was created to be in charge of museums all over the kingdom with the aim of improving museum conditions and spreading museum culture. Unlike the Ministry of Culture, the NFM focuses only on museums and devotes all its energy and financial and human resources to making museums more attractive and well attended. The mission of this new institution is plainly stated as follows:

> Among the main objectives of the Foundation are the democratization of culture, as well as strengthening, preserving and enhancing Morocco's cultural and artistic heritage. This mission requires the establishment of a new approach to modern cultural management, which will make museums welcoming, and attractive public spaces, contributing to the knowledge and understanding of the various aspects of the national heritage.[3]

In accordance with its mission, the foundation has taken a series of actions to promote Moroccan museums. First, it has renovated some museums to meet the international standards of museums. Second, the NFM has built some new museums, such as the Mohammed VI Museum of Modern and Contemporary Art (MMVI) that opened its doors in 2014. Third, the NFM organized many exhibitions of famous international artists to make Moroccans acquainted with these well-reputed artists. Finally, the NFM has also signed several memoranda of understanding with many countries, including the United States of America (the Smithsonian Institution), France (the French Ministry of Culture), and China (China Central Academy of Fine Arts) to provide expertise and to train museums curators and technicians at the theoretical as well as practical levels. Answering a question about what dynamics the foundation fits into, Mehdi Qotbi, president of the NFM, stated in February 2021:

> Nationally, the foundation manages fourteen museums and has renovated two so far. In the next two to three weeks, another museum in Safi will be dedicated to ceramics. This is to provide all cities with museums and to offer each city a specificity.

> Previously, all museums had the ethnographic or archaeological title. Today, we give a specificity for each of them so that there will be a complementarity.[4]

Academic Programs

Moroccan universities started offering courses or degrees concerned with museum studies only in the first decade of the twenty-first century. They were then sensitive to the dynamism taking place in museums and have therefore realized the need for qualified museum professionals. In the academic year 2016–2017, a master's degree in museology and cultural mediation was launched at the Faculty of Letters and Humanities in Rabat thanks to a partnership between the NFM and Mohammed V University in Rabat. A press article, titled "Finally, a Master in Museology in Rabat," describes this event:

> It has finally arrived! The long-awaited "Master in Museology" . . . has just been launched . . . Mehdi Qotbi said: "We are hopeful that in two years we will be able to integrate young professionals into our museums . . . The aim is to train professionals in a sector that is constantly developing." The president of the National Museums Foundation added that this is the first time in Morocco that professionals in modern and contemporary museology will be trained.[5]

It is within this frame of mind that another master's program, "Cultural Policy and Cultural Management," was launched in the academic year 2018–2019. This program, hosted by the Faculty of Letters and Humanities, Ben M'sik, in Hassan II University of Casablanca, aims at

> train[ing] a new generation of researchers, cultural managers, cultural decision-makers and academics capable of contributing to cultural activities in their countries and the Arab region, and of working in a strategic way in the public cultural sector, the creative industries and the independent cultural sector.[6]

Today, there are other bachelor's and master's programs that have included tangible and intangible heritage in their curricula. A remarkable work is being done in museums as well as at universities to redress the situation, which will impact the whole sector positively. Medhi Qotbi, the president of the NFM, is confident in the future: "Today, the number of visitors to museums has increased fivefold. . . . This is unimaginable in this country; it means that Moroccans are now in a mental disposition to go to art and museums."[7]

BEN M'SIK COMMUNITY MUSEUM

It is within these evolving circumstances that the storytelling approach is carried out in Morocco, a logical outcome of the evolutionary dynamic process Moroccan museums are undergoing. In line with its mission, the BMCM, hosted at the Faculty of Letters and Humanities Ben M'sik, Hassan II University of Casablanca, Morocco,[8] was fortunate to embark upon this new experience of collecting stories that portray the social and cultural life of its vibrant community.

Ben M'sik, where the Faculty of Letters and its affiliated museum are located, is today one of the biggest districts of Casablanca with a population of more than one million inhabitants. To the people of Casablanca, the mere utterance of the words "Ben M'sik" would recall Karyan Ben M'sik, formerly one of the biggest shanty towns where more than 100,000 people lodged during the post–Second World War period. Since then, Casablanca has become the economic capital of the kingdom and the locomotive of the development of the Moroccan economy. It attracts 56 percent of industrial labor and contributes to 44 percent of the industrial production of the kingdom.

The economic boom of Casablanca attracted waves of migrants from all over Morocco. They flocked to this city seeking jobs and better social and economic opportunities. Most of the migrants who came from the neighboring rural areas settled first in Karyan Ben M'sik, in slums because they could not afford paying decent accommodations. "As migrants streamed in from the countryside, Casablanca gave the French language the word *bidonville*—'slum'—coined from the laborers' shanties made from flattened tin drums, or *bidons*."[9] Ben M'sik was then one of the underserved and deprived areas of Casablanca. In an article titled "A Community Museum Records Real Moroccan Life," John Thorne, foreign correspondent of the *National*, declares: "In most cases, that experience is migration. For decades, waves of rural poor have landed in Ben M'sik and other Casablanca suburbs, seeking a better life. Ben M'sik represents the dream of Casablanca."[10]

The Bread Revolt

In 1981, a revolt broke out. Under pressure from the International Monetary Fund (IMF), the Moroccan government adopted an austerity plan and reduced its food subsidy. This led to a 50 percent increase in the price of flour in June 1981, which led to a popular uprising and a national strike that paralyzed a number of Moroccan cities, including Casablanca. This social uprising was called "The Bread Revolt." The French newspaper *Le Monde* reported its causes:

> This outbreak of violence recalls the serious riots of March 1965. . . . The two uprisings have the same cause. . . . Thousands of families are crammed into makeshift homes: lack of hygiene, promiscuity and pollution come to join the daily problems of unemployment and the cost of living.[11]

Following this revolt, the government designed a plan to improve the social conditions of the inhabitants. In this respect, to avoid any further social tension, the government gave priority to these underserved and squalid neighborhoods. Therefore, the shantytown Karyan Ben M'sik was demolished and a new modern district, named Moulay Rachid, emerged instead. It was equipped with hospitals, schools, universities, a cultural center, and many other necessary infrastructures and facilities. Describing this big operation, a press article titled "Casablanca: Last Day of the Slums of Karyan Ben M'sik" stated:

> The famous Karyan was the largest and oldest slum in the Kingdom, where thousands of households lived, all of which benefited from a gigantic rehousing project built in particular in the commune of Sidi Moumen and the district of Moulay Rachid of Casablanca. The last makeshift homes of Karyan Ben M'sik will be razed this Friday morning.[12]

CREATING COMMUNITY COLLABORATION PROJECT

The Ben M'sik Community Museum (BMCM) in partnership with the Museum of History and Holocaust Education (MHHE), Kennesaw, Georgia, the United States, embarked on a project entitled Creating Community Collaboration (2009–2010) that consisted of collecting some oral (hi)stories. This project was sponsored by the former Museums and Community Collaborations Abroad (MCCA) program (now Museums Connect), funded by the US State Department's Bureau of Educational and Cultural Affairs and administered by the American Alliance of Museums.

Supported by the Museums Connect grant, the BMCM team collected thirty narrative personal stories about the social and cultural lives of the inhabitants of Ben M'sik. These narrative stories were a pioneering initiative "to give voice to people and communities previously left out of the historical record."[13] More importantly, "this project sought to gather, analyse, and learn from the voices of lived experience and give those individuals a chance to shape the way their his-

Figure 11.1. Al Haj Lamlih, seventy-five years old, photographed while being interviewed by the BMCM team, 2010. Courtesy of Samir El Azhar.

tory is told."[14] Contrary to what one might expect, working on oral (hi)stories was not an easy task. In the United States and Europe, museum practices are anchored in a long museum tradition, and recording narrative stories has therefore become a common practice. According to Leslie Bedford, "[t]he power of narrative is no secret in the museum world where various forms of storytelling have long been employed to engage visitors."[15] The inclusion of personal stories of war, natural catastrophes, strikes, terrorist attacks, economic crisis, to name only a few, has added more credibility to museums as cultural institutions concerned about the communities they serve. However, in Morocco, storytelling is a new approach that Moroccan museums are discovering.

When we first embarked upon this project of recording people's stories, we faced many challenges. In Morocco, people share stories privately with family members, friends, and acquaintances. They tell stories about family life, social conflicts, financial issues, and the like. In my opinion, it is a therapeutic way to unwind so that one can cope with the harsh social reality. However, Moroccans are reluctant to share these stories in public, let alone to sit before a camera and be recorded. According to them, a camera means an official eye of a big brother is watching them.

The second challenge we faced is related to trust and reliability. When we first approached the Ben M'sik people to record their personal narratives, they showed little enthusiasm for this project. They believed that we were politicians hoping to win their support for the upcoming elections. Later, when confidence was established, they revealed to us that they did not trust politicians who were interested in them as votes and not as human beings. They came to see them at the beginning of every electoral campaign, promised them a brighter future, and then disappeared once the elections were over.

Accordingly, the Ben M'sik people were astonished when we told them that we were interested in them not from a political but from a cultural perspective because we believed that they were important. They always thought that the stories of their simple life were meaningless and insignificant. We also pointed out that their greatness was to be found, paradoxically, in their simple life. The attempt to write history from below was a new perspective that paid tribute to these ordinary mortals. The story-gathering approach to social history has its roots in Alltagsgeschichte—a bottom-up approach popularized in Germany in the 1980s. The new German approach Alltagsgeschichte, literally meaning "history of the everyday," focuses on ordinary people. "Using a methodology influenced by anthropology, practitioners of 'every-day history' have utilized memoirs, letters, old photos, and interviews with participant observers in order to evoke the past social life of select groups."[16]

Thanks to the students/members of the museum, the Ben M'sik inhabitants overcame fear and apprehension and excitedly engaged in this oral (hi)story project. The vast majority of students who enroll at Faculty of Letters Ben M'sik are themselves Ben M'sik residents, born and bred in this district. Therefore, our students were our ambassadors who explained the objectives of our project to their neighbors, family members, and friends. They dissipated all worries and convinced them to video-record their stories. Thus, we selected interviewees with attention to diversity in terms of age, level of education, profession, ethnicity, and so on.

During the project, we recorded thirty narrative stories that tell about the interviewees' childhood, adolescence, love, marriage, neighbors, social failures, parents, and more.[17] All the stories are in one way or another interesting. However, because of lack of space, I will refer to only a few stories that show some aspects of these ups and downs of social life in Ben M'sik. The first story is that of Noureddine El Daif, who was born in 1956 in Ben M'sik in Casablanca. The most important part of his narrative is about the Bread Revolt that took place in 1981. Following this social uprising, he was arrested by the police, accused, according to him, "of the guilt of helping an unauthorized picketing," and sent to jail for twenty years. In his own words,

> I was arrested and tortured . . . I didn't know where I was and we spent a period of twenty-eight days of torture because they charged us for being leaders of the

> strike. But we all knew that the real reason was the fact that citizens couldn't afford the high prices, especially in Casablanca. The union was responsible for the strike. The State didn't accept such a thing and they brought soldiers to put an end to the strike.[18]

Thousands of young people from the *bidonvilles* in outskirts of Casablanca formed mobs and destroyed symbols of wealth in the city, including banks, pharmacies, grocery stores, buses, and cars. Police and military units fired into the crowds and arrested hundreds of rioters. There were heavy casualties and damages. To quote the *Washington Post*: "The 'black Saturday' that struck this dusty port city last June with the worst rioting in the [last] 20 year[s] . . . has underlined the desperate economic conditions of much of Morocco's population."[19]

When Noureddine El Daif came back after his twenty years of imprisonment, he found his Ben M'sik neighborhood had completely changed: "I was shocked by the great changes. The open agricultural fields were replaced by concrete buildings. A new district, Hay Moulay Rachid, was built . . . now things are improving, better than they were in the nineties."[20]

In 2004, King Mohamed VI created a human rights commission, called Equity and Reconciliation Commission (ERC), a proof of the country's commitment to human rights and of "Morocco's efforts to acknowledge and address serious human rights violations of the past." According to Human Rights Watch:

> The king made clear that he considered this body a truth commission. Its mandate is to investigate forced disappearances and arbitrary detentions carried out between 1956 and 1999, to prepare a report containing specific as well as general information concerning these violations, and to recommend forms of compensation and reparation for the victims.[21]

Another interesting narrative story is that of Mohammed Zyna, which sheds light on civic and political engagement in Ben M'sik. Born in 1968, Mohammed received his education at Ben M'sik. He got his bachelor of science in physics from the Faculty of Sciences Ben M'sik. After graduation, he found it necessary to take a course in computer sciences. He founded an association to help young people living in his neighborhood acquire computer skills. He is also a member of a political party. When asked how he would solve the problems of his neighborhood, he answered,

> As a social activist and political partisan, I believe in everyday meetings that are related to everyday reality. This neighborhood has its own specificities that must

> be taken into consideration. I believe in the policy of proximity to diagnose social diseases. We cannot bring a specific scheme from the top and implement it here. Any scheme must emanate from the everyday realities of people.[22]

In his association, Mohammed provides one year of training in computer skills, electronics, embroidery, tailoring, ceramics, and more to enable the Ben M'sik people, regardless of their gender, intellectual levels, and social positions, to acquire some skills that would help them sustain their lives. In an answer about the role of the political parties in people's lives, he states:

> Political parties . . . are created to train and raise political awareness of all social classes. . . . Our role, as political parties, is to reconcile people with politics, make them practice politics, make them trust politicians and then we can ask them something else.[23]

Ms. Khadija Ghazali, born in 1965 and brought up in Ben M'sik, narrated the ups and downs of her life in this district. She is a good example of a Moroccan woman who has struggled throughout her life to assert herself and to improve her social position. Being the oldest of her eight brothers and sisters, she helped her mother in the household chores in addition to doing her school assignments. After the death of her father, she was compelled to leave the university to work in a clothes factory to sustain her poor family. After she had worked in several private companies as a typist, she was hired to work in a public institution at the lowest rank. Twenty years later, she returned to the same university she had left earlier and succeeded in getting a BA in Social Development. Thanks to this degree, she succeeded in climbing the administrative ladder. She started work in this public institution in rank 1 and now she is in rank 10.

Khadija adhered to the social programs launched by the National Initiative for Human Development (NIHD). She is an example of a social activist who believes in a noble cause to serve all the members of the Ben M'sik community. An ambitious project, NIHD assists the government in improving inclusiveness and implementing processes at the local level in order to enhance the use of social and economic infrastructure and services by poor and vulnerable groups. When asked about the additions that the NIHD has brought to Ben M'sik, Khadija declared:

> The National Initiative for Human Development was a Royal project launched by His Majesty King Mohamed VI. It was an important and fantastic experience that Ben M'sik greatly benefited from. Several things were achieved thanks to this project, such as youth houses, sport spaces, parks. . . . Concerning youth houses, they host computer labs, libraries, theater workshops, sport rooms, etc.[24]

The thirty stories that we collected and recorded were first conducted in colloquial Moroccan Arabic, *darija*, which only Moroccans understand.[25] Then, they were transcribed in classical Arabic and translated in English.[26] Youssef Sourgo, a member of the Ben M'sik Community Museum, stated:

> My task, along with the other members of BMCM team, has been to transcribe and translate the oral histories. . . . The community members' oral histories, which the previous team had videotaped, have revealed interesting facts that even the students among us who are living in the Ben M'sik neighborhood have not been aware of.[27]

This project of collecting narrative stories culminated in a cultural event, "Coffee and Conversation Program," held in the theater of the Ben M'sik Cultural Centre, Moulay Rachid, on June 5, 2010. It was an opportune occasion "for project participants, both interviewers and interviewees, to share their experiences and showcase the stories gathered during the interview process."[28] In this respect, five panellists shared their stories with more than eight hundred people attending this ceremony. Dr. Kacem Marghatta, professor in the Department of Arabic Literature at the Faculty of Letters and Humanities Ben M'sik, born and raised in Ben M'sik, was then forty-five years old. Dr. Marghatta shared some of his childhood reminiscences with the audience. He recalled that he used to play football in the same spot where the Ben M'sik Cultural Centre: Moulay Rachid stands today. There used to be a well from which he and his

Figure 11.2. Dr. El Azhar supervising the transcription of the narrative stories by the BMCM team, 2011. Courtesy of Samir El Azhar.

friends used to drink cool water once the football match was over. He added that it is marvelous that in the place of that well a cultural institution (referring to the place where the ceremony was taking place) stands today to quench the thirst of the residents of the Ben M'sik for cultural activities. He also remembered the open fields where spikes of wheat grew. He pointed out that it is really wonderful to see that in the place of those green fields two academic institutions stand side by side, the Faculty of Letters and Humanities Ben M'sik and the Faculty of Sciences. In the past, the place provided the population of the area with bread, food for the stomach. Today, the place provides the people of Ben M'sik with knowledge and wisdom, food for the mind.[29]

Immediately after this ceremony, a meeting was held with the thirty interviewees to discuss an important point. According to the terms of the grant, participants had to receive a stipend of fifty dollars each to cover expenses related to their transportation and to thank them for the trouble they took during the interviews. When we finished the interviews, we learned that Moroccan law prohibits Moroccan citizens from receiving cash money from foreign nongovernmental organizations and institutions. We were in an awkward situation, torn between our contract compliance signed with American Alliance of Museums (AAM) and our promise to our storytellers. In this meeting, we informed our narrators about this and suggested that instead of giving this money to separate individuals, the money could be invested, for instance, in a charity project from which the Ben M'sik residents could benefit. We explained "the valid principle that having one's life story recorded for the future is reward in itself."[30] We also made it clear that these recordings would not generate any profits but would be utilized in academic research to help write the social and cultural history of this district. After a long debate where several suggestions were made, we finally agreed that this money would be used to buy computers for a local primary school.

We solved only half of the problem; the other half had to be resolved too. We informed our Kennesaw State University partners, who were concerned about respecting the terms of the contract because this situation might put the whole contract at stake. When they reported the matter to AAM, the case was handled within the framework of culture differences. Apparently, this was not a unique case where AAM had to adjust its contract with foreign museums, bearing in mind that storytelling occurs within a different cultural environment where museum practices are different from those of the United States.

Thanks to this middle ground between the narrators' promised stipends and AAM's legal contract, a computer room was established in a local primary school in Ben M'sik. We were honored in the inauguration ceremony by the presence of an American diplomatic delegation in Morocco. From the Moroccan side, the representative of the Ministry of Education in the Prefecture of Ben M'sik and several local authorities also attended this ceremony. A feeling of pride spread among the interviewees and their interviewers because this project of storytelling led to the creation of this computer room that would serve the community.[31]

The project of collecting narrative stories has enabled us to build strong bonds with our sociocultural environment. Because of these stories, we have a better understanding of the Ben M'sik community. Symbolically, these stories have demolished the wall constructed all around the university that hinders the Ben M'sik inhabitants from participating in any cultural or academic activities organized by the university. Likewise, it has prevented the professors of the university from knowing about the activities organized in the neighborhood. The oral history project Creating Community Collaboration has broken down this metaphorical wall and enabled academics to leave their ivory tower and to go beyond the wall to meet ordinary people. Today, the collected narrative stories are available in the Ben M'sik Community Museum for researchers and academics. They provide valuable information on this crucial period of the history of the district of Ben M'sik and the city of Casablanca as a whole.

To conclude, this chapter has tried to trace the evolution of Moroccan museums with a special emphasis on the storytelling approach. It has also attempted to show the historical, social, and educational environment where these museums operate to reach the conclusion that storytelling is a new approach in Morocco. The stories of individuals and of communities have not yet become a part of standard museum practice in Morocco since only two museums have embraced this paradigm. Nevertheless, we are confident that other museums will follow, as museum culture has agreeably evolved in the last decade. Using these oral stories, the Ben M'sik Community Museum is currently working on a book in Arabic to record the social and cultural life in Ben M'sik. Accordingly, the museum is considering collecting other narrative stories that would focus on some important historical events that Casablanca witnessed in the twentieth century.

NOTES

1. "Museums of Morocco," accessed in 2010, http://www.maroc.net/museums/.
2. Katarzyna Pieprzak, "Introduction," in *Art and Modernity in Postcolonial Morocco: Imagined Museums* (Minneapolis: University of Minnesota Press, 2010), 4–5.
3. Accessed February 25, 2021, http://www.fnm.ma/fondation/presentation-de-la-fnm/ (in French; S. El Azhar, Trans.).

4. Engouement des Marocains pour les musées nationaux, selon Mehdi Qotbi [Interview], accessed February 25, 2021, https://www.yabiladi.com/articles/details/53798/engouement-marocains-pour-musees-nationaux.html (in French; S. El Azhar, Trans.).

5. Enfin un Master muséologie à Rabat, accessed February 26, 2021, https://www.etudiant.ma/articles/enfin-un-master-museologie-a-rabat (in French; S. El Azhar, Trans.).

6. Master en Politiques culturelles et Gestion culturelle: Appel à candidatures à l'Université Hassan II, accessed February 26, 2021, https://lematin.ma/journal/2020/appel-candidatures-luniversite-hassan-ii/339253.html (in French; S. El Azhar, Trans.).

7. Engouement des Marocains pour les musées nationaux, selon Mehdi Qotbi [Interview], accessed February 25, 2021, https://www.yabiladi.com/articles/details/53798/engouement-marocains-pour-musees-nationaux.html (in French; S. El Azhar, Trans.).

8. For more information about the Ben M'sik Community Museum, please see http://bmcm.flbenmsik.ma/.

9. John Thorne, "A Community Museum Records Real Moroccan Life," accessed March 1, 2021, https://readingmorocco.blogspot.com/2009/12/community-museum-records-real-moroccan.html.

10. John Thorne, "A Community Museum Records Real Moroccan Life," accessed March 1, 2021.

11. Les émeutes de Casablanca, accessed February 27, 2021, https://www.lemonde.fr/archives/article/1981/06/24/les-emeutes-de-casablanca_2729314_1819218.html (in French; S. El Azhar, Trans.).

12. Jalil Laaboudi, "Casablanca: Dernier jour du bidonville Kariane Ben M'sik," accessed March 1, 2021, https://www.bladi.net/casablanca-bidonville-kariane-ben-msik,43011.html (in French; S. El Azhar, Trans.).

13. Leslie Bedford, "Storytelling: The Real Work of Museums," *Curator: The Museum Journal* 44, no. 1 (2001): 31, https://onlinelibrary.wiley.com/doi/epdf/10.1111/j.2151-6952.2001.tb00027.x.

14. Jennifer Dickey and Catherine Lewis, "Introduction: The Museums and Community Collaboration Abroad Project," in *Crossing Borders: A Transatlantic Collaboration*, ed. Samir El Azhar (Casablanca: Force Equipment, 2010), 16.

15. Leslie Bedford, "Storytelling: The Real Work of Museums," *Curator: The Museum Journal* 44, no. 1 (2001): 30, https://onlinelibrary.wiley.com/doi/epdf/10.1111/j.2151-6952.2001.tb00027.x.

16. James H. Jackson, "Alltagsgeschichte, Social Science History, and the Study of Migration in Nineteenth-Century Germany," accessed March 1, 2021, https://www.cambridge.org/core/journals/central-european-history/article/abs/alltagsgeschichte-social-science-history-and-the-study-of-migration-in-nineteenthcentury-germany/C073E7B7D14F838F1A535391680F7734.

17. Special thanks must be extended to the BMCM team (students of the Department of English, American Studies program, and those of the Department of History) faculty of Letters Ben M'sik, for recording these narrative stories.

18. Noureddine El Daif, interviewed by the BMCM team, unpublished.

19. John K. Cooley, "A 'Black Saturday' Shadows the Future of Hassan's Morocco," accessed March 2, 2021, https://www.washingtonpost.com/archive/politics/1981/08/25/a-black-saturday-shadows-the-future-of-hassans-morocco/8a5cb6ce-39b4-42b9-bb48-f3a196706961/.

20. Noureddine El Daif, interviewed by the BMCM team, unpublished.

21. Human Right Watch, *Morocco's Truth Commission: Honoring Past Victims during an Uncertain Present*, accessed March 2, 2021, https://www.hrw.org/sites/default/files/reports/morocco1105wcover.pdf.

22. Mohammed Zyna, interviewed by the BMCM team, unpublished.

23. Mohammed Zyna, interviewed by the BMCM team, unpublished.

24. Khadija Ghazali, interviewed by the BMCM team, unpublished.

25. Moroccan dialect Arabic, called in Morocco "darija," is a colloquial language bringing together several varieties of dialect Arabic spoken in Morocco. It is spoken by more than thirty million people in Morocco and by several hundreds of thousands in the countries of Moroccan emigration.

26. Sincere thanks and gratitude go to the BMCM team for transcribing and translating these narrative stories.

27. Youssef Sourgo, "Making Change: Making History," in *Ben M'sik Community Museum: Building Bridges* (Casablanca: Force Equipment, 2012), 53.

28. Jennifer Dickey and Catherine Lewis, "Introduction: The Museums and Community Collaboration Abroad Project," in *Crossing Borders: A Transatlantic Collaboration*, ed. Samir El Azhar (Casablanca: Force Equipment, 2010), 21.

29. Samir El Azhar, Report 6: Activities, taking place on June 5, 2010, performed by the Ben M'sik Community Museum. Unpublished.

30. Donald A Ritchie, *Doing Oral History: A Practical Guide* (New York: Oxford University Press, 1995), 109.

31. Samir El Azhar, Report 7: Activities, taking place on Thursday, October 7, 2010, performed by the Ben M'sik Community Museum. Unpublished.

TURN ON, TUNE IN

A Community Storytelling Project with the New Mexico History Museum

Judy Goldberg and Meredith Schweitzer

> *I liked the challenge of having to seriously listen to others' stories, not interrupt, [and then] repeat [the] story back. That was a very good exercise. Made me realize how often we listen just waiting to tell our story.*
>
> —Storytelling Workshop Participant

In 2018, the New Mexico History Museum in Santa Fe launched an exhibit and series of programs leading with personal stories that encouraged deep and curious listening aimed at bringing to life the region's role in the social and political movements of the late twentieth century. Anchored in storytelling, the museum opened the exhibit *Voices of Counterculture in the Southwest* and hosted a series of public programs to activate fresh interpretations of the era's relevance to contemporary times. Employing the adage "the shortest distance between two people is story," the programs invited participants to bring their stories into the public record.

A STORY HIGHLIGHT—ON CIVIL RIGHTS

Georgina Ortega Angel is a daughter from two generations of migrant farm workers. Activism and community organizing started in her early years.

> In 1964/65 my clearest memory is walking with my mother and protesting with the farm workers and fighting for rights and knowing there were laws to protect us, and they were not being observed. That was the era I came into understanding I had a voice. . . . I remember, when I was growing up, I'd go with my mother and other women door to door. They'd be knocking on doors, getting signatures, talking to people about laws that were going to come. I'm talking about civil rights movements: Headstart, health, education, all of the basic standards for people to live in the United States of America—United States citizens. . . . Most of the migrant camps we worked in were crowded, no water, no sanitation facilities whatsoever . . . but people were very giving, no matter how poor they were, they were very giving. . . . We worked with people from the Southwest, all the way down to the frontera of Texas. We met people all over who worked in these camps with us but were suffering and accepting it. I want you to remember that: accepted it. . . . Coming from the Napa Valley as a migrant worker, it was very difficult. I remember working in a camp in Morgan Hill, California, as a twelve-year-old, picking cucumbers, thinking, "Why are we living like this? Why do we have to put up with this?" One afternoon, I went with my mother to the store . . . and I called the Health Department and I asked them, "Aren't there laws against this?"

To hear more of Georgina Ortega Angel's story, go to https://www.youtube.com/watch?v=UxDkGl7el6E&ab_channel=NewMexicoHistoryMuseum.

BACKGROUND TO THE EXHIBITION AND PUBLIC PROGRAMMING

The late 1960s and early 1970s were a time of struggle and social change in American history. Fifty years after the iconic 1967 Summer of Love, the New Mexico History Museum and Palace of the Governors, in step with cultural institutions across the country—from the deYoung Museum in San Francisco to the Metropolitan Museum in New York City—were designing exhibitions to commemorate the anniversary.

The New Mexico History Museum's exhibition development team worked for two years to develop an approach that sought to activate visitor engagement and break from the object-centric museum tradition to feature personal narratives and the human voice. Curated first-person audio accounts from those who had lived through the era came from new recordings and a robust collection of interviews conducted over several decades by the exhibit's co-curator, Jack Loeffler. Archival images, artworks, and ephemera complemented the recordings and fleshed out the exhibition. This approach, the curators believed, would prompt visitors to consider their own memories and interpretations as well as consider how others see themselves within the scope of history.

From this vision, Meredith Schweitzer, New Mexico History Museum's curator of nineteenth- and twentieth-century Southwest collections, along with Jack Loeffler, created *Voices of Counterculture in the Southwest*, a comprehensive look at the regional social movements and events occurring throughout New Mexico and the neighboring states of Arizona and Colorado. In addition to the preexisting audio recordings, current-day interviews were conducted with seasoned hippies, activists, cultural representatives, spiritual guides, alternative land-based homebuilders and farmers, veterans, commune members, and creatives of all sorts.

The exhibition opened with the voice of Allen Ginsburg reading his iconic poem "Howl" and led visitors through an immersive space filled with regional and historical photography, signature tunes of the times, images projected onto a Volkswagen van (hippies loved their vans!), articles of clothing, and a model geodesic dome. Conical speakers with push button panels invited visitors to listen to the many voices recalling events and reflecting on the times.

In accordance with the New Mexico History Museum's mission, the exhibition extended beyond the walls of the museum to reach its citizenry throughout the state. With personal narratives central to the museum's exhibition, Judy Goldberg, an independent contractor with a background in radio production, community programming, and education, developed an outreach program designed to incorporate community storytelling. Five communities—Taos, Dixon, Las Vegas, Placitas, and Silver City—were identified as "hot spots" during the region's counterculture era. These were places where an influx of hippies, primarily from coastal urban centers, had migrated; where spirituality and intercultural exchanges occurred and where resistance to established political power structures were most active. Imbued with counterculture history, these communities seemed most ripe for collaboration. As the project's coordinator, Judy's first task was to envision how to bring people into the project to be mutually beneficial for institutional collaborators, participants, and the museum.

The project, "Turn On, Tune In: A Community Storytelling Project" (TOTI), was designed to extenuate the enlightenment of the times and to perpetuate the value of collecting New Mexicans' voices as valid accounts of history.

Participants were drawn to this project because of their own connections with the era's themes: civil rights and social inequities; anti-materialism and a break from the status quo; the anti-war, environmental, and women's movements; attraction to alternative lifestyles; and a search for spirituality and propensity toward creative expression and activism. Bringing public programming to regions around the state amplified the presence of the museum, countering perceptions that the state museum serves Santa Feans and tourists exclusively. In post-program surveys, the self-selected participants from the five "hot spot" communities repeatedly noted a genuine sense of feeling heard and believing their stories were important testaments to the fabric of history.

Integral to the TOTI Community Storytelling Project was a suggestion that community collaborators consider integrating public history collections into local repositories. Libraries, institutions of higher learning, regional museums, radio stations, community organizations, and leaders within the five communities were tapped to envision how generating digital stories by and for residents could be beneficial. Could the TOTI project augment or ignite local archive collections, and would locals choose to initiate new community events and activities?

At the core of the outreach program was the intent that communities make the project their own. TOTI facilitators came to honor and celebrate the lived stories of community participants within the context of a specific historical framework.

> *If we all knew each other's stories, we would live in a more empathetic and compassionate world. . . . Even though all of our stories were quite different, we found a commonality, a shared humanity. We drew closer to one another. We were becoming a family. We learned to care for one another.*
>
> —Storytelling Workshop Participant

CONCEPTION TO IMPLEMENTATION

Building community engagement through museum programming takes a lot of planning to establish a foundation of partnerships and collaborators. From the onset, the goal was to be inclusive and representative of multigenerational and culturally diverse populations. The setup required months of recruitment, coordinated meetings, and agreed-upon formats to launch the six distinct regional workshops and their accompanying community listening events. This organizing phase ran from July through October 2016. The museum contributed the workshops and facilitators, and the community partners assumed responsibility for publicity, workshop hosting sites, and venues for presentations. Throughout the project's development, the participating institutions and individuals were integral to the success of the programs.

Once the community partnerships were in place, there were a series of phases to the TOTI project. The first was to identify ten individuals (two from each of the "hot spot" communities) to come to Santa Fe to take part in a digital storytelling weekend workshop with StoryCenter, an organization out of Berkeley, California. The participants would learn software to create videos made from their own written and recorded stories, along with digital transfers of their images. Ultimately, the StoryCenter staff would fine-tune participants' content to incorporate the ten videos into the New Mexico History Museum's *Voices of Counterculture in the Southwest* exhibit. This first phase of the TOTI project occurred simultaneously with the opening of the exhibition in May 2017.

In phase two, museum exhibition co-curator (Meredith) and Judy designed and facilitated five two-day regional workshops and co-coordinated community events at each of the five sites. The facilitators conducted group and partner exercises for participants to hone their stories. At the end of the two-day workshop, participants practiced and recorded their personal narratives. The audio recordings were edited and presented at the community public events.

The regional community workshops ran from September 2017 through January 2018. Prior to these, Judy worked directly with individuals and organizations to affirm commitments and to promote the project's relevance to contemporary history and to our lives today—personally, politically, and socially. Participation by attendees was a big commitment, requiring two full days of workshops and two live presentations. In retrospect, offering stipends to honor and respect their contributions would have been ideal.

In phase three, the stories were made available to participants, community partners, and the general public through online venues.

Nuts and Bolts of the Site-based Community Workshops

To attract volunteer participants to the project, facilitate the storytelling workshops, and coordinate public presentations, work started with several months of phone calls, emails, social media posts, press releases, radio broadcasts, and countless follow-up meetings. This setup clearly illustrated that a community project of this scope cannot be just a "one and done" effort. It needed dedicated coordinators and the resources to support the logistics for the storytelling process to be unencumbered by logistic snafus. This one-on-one contact between Judy as point person and local coordinators and volunteer participants was the backbone to the success of the program.

Each community program started on a Friday evening with either a public presentation by Meredith or a filmed walk-through of the *Voices of Counterculture in the Southwest* exhibit. Saturday and Sunday, from 9:00 a.m. to 3:00 p.m., participants were guided in crafting and practicing their stories through using structured exercises. On Sunday afternoon, stories were recorded and later edited by the facilitators in the span of a week. Then the community was invited to a public listening event, whereby the participants' stories were either performed or played as audio recordings through speakers, with an accompanying visual on a screen. However, for the first two community presentations, when the stories were performed live by the participants, the facilitators found the tellers had trouble keeping to the time limits. Instead, they found there was a certain magic to just listening in a group setting. Like families sitting around the old-time radio consoles in the 1940s, the listening events conjured up a certain closeness, as each audience member imagined their own images from each story. This, in turn, reinforced our original intention to nurture and practice the art of listening. All six presentations generated audience discussions followed by a potluck-style reception. On some occasions musical performances took place and there was always plenty of opportunity for *¡Plática!*; a chance to converse.

A STORY HIGHLIGHT—ON ALTERNATIVE LIFESTYLES

Raised as a hippie kid in Placitas, New Mexico, Rachel Wexler brought a critical eye to the experience of the counterculture era.

> I am a product of a failed experiment and as a result of that I don't fit into mainstream culture. Recently that experiment has been on public display and a lot of emotion is bubbling up around that . . . I found myself in the Community Room at the Placitas Public Library where images of my childhood were on the wall and there were many people in the room . . . all who were very curious about this romantic time in our country. But my experience was that time was not so romantic; I was a child. The ideals and values of that time were imposed on me in a way that was good and in other ways not so good . . . I was asked what it was like to grow up like that and I responded angrily . . . We were looking at a picture of my family doing the hippie thing of building a structure and my father's in the picture and my sister's standing there with her hands on her hips overlooking her

> domain and I'm on a hill scantily clothed (chuckles), [a] pre-pubescent angry-looking girl . . . I knew what was going on behind the scenes; being a nine-year-old child sitting amongst a group of people having a joint passed to me and the expectation that I, as a nine-year-old child, would make a choice, some choice, of what to do with that.

To hear more of Rachel Wexler's story, go to https://www.youtube.com/watch?v=FPU2SlIsdmg&t=133s&ab_channel=NewMexicoHistoryMuseum.

CHALLENGES AND REFLECTIONS

Stories are the most powerful when they immediately connect with the listener. For this project, the greatest challenge was time. Time to properly coordinate, time to properly introduce the structure, time to properly conduct the workshops, and time to produce the content. But time was also the greatest blessing. Participants in the workshops often felt pressured to fine-tune and record a story within the confines of a two-day workshop and to fit their accounts within an eight-minute time frame.[1] This was difficult for many, though in the end almost all appreciated the opportunity to refine their stories. Through the process of designing and facilitating the project, the facilitators stayed tuned in to one another and adjusted strategies. Schedules shifted or participants required flexibility. Accommodations for particular participants were part of the flow.

The scale of this project required at least two people working over its course. The project was designed to divide the tasks according to facilitator's expertise and availability. As a contracted consultant, Judy was able to devote more time to communications, outreach, and workshop preparations. As co-facilitators, mutual support, remaining flexible, and being communicative throughout was essential. The two facilitators' personal ages spanned the two generations of participants, which was also helpful.

At the beginning of the regional workshops, the schedule was too tight, causing unnecessary stress. And for the timing of the workshop activities to go just right, the ideal size was eight participants. Again and again, it was clear that participants appreciated listening to one another as much as, if not more, than telling their own stories. The workshop started with a fundamental guideline: listen to who is speaking and give feedback specific to what that person is saying, rather than draw from one's own experiences or associations for feedback. An example was the occasion a participant stated what became the best illustration of what it meant to listen with full attention. After the introductory exercise of telling one's condensed personal biography in two minutes to a partner and having the listening partner introduce the "telling" person back to the group, the one whose story had been told by another wasn't satisfied. "You told only the parts of the story that related to *your* life, and you left out details that happened in *mine*," she stated. This honesty brought the group closer, and the intent to listen, without triggering one's own experiences, took effort and reaped rewards. Clearly, the success of the project hinged on the conscious practice of gracious listening. When participants responded specifically to what the given teller said, the feedback proved to be most useful. This step was invaluable in the story creation process.

Feedback from Participants

As part of the project, the program asked participants to fill out a ten-question evaluation reflecting on the workshop and listening event. Out of the twenty-seven anonymous evaluations, here are selected highlights responding to the TOTI Community Storytelling experience:

> I began to see, in a way, that all people in their own way, live a counterculture experience. It made me realize how much society discounts our uniqueness in its pursuit of a homogeneity.
>
> I came into the group expecting my story to be unique and to stand out, but I was so proven wrong. Each person's story stretched me, filled me with wonder, and really, mostly humbled me. I am so grateful for that experience.
>
> the importance of volunteering, staying engaged and standing up for what is right, even if you're standing alone.
>
> I had an opportunity to reflect on my own experience and how it was part of a larger tapestry of the counterculture experience. My interactions with my fellow workshop participants gave me a sense of belonging and validated my experiences.
>
> It helps me value my story more, and strengthens my belief that there is value in helping others tell their stories. . . . Things I learned will probably weave their way into the work I do with women veterans.

(referencing another participant's story about having hippie parents) It's interesting how people can more easily learn from those we're not so closely related to and entangled with.

As a litigation attorney, we tell stories in trial all the time, but I've never had any formal training in it. What I say is not necessarily what a juror will hear.

The value that I found is that all of our stories have a connecting theme and that is a search for justice, love, and acceptance.

Successes

The program fostered new partnerships with eighteen community organizations (libraries, museums, radio broadcasters, and cultural community groups).

Fifty-two community members participated in six workshops resulting in fifty regional stories. Participant profiles included:

- Ages spanning twenty-five to ninety-one;
- Demographics including Hispanic, African American, Native American, and those of Anglo descent; Indigenous New Mexicans including fifth- and seventh-generation Hispanic families; men, women, and transgender participants;
- New Mexicans, New Yorkers, Californians, Midwesterners, and Europeans; and
- Range of socioeconomic origins, including migrant farm workers, scholars, artists, writers, musicians, health care providers, farmers, educators, professionals, and students.

Eleven public events were attended by a total of 462 visitors, including two events in each of the five communities, plus one at the New Mexico History Museum on the day of the exhibit opening.

> *The workshop helped me see how much we all need to connect, share experiences, knowledge, and ideas, in order to learn more and move forward and contribute something during these more modern and troubled times. . . . Realized that we rarely tell meaningful stories of our lives to each other.*
>
> —Storytelling Workshop Participant

Site-based Outcomes

Creating a public program around listening was novel and offered a unique experience. Many participants who initially hesitated in committing to the required two days, and two presentations came back to say they were very pleased with their decision, as they had no idea how worthwhile and even—for some—therapeutic it would be. One participant went as far to say, "I chose to participate for several reasons. I love New Mexico and I love the counterculture. I also felt I had an important story to share. I am not sure what my expectations were, but the event turned out to be my favorite thing I have attended in Taos in seventeen years."

Like any new project, the structure of the programs evolved iteratively. The shift from live performances to the public listening event was a worthwhile revision, given the time constraints of the project. Listening to each story within the context of the counterculture era and among the others broadened the power of the stories and perceptions; proving the sum is greater than its parts.

Impacts of the project varied by location, reflecting regional and demographic differences:

Las Vegas: Eight of the nine participants, now in their seventies and one in his eighties, were of Hispanic descent and had grown up together, either as friends or acquaintances. As a result of the workshop, they expressed how they connected with one another at a deeper level; more unified and coalesced. Many were involved with Casa de Cultura, an educational nonprofit, and saw how the TOTI project fit within their purposes in community outreach. The New Mexico Highlands University Donnelly Library and the Las Vegas Museum and Rough Riders planned to archive the stories for patrons. There was interest, on the part of some storytellers, to bring their stories into high school or university classrooms to further conversations about culture and identity.

Silver City: This was the most diverse group; participants from ages twenty-five to ninety-one, including a graduate student, a librarian, authors, academicians, travelers, a transgender individual, a pastor, therapists, artists, a curator, and educators. The group was formed, to a large extent, thanks to a dedicated local volunteer. After the public listening event at the Western New Mexico University's Miller Library, some audience members joined with participants to form an ongoing oral history group. Additionally, the university media department videotaped the event, calling it "Turn On, Tune In, Act Up." The video was edited, distributed to the participants, and broadcasted on Grant

County's local community TV station, CATV. The collection of stories would be made available at the Miller Library and at the Silver City Museum, another key partner.

Taos: There was extensive local media coverage with a featured article in the *Taos News* Tempo edition about the culminating TOTI Community Listening event. Additionally, key partner representatives from University of New Mexico Taos Library and Digital Media Arts expressed interest in future collaborations with the New Mexico History Museum. One of our participants, Tiffany Jama, made new connections with the Taos veterans' community through the telling of her story. Tiffany's father, a Vietnam veteran, had been pulled away from a mission at the last moment when he was stationed in South Vietnam. His two colleagues were fatally wounded, one of them a father to a half-Vietnamese son. Through Tiffany's connection with the era and closeness with her father, her research located someone searching for information about one of the dead servicemen. He was the very son left behind. He had grown up in the States and had said, "Father's Day was always a dark day for me." Tiffany struck up an email, then phone and correspondence, and they became fast friends. She finally bridged the chasm to make introductions with her father. At the end of her story, she told the group of an upcoming reunion for the three of them when they planned to meet in person on Father's Day at the Veteran's Memorial in Angel Fire, New Mexico. The gift of this story at the TOTI Listening event was momentous, but more significant (after the project), Tiffany and her newly found best friend went together to visit Vietnam.

Dixon: Interest in continuing to collect oral histories and to make them available online and for check-out at the library has been an ongoing project at the Embudo Valley Library. Prior to TOTI, Judy was hired to help facilitate residents in editing their StoryCorps recordings into a radio series, "Nuestras Historias," and was asked to evaluate a New Mexico Humanities Council grant for another oral history project, "Nuestras Acequias." This is an example where the TOTI program aligned with and augmented a growing interest in Dixon for public history collections and community listening events.

Placitas: The last workshop and the largest attended event was in Placitas. It was created in tandem with the Placitas Community Library and the local community radio station, KUPR. Similar to Dixon, the community was already involved in oral history collections, and the TOTI project gave more fuel to those efforts. The TOTI story collections were recorded by the radio station and incorporated into their community archives as well as broadcasted on KUPR.

FINAL TAKEAWAYS FOR MUSEUM PRACTITIONERS (FROM THE CO-FACILITATORS)

1. Hire a project coordinator. If a designated person within the museum can allocate the requisite time to a project like this, great! But we believe our success hinged on the fact that the coordinator devoted time engaging with potential participants and developing institutional partnerships.
2. Any community project will look completely different from the initial conception, and you should allow space to be comfortable with the shape and form of the final project differing drastically from the original idea. The community becomes a curator, and as content-makers the aesthetic choices and the moral compass for the process change with their participation. To truly be inclusive, the project must embrace who and what comes forward from the public participants.
3. Total budget allocation for the community storytelling project was forty thousand dollars. Expense totals came in slightly under budget. We want to reiterate our recommendation to budget for participation stipends, rather than rely upon people donating their time. The self-selection of participants in this project was fortunately diverse. Yet people's lives are complicated and overprogrammed. If you want to represent a wider cross-section of the communities you serve, honor and value people by paying them for bringing their expertise and experience to their public institutions.
4. By extending the walls of the museum or institution of learning, you welcome participants who may never have set foot into the museum. This kind of project not only brings new patrons, but also, as was demonstrated in our public events, brought families and friends who otherwise were yet to form a relationship with the richness a cultural institution can offer. Our audiences were primarily filled with family members and friends of the community storytellers.
5. The product is not necessarily the proof of the project's value. In the process of conducting the workshops and creating the community listening events, the project facilitators realized the true impact was in the moments of creation. Though museum practitioners' eyes are most often on historical context, relevance, and quality of content, this kind of project truly celebrated the moments within the project experience. Strangers became friends; people who had known one another for decades claimed to appreciate one another in new ways; relationships were more authentic and deeper by accessing one's history and connection to place and time.

The fact that some remarkable stories surfaced and were well crafted was almost a by-product. It was a very "now" kind of impact, which aligned well with one of the counterculture's iconic philosophies: *Be, Here, Now*.

6. The life beyond the project continues in unanticipated ways. Families contacted the museum in order to access the digital stories for memorials when family members passed. People wanted to start their own community oral history projects.

Overwhelmingly, the importance and power of personal storytelling proved itself over and over throughout the project. The response to the public events and, more specifically, to the content of the produced stories, was moving and celebratory. The participants in the workshops consistently found value in their participation; surprised by the connections they felt with one another and by the power of documenting a slice of their own history in the context of the larger story of the times. Consistently, people reported they thought they had a unique story, yet when it became part of the larger story, they realized the commonality and universality of their own experiences. For some who had repeated telling their stories over the years, listening to others made the workshop experience most worthwhile.

The inception of this project stemmed from the vision and commitment to the belief that people make history. Though we are a celebrity-focused society, it is of utmost value that "regular people" have the opportunity to express themselves and be heard. This project relied on participation by those already inclined to dedicate themselves to acknowledging the stories of unsung heroes as a means to deepen our connections to one another and to broaden our understanding of humanity.

In the end, it was the act of storytelling that made this project successful. Storytelling, at its core, requires a partnership between a teller and a listener. It requires engagement. What better way to celebrate an era of history that is still trying to reckon with itself today? When we can listen, we invite new perspectives on systemic structures, and we foster opportunities for a more peaceful and equitable society.

NOTE

1. The facilitators chose a time limit of eight minutes for participants' narratives as a way to contain the stories. Because our intention was to both record history and host a listening event, we struck a happy medium between a radio piece, generally less than

three minutes, and the ramble a podcast may take. Listening in a group is an unusual phenomena, so we didn't want to exhaust our audiences, nor did we want to constrict the participants. With eight participants the presentation would be roughly an hour, which left time for questions and comments from the audience and to fuel conversations during the potlucks.

13

QUEER MUSEUM NARRATIVES AND THE FAMILY AUDIENCE

Margaret Middleton

Each year in June, more museums debut temporarily rainbow-colored logos, fly the Pride flag, and host LGBTQ[1]-themed programming. Yet queer[2] narratives remain rare in permanent exhibits. When I ask my museum clients and colleagues why this is, the answer I most often hear is that their museums serve family audiences and school groups, implying that the content would be inappropriate for children. They usually follow up quickly by assuring me that this is not representative of their personal views, but the views (real or imagined) of a stakeholder, such as a board member or funder. Regardless of who they attribute these views to, museum professionals choose to take them seriously by omitting queer themes from museum content. This choice lends the museum's authority to a larger narrative that asserts queer themes are not appropriate for children, a homophobic and transphobic narrative that continues to drive stigmatization and discrimination against queer people of all ages.

Museums have an opportunity to counter this harmful narrative by creating queer content specifically for families with children, contributing to an actively queer-positive narrative by centering the care and safety of queer people. This chapter begins by describing the dominant narrative about queer themes and young children, detailing three of the most common arguments used against the inclusion of queer content in museums: that children must be protected from queerness, that queer themes will confuse them, and that gender and sexuality are inappropriate topics for children. I challenge each of these arguments by demonstrating the significance and relevance of queer themes to young visitors. The chapter concludes with strategies for presenting queer content in museums for preschoolers and elementary-age children (age ten and younger) and their caregivers in ways that prioritize queer children and queer families.

THE DOMINANT NARRATIVE

The term "family audience" is commonly used in museums, but not commonly defined. There seems to be an unspoken consensus in the field that "family friendly" exhibits and "family programs" are intended for young visitors and their caregivers. Dominant culture designates a range of themes that are not "age appropriate" for children, including (but not limited to) racism, sexuality, drug use, and violence. Behind this belief is a tacit assumption that children have no experience with these concepts and that their lives align with the dominant culture. As a result, "family friendly" can be code for content that does not center marginalized people. Broadly, "family" is commonly used as shorthand for "nuclear family," which connotes a family with children and their two heterosexual, married parents.[3] Specifically, the word "family" has historically been taken up by conservatives to promote heterosexuality and traditional gender roles in their anti-gay and anti-trans agendas. As scholar Jules Gill-Peterson writes, "Children, by design deprived of civil rights and infantilized, are easy targets for political violence-just as easily, it turns out, as concerned adults can claim them for protection."[4]

Though museum professionals may not be using the Christian right's political notion of family, it is important to be aware of the assumptions communicated to visitors in museum experiences. These include filling out family memberships forms with fields marked "mom" and "dad," reading labels and hearing announcements addressed to "parents," and using family bathrooms indicated with an icon of a man and woman holding hands with a child between them. Assumptions about what it means for a museum to be "family friendly" have been influenced by a dominant narrative that has been shaped by queerphobic talking points. The following three arguments exemplify the dominant narrative, and challenging them requires challenging these underlying assumptions.

"We need to protect the children"

On its face, the statement "we need to protect the children" is hard to disagree with. However, in the context of the discussion of queer themes, the statement "we need to protect the children" suggests that queer themes pose harm to children and adults have a responsibility to shield them from that harm. Conservatives have long used potential threats against the "purity" and "innocence" of children to further white supremacist goals[5] and fuel moral panics. To make political gains,[6] they weaponize childhood against the specter of the predatory homosexual, cast in their narrative as a form of "folk devil."[7] This strategy is currently being employed in efforts to legally block trans children from receiving gender-affirming care, bar educators from broaching queer topics with their students, and prohibit queer prospective parents from adoption, fostering, and acquiring fertility treatments.

The rhetoric used today is nothing new. The Lavender Scare of the 1950s, which coincided with McCarthyism, brought about propaganda like *Boys Beware*, the cautionary film for young people that characterized gay men as sexual predators. The rise of the Christian right in the 1970s saw the formation of Save Our Children, a group led by Anita Bryant to fight an antidiscrimination ordinance in Florida by claiming gay men recruited, seduced, and molested children. In the late 1970s and early 1980s, the Christian fundamentalist groups Focus on the Family and the Family Research Council[8] were founded, contrasting their narrow idea of family with homosexuality in their anti-gay lobbying efforts. In the 1980s, the AIDS panic led to the enactment of numerous "no promo homo" laws in the United States as well as Section 28 in the United Kingdom, forbidding teachers from discussing LGBT topics and students from starting Gay Straight Alliances. Though many of these laws have recently been overturned, queer teachers today still report discrimination and scrutiny from administrators,[9] colleagues, and students' parents who accuse them of trying to turn their children gay.[10] The same "predatory queer" narrative is behind the current spate of anti-trans legislation in the United States, with the proponents of the bills having re-cast their folk devil as a trans activist seeking to coercively turn children transgender. As I write this, at least twenty-five state-level bills have been introduced in 2022, most of them aimed at blocking transgender children from receiving gender-affirming healthcare and from participating in school sports. Meanwhile in the United Kingdom, the 2020 amendment of the Gender Recognition Act kept in place medical diagnosis requirements for gender marker changes instead of opting for a self-determination policy, and the Bell v. Tavistock decision of the same year has made it more challenging for people under age eighteen to access puberty blockers. In April 2022, the UK government announced that a proposed ban on so-called conversion therapy would not include transgender people.

Children's access to queer media also continues to be restricted systematically through initiatives like Florida's Don't Say Gay Bill and dubious bans on "Critical Race Theory." In 2019, eight of the top ten banned books in the United States had "LGBTQ themes," and the American Library Association noted "a rising number of coordinated, organized challenges to books, programs, speakers, and other library resources that address LGBTQIA+ issues and themes."[11] These challenges claim to be on behalf of the well-being of children. This undoubtedly has a chilling effect on all would-be producers of queer content for children, including museums, who fear public scrutiny. Pushing back on arguments about "protecting children" involves looking critically at why some people view discussing queer topics as posing a threat to children.

"You're confusing the children"

The argument that children will find queer themes confusing is predicated on the idea that children have little understanding of gender and sexuality, and it neglects the fact that many children have queer families and still more have significant relationships with queer people in their lives. This statement also suggests that confusion is a bad thing. Confusion when encountering something new is a common reaction, and it often sparks curiosity. Studies have shown that preschoolers spend more time with an activity when they encounter confounded evidence.[12] Knowing this, children's museum exhibit developers include surprises and puzzling phenomena (for example, two identical-appearing balls, one that floats and one that sinks) to inspire and extend exploratory play in exhibits—essentially designing for productive confusion.

Perhaps more confusing is the contradictory popular understanding of children's relationships to their own genders and sexualities. "There is currently a dominant narrative about children," write scholars Steven Bruhm and Nat Hurley. "Children are (and should stay) innocent of sexual desires and intentions. At the same time, however, children are also officially, tacitly, assumed to be heterosexual." This assumption persists even though many adults, queer and otherwise, report having a sense of their own gender and sexuality as children. The lesbian art collective fierce pussy was inspired by their queer childhoods for a series of posters they produced in the 1990s featuring their own baby pictures paired with the typewritten words "lover of women," "muffdiver," and "bulldagger." "It was very satisfying to us and to our tribe to say 'we are here and this little kid in the little dress is a dyke,'" the collective said in an interview.[13] "Also, the idea of the future manifested in the installation because it's not just about our past as children and our baby pictures but this child could grow up to become a dyke." The confrontational nature of this piece is rooted in the

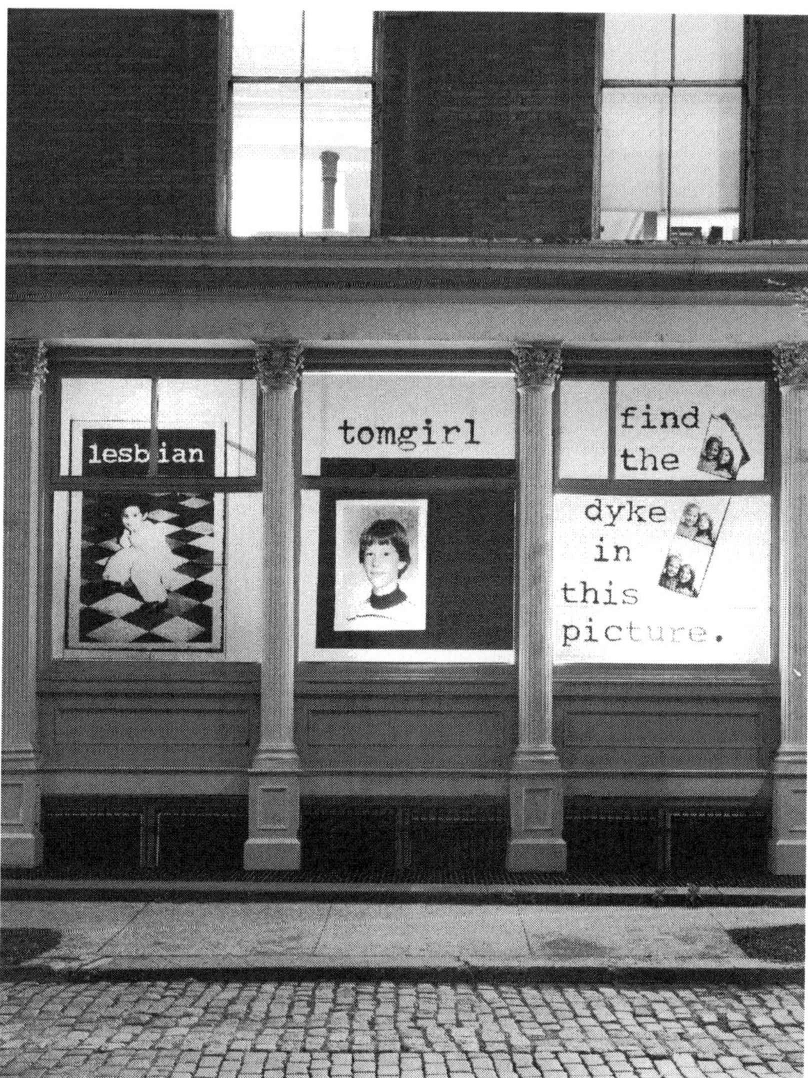

Figure 13.1. fierce pussy, AND SO ARE YOU, Ink on paper, site-specific window installation. Leslie-Lohman Museum of Art Facade Comission, 2018. Photo: © Kristine Eudey, 2018.

dominant assumption that children, including the ones in the pictures, are both straight and asexual. Not only do queer children exist, they face discrimination from peers, teachers, and their own families. LGBT and gender-nonconforming children suffer child abuse at higher rates and are four times as likely as their straight and cisgender peers to take their own lives.[14] Queer youths face higher rates of mental illness and suicide,[15] and estimates suggest they make up 20 to 40 percent of the adolescent homeless population.[16] Regardless of how uncomfortable it might make some adults, the reality is that children do have sexualities and some of them are queer. For children who have begun to come into their own queerness or who have queer friends and family members, encountering queer themes does not evoke confusion but recognition.

"Gender and sexuality are inappropriate topics for children"

Gender and sexuality are themes generally relegated to the "difficult topics" list deemed appropriate for adults only. This is likely because of their association with sexual acts and the taboos around children's interest and participation in sexual acts. But the ways that people of all ages experience gender and sexuality are not limited to sexual acts. In fact, gender and sexuality are frequently discussed in museum offerings for family audiences; they just go unnoticed because cisgender and heterosexual themes are presented as "normal."

Biographies of straight historic figures and artists usually include mention of marriage, love, and lineage because a person's romantic and sexual partnerships are culturally significant and help us understand their life. Museum label copy identifies the genders of everything from historic ships addressed as "she," to live animals in an enclosure, to visitors when they are sorted into gendered bathroom facilities and addressed by tour guides and loudspeaker announcements as, "ladies and gentlemen, boys and girls." This emphasis on gender communicates a shared understanding of the importance of gender to a person's identity. If romantic relationships and gender identities are important to recognize in museum content and museum visitors, surely that should apply to all relationships and identities.

CHANGING THE NARRATIVE

Even though museum professionals may not agree with the aforementioned arguments, cultural assumptions about what it means to be family friendly and whether queer content is appropriate for children will come through in the visitor experience unless content developers intentionally subvert them. As

Steven D. Lavine and Ivan Karp write, "Every museum exhibition, whatever its overt subject, inevitably draws on the cultural assumptions and resources of the people who make it."[17] Content developers can directly counter the dominant narrative by creating new narratives in their exhibits.

Museum visitors report "learning about others" as a top reason for their visits,[18] and lesbian, gay, and bisexual museums visitors report feeling a sense of affirmation when seeing their communities represented.[19] Scholars of children's literature describe stories about people from outside the dominant social group as acting as "windows and mirrors." Queer stories in museums can act as mirrors for children who have queer friends or family members, or who have already begun to come into their own queer identities. For other children for whom queerness is not visible to them in their lives already, queer stories in museums can be windows into another person's life. Dr. Rudine Sims Bishop, champion for multicultural children's literature, first introduced this concept. Bishop explained that readers needed a balance of windows and mirrors—without mirrors, children outside the dominant social group feel devalued, and without windows, children from the dominant social group feel an inflated sense of their own importance.[20]

Museums often respond to calls for representation of people outside the dominant social group by creating programming. In traditional museums, offerings for families with children tend to be programmatic, like craft-making and stroller tours.[21] Similarly, studies have shown that equity and inclusion efforts in museums (which is how museums often categorize queer content) consist mostly of programming.[22] Queer-focused programs in museums frequently take the form of special-interest tours, lectures, and evening events. Queer-focused programs for young children and their caregivers sometimes include rainbow-themed art projects or Drag Queen Story Hours, where storytellers dressed in drag read from picture books, often with themes of queerness or inclusion.[23] While these programs are often popular and meaningful for participants who seek them out or happen upon them, they are singular and ephemeral and limit engagement by limiting attendance and requiring reservations if not also separate fees. Cocktail parties and other alcohol-focused programs require guests to show IDs, which can be a barrier for participation for transgender attendees, whose names, photographs, or gender markers do not match their current presentation.

Programs are also limited in reach because they do not tend to leave a lasting effect on the museum that hosts them.[24] Often developed in isolation by siloed teams, programs may not involve upper management or benefit from larger budgets reserved for more permanent museum installations. Purposefully inclusive permanent exhibits and facilities are more effective methods of meeting diversity and inclusion goals than programs because they engage more visitors over time and are available to all visitors, year-round, demonstrating a stronger commitment to the content and the audience. Still, diversity and inclusion work is challenging to advocate for in institutions, and every program that centers marginalized audiences represents a hard-won success. Programs and other temporary experiences are an important part of a larger commitment to queer inclusion.

With the concept of windows and mirrors in mind, in 2015 I designed a temporary traveling exhibit for Boston Children's Museum about a family with a transgender grandparent. *Mimi's Family: Photography by Matthew Clowney* featured a series of photographs of local transgender woman Erica Tobias with her children and grandchildren (figure 13.2). In the following section are three strategies we used in this exhibit to counter the narrative that queer themes are inappropriate for children and to make sure families felt as welcome and comfortable as possible in the exhibit: story sharing, providing resources, and rethinking content warnings.

Share Stories

Thoughtful and intentional storytelling is an essential part of constructing new narratives. Museum exhibits can tell stories and they can encourage visitors to

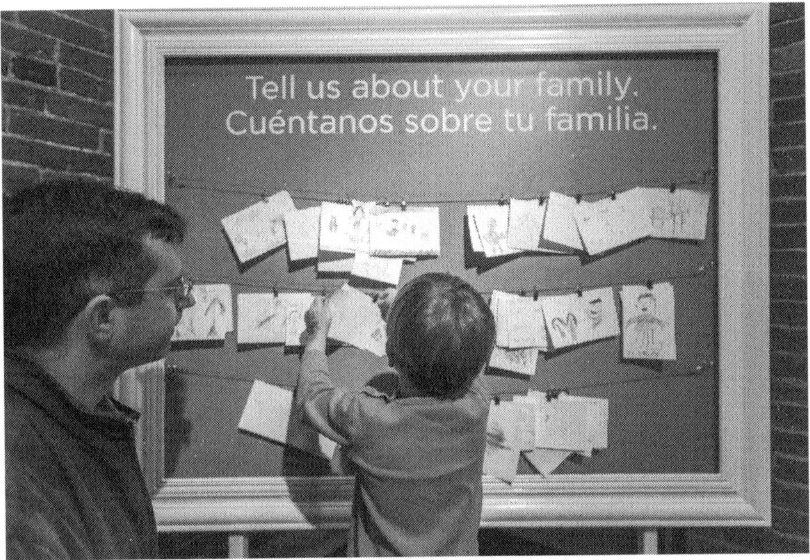

Figure 13.2. ***Mimi's Family,*** **at Boston Children's Museum. Photograph by Matthew Clowney.**

tell their own stories. In an exhibit that tells a story, caregivers fall easily into the role of narrator and help to guide their children's learning experience. This relationship between child and adult is the hallmark of family learning.[25] Significant adults in a child's life have a past and future with the child they are visiting with, so they can help interpret exhibit content by comparing it to their own lives ("that dog in the photo looks just like Max") or relating it to shared memories ("this garden reminds me of *Peter Rabbit*"). They also can reminisce about their time together after their visit, strengthening their learning retention. When visitors tell their own stories to one another, they relate to the content, make connections with it, and construct personal meaning.[26] Exhibits leverage this technique by using label copy to encourage dialogue between visitors and sharing stations that prompt visitors to respond to a question and leave their stories for others to see.

Prioritizing pre-readers, *Mimi's Family* relied on large-scale, full-color photographs to create a visual narrative with very few words. We hung the pictures low for optimal visual access for five-year-olds and paired each image with a question like, "How has your family changed over time?" and "What makes your family special?" As exhibit planner Judy Rand writes, "Labels rooted in real-life experiences can—and do—start lively family conversations."[27] We also included a sharing station with child-sized table and chairs with drawing materials under the prompt, "Tell us about your family." Visitors were encouraged to draw or write a response and add it to the exhibit by clipping it up in an oversized picture frame. The responses from children mostly came in the form of family portraits. Beverly Serrell, the author of *Exhibit Labels*, recommends exhibit developers use talk-back boards to ask questions they care about the answers to.[28] In this case, the pride and sincerity in these little drawings that appeared every day heartened staff and reassured us that the exhibit was resonating with visitors.

Provide Resources

Some visitors may not be prepared to have conversations about queer topics with their children, so it is important to provide such resources as glossaries, books, explanatory text, and well-trained staff who can jump in and help if they get stuck. For *Mimi's Family*, we worked with community partners with trans experience and expertise to create a resource guide with a glossary that we included in the gallery for visitors to refer to and take home. Like the exhibit labels, we wrote the glossary for adults, but at a vocabulary level accessible for young children so adults could use it to explain concepts to their children. In addition to the glossary, the guide included two reading lists: one, a list of websites and books where adults could get acquainted with local queer and transgender groups and learn more about transgender topics, and the other, a list of children's picture books about gender. We also created a book nook with a cozy sofa to snuggle up on with a basket of children's books about gender expression and queer families. Reading books together is an effective way for adults to bond with their children and instruct them, especially when they may not feel equipped to talk about a particular topic unaided.

Staff need resources too. Aware of the common arguments against discussing queer content with children, the exhibit team created an FAQ sheet for internal use with answers to some of the questions we anticipated from visitors ("Why is Boston Children's Museum showing this exhibit?" and "Isn't this topic too mature for children?"), led an in-exhibit training for play guides who would be staffing the exhibit, and hired Tre'Andre Valentine from Boston-based organization Network La Red to lead Trans 101 trainings for all staff. The resources we provided helped staff feel supported, knowledgeable, and prepared to help visitors have a positive experience when the exhibit opened.

Rethink Content Warnings

Weeks before we were set to install *Mimi's Family*, some museum staff asked us to put up a warning sign so visitors could choose to avoid the gallery if they objected to the content. This is a common inclination with exhibits featuring queer themes, but when museums choose to flag queer-themed exhibits with a content warning it betrays an expectation that the visitor is straight and worse, it acts as "a technology of covert censorship,"[29] perpetuating stigma by reinforcing the narrative that it is acceptable to find queerness objectionable.

At the same time, in the way that some straight content may be inappropriate for young children, some queer content may not be appropriate for young children. Sex, sex work, and kink are all significant themes in queer life and history. Many queer people have purposefully fought to create their own space free from heteronormative expectations of marriage and children. Thrown out of the house as teenagers, estranged from homophobic family members, or suspected of pedophilia, they create chosen families with other queer adults, and their childfree lives are proud assertions of their identities. As a population victimized by hate crimes and state violence, queer people have some brutal stories to tell, and so a warning may well be warranted for some exhibits.

Effective content warnings do not dictate how visitors should decide to view an exhibit, but instead describe the content and let visitors make up their own minds. When writing a content warning, be as descriptive as possible. Instead of using vague language ("sensitive topics," "potentially disturbing"), tell visitors what to expect ("depictions of sex acts," "discussion of suicide"). Do not speculate who might find the content challenging ("viewers with PTSD" or "children") or who it is best suited for ("adult" "18+" or "mature" audiences). Instead, let visitors use the information in the description to decide whether to view the content and offer alternative routes should they wish to avoid it.

Thankfully, the education staff at Boston Children's Museum recognized the stigmatizing power of the content warning and instead wrote a letter of support which we framed and installed in the exhibit. Addressed to visitors, the letter explained why the education team believed the content of the exhibit was important and how it related to the museum's mission:

> A Note from the Educators
>
> Boston Children's Museum is committed to helping children develop a strong foundation of knowledge and skills that can contribute to their ability to navigate a wide range of experience over time. We work to support an inclusive community across all of our exhibits and programs.
>
> Within the safe and accessible context of a children's museum, *Mimi's Family* offers important opportunities for us to support our visitors who see themselves reflected in the exhibit and foster perspective taking, empathy, and understanding in developmentally appropriate ways.
>
> Thank you for visiting. We hope you enjoy the exhibit.

By explaining how content developers created the exhibit specifically for young visitors and their caregivers, this note became an anti-content-warning. Instead of supporting the assertion that queer themes are inappropriate for children by using a warning or passively resisting the dominant narrative by omitting a warning, the education staff decided to create a new narrative asserting that queer themes are for everyone.

CONCLUSION

Museum professionals must reexamine their assumptions about what content is appropriate for young audiences and think critically about how queer themes fit into "family friendly" museum offerings. The dominant narrative that queer content is threatening to children has real consequences. The needs of children are no excuse to omit queer themes from museums—in fact, they are the reason queer themes are so vital for museums to include.

When I was planning *Mimi's Family*, there were no permanent museum exhibits for young children about LGBTQ people. Six years on, that has not changed. This temporary exhibit was on view for one week at the Provincetown Library and six weeks at Boston Children's Museum. After keeping the exhibit in storage for several years, the museum eventually disposed of it. I say this not to diminish the success of the exhibit but to emphasize the need for more queer content for young museum-goers, particularly in the form of permanent exhibits and inclusive facilities. Museums have an opportunity to support queer visitors, especially queer children and children with significant queer people in their lives, and contribute to creating a new, queer-positive narrative.

Thank you to Jamie J. Hagen for her essential editing support and to Sacha Coward for helping me frame the arguments.

NOTES

1. Lesbian, Gay, Bisexual, Transgender, and Queer.
2. I use "queer" in this chapter to describe people who are not straight and/or cisgender and content and themes related to those people.
3. R. Kinsley, M. Middleton, and P. Moore, "[Re]Frame: The Case for New Language in the 21st Century Museum," *Exhibition* 36, no. 1 (2016): 56–63.
4. Gill-Peterson, Jules. Histories of the Transgender Child. Minneapolis: University of Minnesota Press, 2018. 2.
5. Greenesmith, Heron. 2019. Best Interests: How Child Welfare Serves as a Tool of White Supremacy. Political Research Associates, November 26, 2019. https://politicalresearch.org/2019/11/26/best-interests-how-child-welfare-serves-tool-white-supremacy.
6. A. Niedwiecki, "Save Our Children: Overcoming the Narrative That Gays and Lesbians Are Harmful to Children," *Duke Journal of Gender Law & Policy* 21 (2014): 125–75.
7. Kerry H. Robinson, "In the Name of 'Childhood Innocence': A Discursive Exploration of the Moral Panic Associated with Childhood and Sexuality," *Cultural Studies Review* 14, no. 2 (2008): 118.
8. Family Research Council is classified by the Southern Poverty Law Center as an anti-LGBT hate group.
9. S. Woolley, T. Quinn, and E. Meiners, "The Gender, Sexuality, and Queer Milieu," in *The SAGE Guide to Curriculum in Education*, ed. M. Fang He, B. D. Schultz, and W. H. Schubert (Los Angeles: SAGE, 2015), 351–57.
10. Tiffany E. Wright and Nancy J. Smith, "A Safer Place? LGBT Educators, School Climate, and Implications for Administrators," *Educational Forum* 79, no. 4 (2015): 400.

11. American Library Association, "Issues and Trends," April 12, 2020, accessed May 10, 2021, http://www.ala.org/news/state-americas-libraries-report-2020/issues-trends.

12. Laura E. Schulz and Elizabeth B. Bonawitz, "Serious Fun: Preschoolers Engage in More Exploratory Play When Evidence Is Confounded," *Developmental Psychology* 43, no. 4 (July 2007): 1045–50.

13. "Interview: Fierce Pussy," *Curve Magazine* 31, no. 1 (2019), accessed June 30, 2021, https://www.curvemag.com/blog/art/interview-fierce-pussy/.

14. The Trevor Project, "Strategic Plan and Mission," https://www.thetrevorproject.org/about/strategic-plan-mission/.

15. Youth.gov, "Behavioral Health," https://youth.gov/youth-topics/lgbtq-youth/health-depression-and-suicide.

16. Youth.gov, "Homelessness & Housing," https://youth.gov/youth-topics/lgbtq youth/homelessness.

17. I. Karp, S. Lavine, and Rockefeller Foundation, *Exhibiting Cultures: The Poetics and Politics of Museum Display* (Washington, DC: Smithsonian Institution Press, 1991), 1.

18. Margaret Middleton, "Queer Possibility," *Journal of Museum Education* 45, no. 4 (December 2020): 429.

19. J. Heimlich and J. Koke, "Gay and Lesbian Visitors and Cultural Institutions: Do They Come? Do They Care? A Pilot Study," *Museums and Social Issues* 3, no. 1 (2009): 93–104.

20. Rudine Sims Bishop, "Mirrors, Windows, and Sliding Glass Doors," *Perspectives: Choosing and Using Books for the Classroom* 6, no. 3 (1990).

21. S. Erdman, N. Nguyen, and M. Middleton, *Welcoming Young Children into the Museum: A Practical Guide* (New York: Routledge, 2021).

22. Natalie Sweet and Adina Langer, *The Southeastern Museums Conference Equity and Inclusion Survey Report*, 2019.

23. Harper Keenan and Lil Miss Hot Mess, "Drag Pedagogy," *Curriculum Inquiry* 50, no. 5 (2021): 448–49.

24. Margaret Middleton, "The Queer-Inclusive Museum," *Exhibition* (Fall 2017): 81.

25. Lynn Dierking, "What Is Family Learning?" *Engage Families*, https://engagefamilies.org/family-learning-101/what-is-family-learning/.

26. Nina Simon, *The Participatory Museum* (Santa Cruz, CA: MUSEUM, 2010), ii.

27. Judy Rand, "Write and Design with the Family in Mind," in *Connecting Kids to History with Museum Exhibitions*, ed. D. Lynn McRainey and John Russick (Walnut Creek, CA: Left Coast Press, 2010), 266.

28. Beverly Serrell, *Exhibit Labels: An Interpretive Approach* (second edition) (Lanham, MD: Rowman and Littlefield, 2015), 188, https://rowman.com/ISBN/9781442249028/Exhibit-Labels-An-Interpretive-Approach-Second-Edition.

29. Nikki Sullivan and Craig Middleton, "Warning! Heteronormativity," in *Museums, Sexuality, and Gender Activism*, ed. Joshua G. Adar and Amy K. Levin (London and New York: Routledge, 2020), 33.

14

FROM A SINGLE FAMILY'S STORY TO DIVERSE STORIES OF IMMIGRATION AND WORK IN THE RONDOUT

Sarah Litvin

At the Reher Center for Immigrant Culture and History in Kingston, New York, we have used a single story, that of the Reher family, who once operated a small bread bakery in our site and lived upstairs, to inspire a new and rapidly growing multidisciplinary institution that works as a historic site, an innovative new museum, and a grassroots community organization. Our interpretive strategy is to tell the Rehers' story, but not in a tone of reverence or nostalgia. Rather, their story serves as a launch point for our programming, which we have developed around the core ingredients of the Rehers' story: immigration, community, work, and bread. Tours, exhibits, and programs on these themes draw diverse people into the same room to discover and share how those themes resonate with their own experiences and family history. In the process, we foster appreciation for our city's history and invite visitors to find connections between past and present.

For thirteen years, from 2004 to 2017, the Reher Center was an all-volunteer building preservation project that offered sporadic off-site programs and an annual multicultural festival. In 2017, under my professional leadership, we wrote our mission, "to preserve and present stories with universal appeal about immigration, community, work and bread. [The Reher Center] uses its historic bakery building in Kingston's Rondout neighborhood to forge emotional connections among all peoples through tours and programs." Since then, we have hosted seven gallery exhibits and over forty public programs, including three citywide community craft projects and a yearlong collaboration among three local schools. In July 2021, we launched our public historic bakery tour program, and we will pilot field trips to our historic bakery in 2022. This chapter will share how our mission emerged out of the Reher family's story and how that single story led us to identify and uplift new stories of our local history; attract folks from different backgrounds into our project as staff, program partners, volunteers, and visitors; and create a vital new space where diverse Kingstonians connect with one another.

In her famous 2013 essay "The Danger of a Single Story," Chimamanda Ngozi Adichie shares the repercussions of using a single-story when it's told by an authoritative voice and becomes the stand-in for a whole group's experience. She argues, "It is impossible to talk about the single story without talking about power. . . . Power is the ability not just to tell the story of another person, but to make it the definitive story of that person."[1] We easily might have fallen into the trap of offering a "single story" in our interpretation of Reher's Bakery. For example, we could have offered up a very specific story focused on the details of the Rehers, or suggested that the Reher family's experience was a stand-in for the Jewish immigrant experience, or the family bakery experience, or "the immigrant experience" overall. Any of these approaches could teach something, if generic: Many Jewish Eastern European immigrants were business owners; the Rehers' story represents "the" immigrant story (implying there is only one way to be an immigrant); to operate a bakery requires a particular division of labor, and so on. In these scenarios, the museum plays the role of authority helping the visitor to make sense of a particular place and time by offering up a singular translation of the Rehers' story.

Our interpretive approach to offering a single story differs. We use our historic site and the Rehers' story to help visitors find shared experiences. From the single story of the Reher family, we have exacted four universal themes: immigration, community, work, and bread. We treat these themes as points of entry for visitors and community members to share their own knowledge and point out variations. For example, we begin our Historic Bakery tours by asking visitors where they purchased bread growing up. This indicates from the start that neither Jewish visitors nor museum staff will be the authoritative voices on this tour. Rather, we are all in a process of discovery together. We are creating a sense of kinship where participants understand that their own personal experience is sufficient authority to contribute; and where we are exploring differences on the individual level, not the group level.

By creating opportunities for our community to share and hear one another's stories, we not only discover points of variation, but also new and unexpected points of connection. On one tour, we learned that older visitors, regardless of their identity or geographic background, shared a memory of going to a family-run bakery, while younger visitors shared memories of supermarket bread. On another tour, we discovered that a child of an Indian immigrant and a child of a Chinese immigrant both shared a similar memory of being shocked to discover the popularity of sandwiches among their classmates at school, since it was not a staple in either of their homes. By zooming out to universal themes and inviting all to share how they relate, we cede authority and discover intersectionality. In this way, we are using the Reher family's story to undo the dangerous othering work of the single story Adichie describes.

HISTORY OF REHER'S BAKERY—OUR SINGLE STORY

On May 11, 1908, Ada Adushevsky Reher, a Russian Jewish immigrant, purchased the buildings at 99–101 Broadway in Kingston, New York, for $3,500. This was a hefty sum at the time—accounting for inflation in housing, it would be 346,892.81 in 2021 dollars.[2] Ada, her husband, Frank, and nine children (six of their own and three from Frank's first marriage) eventually lived in the second-story, two-bedroom apartment. The family opened a bread bakery on the ground floor and operated it together for the next eighty years.

The neighborhood, which is called "the Rondout" or "Downtown Kingston," was packed with the descendants of Irish and German, Italian and Eastern European immigrants who had been drawn there since the early nineteenth century for jobs in waterfront industries such as brick-making and shipbuilding. The buildings at 99–101 Broadway were built by the Irish immigrant Cloonan family in 1877 when the neighborhood was the major transfer point for coal making its way from western Pennsylvania, via the Hudson and Delaware Canal, to New York City. Kingston was the third-busiest port on the Hudson River. By the time the Reher family moved in, Kingston's heyday as a port city was past; the railroad opened in town in 1883, displacing water-based transportation and bringing in new industries such as bustling garment and cigar factories in the midtown neighborhood, just north of the Reher family's buildings. Many of the families who rented the third-floor apartment from the Reher family worked in these midtown factories.

On the second floor, six of the Reher siblings lived together in the two-bedroom apartment for their entire lives; four sisters slept side by side on single beds while the brothers shared the other room. They also worked together to operate the corner store and bread business, which produced, sold, and delivered rye bread on Wednesday, challah on Friday, and rolls each Sunday. This was an Orthodox Jewish family, and the bakery closed only during the Jewish Sabbath each Friday evening to Saturday evening, on fall High Holidays, and during the week of Passover, when Jewish people are prohibited from eating or selling bread. The family kept this up until their health failed. In the early 1980s, they closed the business and retired upstairs.

HISTORY OF THE REHER CENTER

A farsighted group of volunteers led by Geoffrey Miller peered into the window of Reher's Bakery in 2002 and discovered a time capsule; yellowed newspapers on the racks, a 1980s calendar on the wall, rusty cans on the shelves. Family-friend Barbara Blas approached Hymie Reher in 2002 to inquire about his plans for the building, and she shared Geoff's idea: to preserve the space as a vital vestige of the "live to work" environment in which so many immigrant families to the Rondout neighborhood had built their lives and of the vibrant multiethnic, multiracial community that had lived in the area for over one hundred years. An urban renewal project had destroyed 427 buildings in the neighborhood between 1967 and 1970, scattering its community. So though that community lived on in the memories of many who grew up there in the 1950s and 1960s, there were few physical spaces left to commemorate it.

In 2004, Hymie Reher, the youngest in the family, donated the building to the Jewish Federation of Ulster County just before he passed away. After the committee arranged for the property to be deeded to the Jewish Federation, Geoff assembled a group to preserve the building. Between 2004 and 2017, they raised over $750,000 in grant funding from state and county sources to conduct archeology, improve drainage, reconstruct the storefront, replace the roof on one of the buildings, and more. Geoff envisioned a multicultural center dedicated to celebrating the rich diversity of the various ethnic groups in the Hudson Valley both historically and today. The committee organized programs such as the Kingston Multicultural Festival, which brought together performing and cultural groups from various backgrounds from across the Hudson Valley, and a series entitled "Immigrant Gifts to America" that featured arts and comedy of contemporary immigrants.

By 2017, Geoff and the other museum founders expanded their committee to include people with museum, marketing, arts, and business backgrounds. Together, the group determined that it was time to hire a professional who could direct the project.

RESEARCHING AND REFINING A SPECIFIC STORY OF REHER'S BAKERY

I got involved in the project as an interpretive planner in 2017, thanks to my background at Manhattan's Tenement Museum. Just as that museum uses re-created apartments of former residents of the building as the setting for guided tours, so, too, did the Reher Center committee see the potential to develop a similar interpretation in the historic bakery. The committee had tiptoed around the artifacts that the Reher family left strewn about the bakery retail shop in an effort to preserve the "time capsule" appearance. But in order to make a meaningful museum out of the site, I argued that the first step (after taking copious photos!) was to remove those artifacts from the space to study and catalogue them.

Summer 2017 grants from Arts Mid-Hudson and Humanities New York supported the work of archivist Samantha Gomez-Ferrer and myself to catalog and study the Reher family's artifacts that had been left in plastic bags and bins as well as on the shelves. We moved light-sensitive old newspapers and documents into archival boxes out of the sun and poured over snapshots, handwritten Yiddish letters, tax receipts, boxes still filled with seeds, business cards for flour purveyors, oil cans, and so much more. Samantha delved into the details of faces and catalogue numbers. I zoomed out, interviewed the Rehers' last remaining nephew about his memories, and used the various clues we found to weave together a story that would have resonance and significance beyond just the story of one corner store and bakery.

As we made our way through, one document piqued my curiosity: a brown paper bag with a handwritten list of names that were remarkably diverse: Polish, German, Italian, Irish, Dutch. "Sunday List" was written with an underline at the top. The committee helped me to blast digital images of the bag via Facebook. We invited those whose names appeared there to get in touch with us and share their memories. We learned that the list is a "who's who" of the parishioners at three surrounding Kingston churches circa the late 1950s: St. Peter's, which was German Lutheran; St. Mary's, which was Irish and Italian Catholic; and the Immaculate Conception, which was Polish Catholic. These folks flocked to Reher's Bakery each Sunday following services, and the specialty "bump" or "smooth" rolls that Reher's produced were a staple of their Sunday-morning family breakfast traditions. The Reher family's kosher bakery, it turned out, was producing rolls that were the perfect size for sausage patties or slabs of bacon—non-kosher staples of Christian Kingston's Sunday breakfasts. At the end of that summer, I used oral histories from former customers to create a digital project that linked the oral history videos with the names on the list. It is still available online, at SundayList.org.

Soon after I began this research, I had a frank talk with the Reher Center committee: this project, if it were to work, could not succeed as a project of the Jewish Federation of Ulster County. Because the Reher family was Jewish, and the Reher Center was a project of the Jewish Federation of Ulster County, the public assumed that we were building a Jewish-oriented museum. But the Sunday List had taught me that the story of Reher's Bakery could attract a more diverse audience of Kingstonians. The former customers who came out of the woodwork to share their memories of Sundays at the bakery clearly felt that the bakery was a vital part of their lives and community growing up. I wanted them to see the potential of the Reher Center to serve the same role in their lives today and to recruit this well-connected group of diverse, lifelong Kingstonians as advocates of the project. For the next two years, we began the slow, often painful process of breaking off and incorporating as an independent organization. As part of that process, we took what we learned from the history of the building to define our mission statement.

After much thought and discussion, we settled on immigration, community, work, and bread as our core themes; they were defining features of the specific story of Reher's Bakery that also had the potential for nearly anyone to find a way to connect their own experience or family story. Though our institution began as a preservation project, we wanted to bake change and responsive design into our mission and interpretive strategy. Preservation of the space and the story of the Reher family would keep us anchored in a particular history and appeal to audiences of folks who remember Reher's Bakery or are particularly interested in historic house museums, the Rondout neighborhood, or the history of this time or era. But our central themes offer us far more ways to respond dynamically to the needs of community stakeholders who are always changing as the community grows and shifts. The next step was to ask our community what types of programming they wanted or needed.

PROGRAMMING AROUND IMMIGRATION, COMMUNITY, WORK, AND BREAD

In the summer of 2018, we opened the doors to our building for the first time to offer two "Open House" experiences and several "sneak peek tours" where we invited small groups of community stakeholders to learn the story of Reher's Bakery and to share with us what they would want to see us do, around these themes of immigration, community, work, and bread. We posted boards with posters saying "My vision for the Reher Center is . . ." and invited visitors to add their thoughts on a sticky note. There were thirty readable notes: nine called for more tours, eight wanted a bakery and/or an ethnic culinary center offering classes, two suggested an ethnic food festival, one wanted school programs, three suggested arts experiences, one called for part of the space to be used for affordable housing, and one for accommodations, two wanted the Reher Center to coordinate with other historical sites in the area, two called for support of local immigrant organizations and businesses, and one wanted event space.

Over the past five years, our four themes and the above suggestions have shaped our programs. What has resulted is an interdisciplinary array of offerings that make space to discover, connect, and uplift stories from different groups, times, and places. What follows are just a few examples of the programs these themes have inspired.

The Story Continues and *Life above the Store*

We built the Reher Center Gallery on a shoestring budget in summer 2018 and created a photography exhibit and program that explored how contemporary Kingstonians live aspects of the Reher family's experience. *The Story Continues* shared portraits in text and photographs of the immigrant stories of the contemporary shopkeepers along lower Broadway today. *Life above the Store* brought together contemporary Kingstonians who live now, or grew up, above the store their family operated. Whether it was a Chinese laundromat, a German hotel, or a Jewish optician, they all shared common experiences of being always on call, growing up doing homework in the store, and feeling deeply connected to their local community.

The Spaces Between

In the summer of 2019, we hosted a series of four exhibits and twenty public programs to explore "the spaces between" various identity categories. The series, which was co-curated by Dr. Elinor Levy of Arts Mid-Hudson and Susie Ximenez of The Latinx Project, grew out of the idea that the six Reher siblings who ran the bakery were the children of immigrants, not immigrants themselves. This series was also designed to help complicate the idea of "multiculturalism" as more than just Jews getting together with Italians or Argentinians. Rather, this series made explicit space for the people who live on the margins between groups, including folks who are mixed-race, adopted, children of immigrants/1.5 generation, interfaith, and more.[3]

Programs drew in Kingstonians from diverse backgrounds, who were surprised to discover how much they shared. One talk on DNA testing ended in an older, Kingston-born woman and a young recent transplant hugging and in tears over their shared experience of being adoptees and receiving their DNA test results. Another program featured restauranteurs from the American South, Japan, Italy, and Guatemala sharing and comparing how they have changed their recipes to adapt to the ingredients available in Kingston and Kingstonians' palates. Before the program, I led the restauranteurs on a tour of historic Reher's Bakery. They each found and shared their own connections to the story of Frank Reher using a recipe he brought with him from overseas to start a business and support his family.

The World Kneads Bread and Reher Rolls Revival

Bread is such an integral part of the Reher family's story, and perhaps the most universal point of entry for people from diverse backgrounds. Yet creating programming around this theme has been challenging, since the Rehers did not leave their bread recipe behind, and we do not currently have a functioning kitchen space on-site. *The World Kneads Bread*, a yearlong collaboration from May 2020 to June 2021 between the Reher Center and the Culinary Institute of America's Applied Food Studies program, was one solution. Each semester, students in Dr. Willa Zhen's class chose a bread tradition from a different culture and presented research into that culture and tradition, the history of immigration from that place to the United States, and a recipe. Students who did exceptional work were invited to create a short video for the Reher Center to blast via social media and add to the "Bread Stories" section of our website. Further, Dr. Zhen and one exemplary student, Celia FlorCruz, each led an online Zoom workshop featuring two particular bread traditions: Chinese Fa Gao and Italian Easter Bread. The Reher Center partnered with Think! Chinatown and the Italian-American Foundation to bring these two Zoom programs to broader audiences and to bring those audiences into the Reher Center's work.

We've also maintained close connections with former Reher's Bakery customers, and we brought local bakeries and culinary students into the project through our Reher Rolls Revival, our ongoing attempt to reverse-engineer the lost recipe for Reher's rolls. In March 2021, we solicited donations from eight local bakeries and invited former customers and the general public to pick up the rolls from in front of Reher's Bakery. They then Zoomed into our taste test panel of former customers and baking experts. As a follow-up, bakers will use the former customers' feedback to attempt a Reher roll replica. Whichever wins the most former customers' stamps of approval, we will commission to create for future historic bakery tours.

Community Craft Projects

The Reher Center has created three significant community craft projects to engage students and the greater public in their ideas about community and to amplify the cultures of contemporary immigrants in our city. These projects were born out of the necessity to develop digital and socially distant, outdoors programming during the pandemic. But they serve as great models for our future programming. In 2020, we created a Digital Cultural Quilt of the Hudson Valley project. Over 150 community members contributed by creating a square to reflect their own cultural identity and uploading it to Instagram with the hashtag #culturalquilthv. The app tiled the squares together into a digital quilt that showcased our diversity and was the centerpiece of our eighth annual (and all digital) Kingston Multicultural Festival. During summer 2020, we worked with students and visiting artist Julia Vogl to design a community mural. Students devised three multiple-choice questions about the Kingston community that we then keyed to colors and stencils that Vogl designed to represent local history. Over two August days, 148 Kingstonians visited our courtyard to answer the students' questions and use spray paints and stencils to mark their perspectives on our courtyard wall. The mural, entitled *Our Community Rolls*, reflects our diversity and all that we share.

In spring 2021, we began an ongoing project, Worry Doll Project/Proyecto Muñecas Quitapenas, to focus more closely on immigration, and particularly the growing Guatemalan immigrant population in Kingston. An ancient Mayan legend says that if you have a worry, then create a small doll and put it under your pillow at night. In the morning, you will know how to address the worry. We worked with a storyteller and a Guatemalan cultural consultant to compose a story around the myth of the worry dolls to highlight aspects of Guatemalan culture. We recorded the story in English, Spanish, and the Indigenous language

Figure 14.1. In August, 2020, the Reher Center safely engaged a visiting artist and 148 community members to create a mural for our courtyard wall entitled *Our Community Rolls*. The mural offers a visualization of our community's experiences of our core themes: immigration, community, work, and bread. Courtesy of Verofass Photography.

Q'uechi' and made it available on our website, along with lessons on how to make a worry doll out of pipe cleaners or popsicle sticks. We also brought this project into thirty-three classes in two elementary schools in spring 2021, reaching nearly nine hundred students. We plan to bring it into Kingston's remaining five elementary schools in coming years. The project not only uplifts Guatemalan culture, but also gives everyone, regardless of background, a way to cope and to connect with each other.

Stitched Together and Sewing in Kingston

Kingston was a regional hub of the garment industry from the late-nineteenth through the late-twentieth centuries, though this story has never been told in a scholarly way or through a public exhibition. A two-year project to discover, uplift, and retell the stories of workers—especially immigrant women—in the city's garment industry, both historically and today, uses our core theme of "work" to bring many new audiences into our project. In June 2021, we opened a collaborative student exhibition titled *Stitched Together* in our courtyard and front windows. It features the work of three groups of students, from Kingston Catholic School, Rhinebeck High School, and Ulster BOCES. Throughout the year, they researched and retold—through writing and sewing—the stories of nine women who worked in one of the city's blouse factories in 1918. One hundred fifty students and parents registered to attend the opening reception. The second exhibit, opening in 2022, is a history show that shares the stories and artifacts of local community members who worked in the garment industry in the past or work in it today. More than thirty community members have shared artifacts or oral histories, and a local developer who now owns one of the former shirt factories is interested in permanently displaying the exhibit in the hallway.

HISTORIC BAKERY TOURS: CHANGING OUR BUILDING TO BETTER SHARE ITS HISTORY

Ironically, because we were unable to open our doors for a year due to the COVID-19 pandemic, our historic bakery tour program, which gave birth to our core themes, only opened to the public in July 2021. The small group–guided storytelling experience features a visit to the historic retail shop of Reher's Bakery, partially furnished to look like a Sunday morning around 1959. Using oral histories, photographs, objects, and ephemera, we discuss the diverse community of the Sunday List, the family dynamics of the Rehers, as well as our ongoing process of building preservation, discovery, and reinterpretation. Through a visit to the preserved Oven Room, we explore the Reher family's work, tools, and division of labor as well as changes over time to the neighborhood, clientele, and immigrant communities of Kingston.

Even while the building had to be shut due to COVID-19, the Reher Center's mailing list more than quadrupled in size in 2020–2021. This is because the four key themes that we extracted from the story of Reher's Bakery were resonant enough to inspire online and outdoor programming that drew community members, school children, and tourists into our project.

Now that we have this experience of using our themes to generate meaningful programming for our community off-site, we are finding that we need to re-shape areas of the building to make it more suitable for our offerings. Just as we had to disturb the "time capsule" of the retail shop in order to study it and re-create a space that tells a meaningful story, so too do we need to make changes to other parts of our building. For example, we are covering over some of the historic brick walls of the Gallery space in order to make it useful for hanging art shows and hosting school classes.

Each space requires its own treatment. For example, everyone wants to know if we'll get the 1916 coal-fired oven back up and running. Though it would certainly help us to tell the story and bring audiences into the space, doing so would also ruin the vital aspect of history. By making the necessary updates for it to become functional, we would lose the historic look of the space that is, quite literally, baked in through decades of laboring Rehers. Instead, we will preserve the oven room as it is and instead raise the funds to build a new space that will function much more efficiently and effectively as a contemporary kitchen where we can lead immigrant baking and cooking experiences and school partnerships.

MUSEUM IN THE COMMUNITY, ROLE OF OUR COMMUNITY IN THE MUSEUM

Our museum is based not on a model of "visitors," or members, but rather on a community of informants or co-curators whose contributions become a part of our offerings. Former customers, contemporary immigrants, or former factory workers themselves are offering personal and firsthand knowledge, which is then making its way into the exhibits and programs we create. As we open our bakery tours up for the public to come and learn these stories, they, too, will take on that role—by sharing their own connections to immigration, community, work, and bread. The stories they share will make their way into the narratives our guides tell to future visitors. Thus, the number of stories and storytellers that our tours include will continue to grow as time goes on. This model is inherently responsive to neighborhood change, as the connections and directions our programs take will evolve as the visitors who attend our site change.

At the Reher Center, then, we are using a single story as a way to disperse, not consolidate, curatorial authority and power. That is because the story of Reher's Bakery inspires us to create new programmatic structures, rooted in our core multidisciplinary themes of immigration, community, work, and bread, to solicit and uplift the knowledge that folks in the community have to share. These might take shape as a cooking class, a community mural, or a gallery exhibit. Contributors to these programs want to see their work on display, and they become our audiences. And once they come, they want to come back. While on-site, they meet and befriend people who are quite different from themselves yet who were looped in for their own knowledge of immigration, community, work, or bread. In creating these structures and platforms for sharing, inspired by a widely resonant single story, we are making our community stronger through building this dynamic new institution.

NOTES

1. Chimamanda Adichie, "The Danger of a Single Story," TED video (filmed July 2009, posted October 2009), 18:49, accessed March 28, 2016.

2. "$3,500 in 1908 → 2021 | Inflation Calculator." Official Inflation Data, Alioth Finance, August 10, 2021, https://www.officialdata.org/us/inflation/1908?amount=3500.

3. Rubén G. Rumbaut, "Ages, Life Stages, and Generational Cohorts: Decomposing the Immigrant First and Second Generations in the United States," *International Migration Review* 38, no. 3 (2004): 1160–1205, JSTOR 27645429.

15

THREADS IN THE FABRIC OF LEGACY

The Stories in the Exhibit *Chinese Medicine in America: Converging Ideas, People, and Practices*, Museum of Chinese in America, New York City, April 2018

Donna M. Mah

ORIGINS

The Museum of Chinese in America (MOCA) in New York City is located within walking distance of the streets where the early Chinese migrant sojourners resided within the notorious "Five Points" of Lower Manhattan in the 1800s. That settlement, comprised predominantly of men, typified what was found of Chinese migrants across the world and is oft characterized as "bachelor societies." Not thus named as a function of marital status but for those men who came alone, first leaving their families and homeland in search of work, and further bound in the United States by the quota limits of the Chinese Exclusion Act of 1882 set to prohibit the influx of Chinese. In the postwar decades of the twentieth century, this settlement in New York would evolve and become Chinatown, as the population grew with the easing of legislative restrictions that allowed women, children, and families to immigrate, and for the socioeconomic infrastructure of a neighborhood to take shape. MOCA emerged by 1991 from the foundations of the New York Chinatown History Project that aimed to preserve the artifacts and experience of the first waves of the Chinese immigrant community. Rooted in this history of archiving family stories, the museum creates a connection both to the immigrant experience itself and as it is revealed within the broader context of America's "becoming" amid global geopolitical forces; ultimately offering a space to contemplate the historical and contemporary perspective of our collective American experience.

As the guest curator to the 2018 exhibit titled *Chinese Medicine in America: Converging Ideas, People, and Practices*, I was neither a museum nor curatorial professional. As a member of the Chinatown community, I knew the work of the museum first as a neighbor. I witnessed the museum's evolution and its growing importance in sharing dimensions of the Chinese immigrant experience and the Chinese American story. I understood the importance the museum played as ambassador within the community and for the community. Growing up in Chinatown amid three generations, I also found the many threads of my family's Chinese American experience reflected through the larger arc of our community history told within the museum's walls. Most recently in my work as a practitioner and educator in the field of Chinese medicine, the museum has been an important destination to frame the context of Chinese medicine practice in America and how this lineage connects to a medical and philosophical foundation that encompasses more than three millennia of recorded human history, and beyond.

It was a distinct privilege to work with the Museum of Chinese in America, in particular, the curatorial team led by Herb Tam (curator and director of exhibitions) and Andrew Rebatta (associate curator).

STORY

"Story" served as both impetus and guide to the unfolding of the Chinese medicine exhibit. To start, there is the origin story about an introductory meeting to explore a modest community-based collaboration. I was working at Kamwo Meridian Herbs, which is located a few blocks away from the museum and is the oldest and largest Chinese herbal dispensary on the East Coast. Kamwo, like MOCA, was the frequent destination in the spring season for grade-school field trips for those classes learning about China and Chinese culture, and I sought to explore and formalize that connection we shared. In addition, I had an idea about a simple enhancement to one of the displays in MOCA's permanent exhibit. One part of that exhibit re-creates the interior of a traditional Chinatown neighborhood store of a bygone era that served as grocery, post office, apothecary, and community center, and it included a display of Chinese herbs in both raw and patent form. While historically accurate, my hope was to bring Chinese herbs forward into the present and to highlight this rich tradition in their use in contemporary culinary and medical practice.

The meeting took a turn when MOCA curator Herb Tam surfaced a counter-proposal and said, "I think we should do a whole exhibit about Chinese medicine." This both caught me by surprise and made perfect sense. Through the stories we told in that first meeting—including how I came to study and practice Chinese medicine and what we each witnessed and understood of the Chinese in America through our lived experience and academic inquiry—something bigger was expressed as we just talked, asked questions, explained, wondered, thought-through, and made connections. In our conversation, we together started to tell and see the story of Chinese medicine unfolding through the prism of the larger context of the Chinese American experience.

The telling of a story set the pulse of that first meeting, and that story itself was infused with a series of stories. These stories reached back to the conceptual foundations that reflected early human sensibilities in their connection to the earth below and with the heavens above and in their observation of the patterns revealed in nature, well before there was a written language. Stories revealed how worldviews framed ideas and how ideas inspired and were tested through innovation, as technologies emerged and evolved through the stone age, the first agricultural revolution, the bronze age, and into the digital age. The stories crossed rivers and oceans, over continents and through time, and expressed themselves through the lens of different cultures. Concepts in medicine emerged over the course of human evolution and evolved in response to the nature of illness and disease. Details were revealed through the experience and innovation of individuals, both notable pioneers and the many who are links in the chain though unknown and uncelebrated. Short of simply stacking books, digital files, and artifacts, "story" proved to be the only way to fit thousands of years of human history into a room that measures just 44 feet by 22 feet by 11 feet. Within these physical limits, it proved as important to create space that we could move through as it was to curate the content and display that hung on the walls. As a musical score combines the space between notes to create song, likewise "story" incorporates space to allow us to digest and integrate the most profound accounts of our human experience.

AUDIENCE

Storytelling isn't just a vehicle and what we tell isn't just about expertise; it implies an audience and as such, the storyteller has a contractual responsibility to both the story and to the audience. I had attended a few other Chinese medicine exhibits in different parts of the world, and I was pretty sure that these were mostly interesting to me because of my perspective as a student and practitioner of Chinese medicine. As such, the concept of audience weighed heavily on our minds as a curatorial team, and we felt accountable to the many layers of our community and those to whom we wanted to introduce these stories. We held an awareness of the need to meet those who would be new to this material, those who were poised with curiosity and skepticism, and those who were steeped in expertise from lifelong scholarship and practice. As such, the stories we told needed to resonate and reflect into the different dimensions of our audience experience.

At any one time, my mind was literally crowded with members of our audience, people to whom I felt personally accountable both hypothetically and in a very real way. There were my teachers from China who studied this medicine in a language and perspective very different from my own. There were my American-born teachers, scholars and practitioners with decades of in-depth studies and clinical experience. There were my parents, grandparents, and great grandparents, who carried sensibilities of the medicine etched deeply and revealed simply through cultural norms in our culinary traditions, seasonal specialties, movement practices, or common "first aid" methods. There were the pioneers who first practiced Chinese medicine in America well before there was licensure, first ensconced within the Chinese community and then venturing more broadly across the cultures of both ethnic and medical systems. There were those patients who benefited from the medicine interested to understand more. There would be cynics and skeptics, and those who question the validity or science of Chinese medicine as juxtaposed against the modern measures of technology. There were contemporaries and peers, who might or might not see this world or order the narrative as I saw it. There were students who likewise were striving to make connections and committing themselves to share what they were learning. I held questions of how best to manage these voices and these perspectives, how to negotiate and hold these tensions; could they all be satisfied, and how could they be reconciled.

There was also a sense of responsibility to the stories themselves, and all they contain of what and who came before. This perhaps echoes the concepts of ancestry in the way that the tradition of lineage systems has long defined training and teaching in Chinese martial arts and medicine. Thus, in terms of content, I thought a lot about the stories of those who came before us and who would be best featured within the network of the story arc, and likewise, who would be left out.

CURATOR, CURATION, TO CURATE

It was about two years from that first meeting until the exhibit opened in April 2018. Early in our discussion, the MOCA team reviewed different ways to approach and structure the resources needed, including to bring in a subject matter expert and/or work with an advisory panel. When I was invited to serve as guest curator, I was naive to this realm and had to ask both what that meant and what the job entailed. I went so far as to look the word up in the dictionary. As is my practice, I checked on the etymology of the word and settled on the idea of "guardianship" and saw that it wasn't until the seventeenth century that the term would be applied to libraries and museums. During the course of the project, I often thought about that idea of guardianship, and I liked it for that fraction of something sacred implied—not in a sanctimonious way, but in being about something bigger than yourself. Further wordplay associations from "sacred" to "holy" evoked the idea of there being a spark of life and love in each story, object, or idea. Moving then from "holy" to "wholly" to "whole" surfaced the concept that each story would be part of a greater whole, and this made explicit the importance of each part in a holistic way. Altogether, this proved to be both overwhelming and reassuring. Ultimately, ideas about the role helped to define how the task was undertaken.

The verb "to curate" made explicit the concept of "selection" and, in particular, in the service of the story. With the great expanse of historical and scholarly material available about Chinese medicine, it was clear that the selection process would be heavily weighted on what would be left out rather than on what to include. This felt extraordinarily painful particularly at the initial stages, but in the process, the story line was more clearly expressed and ultimately gave guidance to what was needed in both a methodical and organic way. I began to think of curation as an art form itself, perhaps in the tradition of bonsai, where the master shapes the form of the tree not by the master's will, but by the life force of the tree that is both already present and is meant to be expressed at a particular time and place. In this respect, the story line that emerged was the essential, or life force of the exhibit in this time and place, and the details of the story were selected to create an experience for the audience to connect to the story line. In this way, even those stories that are omitted are accounted for. The story line that evolved was linear and had a waveform. There was a conceptual beginning and end, yet participants could attend from any point and be dropped into the big story from any one of the chapters and move in either direction.

TIME, TEAM, AND PROCESS

What was clear from the beginning was that this endeavor would not be taken up alone. My role as a subject matter expert would not be taken up independently, but as conduit to a network of expert resources with whom I could routinely confer. This included colleagues, scholars in the field, teachers, friends, members of the community—not only as experts but as participants in a dialogue in co-creating a narrative for our audience. Within the museum, I participated as an active member of the curatorial team, working under the guidance of and providing guidance to Herb Tam and Andrew Rebatta, and we were supported by interns and personnel at different stages of a collaborative process. We assembled a formal advisory board and held two meetings in which we discussed what members saw as the critical historical and contemporary elements in Chinese medicine.

Our team decided to meet on a weekly basis, and this discipline allowed the flow of a creative process that emerged early on and into a series of decisions we made together that were formative to the shape of the exhibit. One of the earliest and most important conversations we had was in setting the framework through the naming of the exhibit. Rather than attempt to create a comprehensive exhibit about Chinese medicine, we decided to leverage the museum's identity as it is encoded in its name and focus our attention on the expression of Chinese medicine in America. In this way, the Chinese medicine exhibit would sit squarely within and in relation to the museum itself. Our exhibit held a contextual focus that moved in tandem with the museum's long-term exhibit entitled *With a Single Step: Stories in the Making of America* (2009–2023) that presents the diverse layers of the Chinese American experience from its historical roots to its contemporary expression. In this relational focus, the aim was resonance rather than replication, and, in so doing, we created an opportunity for conversation and discovery to take place both within and between the exhibits.

An additional degree of focus would be honed as we defined the main themes that would run through the narrative arc of the exhibit as "ideas," "people," and "practices," and in how these themes would relate to one another. There was an animated discussion over coffee on whether the themes would be set to "intersect" or "converge," and again the dictionary came out, along with a debate and sketches on napkins as to what "intersection" looked like, versus "convergence." We settled into the idea of "converging," which proved to also be the best word choice, with an active form of the verb to acknowledge an ongoing and dynamic relationship between these themes and the nature of the story and stories themselves as a contemporary and evolving experience. Our process also informed the conceptual layout of the exhibit, which proved to be cleaner in the perception of running along parallel lines and coming together, rather than through the specificity and fixed nature of intersection. This allowed us to further discern what stories we would tell as it allowed for a less specific but more powerful connections to be drawn.

Early on, this investment in time and process defined the standards of collaboration that would characterize how we worked and negotiated together as a team through the duration of the project, including the choice of paint color for the wall, and into installation. The collaborative process further allowed us to consider and work through the multiple dimensions of story and audience from multiple perspectives and to trust one another to together hold our work accountable to the story we were telling.

CONFLICT AND CONVERSATION

There was an early conversation within the curatorial team as we stood within the empty walls of the exhibit space trying to imagine what shape things would take in the transformation of the bare rectangular room. At this stage we had already decided to set the frame and title of the exhibit, but now we had to think about how that would happen in this space. We talked about past shows, ways to optimize wall space, creating more wall space, zig zags, booths, open space, flow. For me, every exhibit in every museum that I could recall came to mind. Most recently, I had attended the Metropolitan Museum of Art exhibit *Michelangelo: Divine Draftsman and Designer*, and we had together visited the Museum of the City of New York. As a native New Yorker, the city's museums were both my landscape and playground, and my experiences there over decades were a reservoir of inspiration. I remember this moment distinctly for both the excitement and anxiety that bubbled up as I felt confounded by the swirl of ideas that had finally begun to take shape, but I could not yet see or imagine how these would translate in physical form in a physical space.

Seemingly out of nowhere, Herb asked me something like "so, where is the conflict in Chinese medicine in America?" Up to this point in the outside world, maybe even by birthright as the middle child, I had become accustomed to think more about integration and cooperation, especially in an attempt to move beyond the stereotypical battlelines of East versus West or modern versus traditional, whether we were discussing culture or medicine or politics. I replied,

"Conflict? There's no conflict." But I felt at once that this had come out too fast, as if I had bypassed any thought whatsoever. So, I slowed it down, took a breath, and asked, "So, actually, why are you asking that question?" I can't quote him exactly, but in Herb's response I heard the idea that sometimes naming the conflict and knowing the tensions up front can lead to the most interesting dimensions of an exhibit, and it doesn't even have to be explicit in the way we are accustomed to seeing things or on display, but it's there. I could see it then as the armature of a sculpture, a tension that both pushes and pulls, a dynamic force that defines form, that creates structure and stability, that allows the reach of an arm, the point or touch of a finger.

Once I gave myself permission to think about conflict and that which comes before resolution and evolution, several ideas came to mind. The big idea that we settled into was one that had surfaced in my earliest investigation into Chinese medicine that sought to differentiate Chinese medicine from biomedicine. I told the story of an early reference text that contrasted the anatomical model and physician of Eastern versus Western medicine systems, presenting the idea of a landscape and the gardener versus a machine and the mechanic, respectively. While I aligned in part to these models of contrasts, they did not wholly relate to my lived experience of these medical systems. I have more often considered these systems to be something like the lenses of the ophthalmology phoropter—that device set before our face during an eye exam— whereby each system contributes different lenses that can be dropped in a variety of combinations to determine one's vision prescription. In this way, we consider what lens or combination provides the best or needed view in the context and service of the situation at hand. As such, instead of seeing these systems as sequential (traditional versus modern), or purely oppositional, could we represent them as coexisting? Can we enhance the concept of "either or" and encompass a perspective to consider "both and"—much in the way that I have contemplated my identity as neither fully Chinese or just American, but as Chinese American, and more. Could we look at medical systems as models of the body that we have the capacity to consider concurrently and aligned to give us the best perspective in the service of health and healing processes?

Through this thought process and conversation, we enacted and defined what we most wanted to create—a space that could contain it all, as a space for conversation, a space where questions could be surfaced and just held, a space to show us some ideas and people and practices to think about and take away with us, a space to explore, discover, and negotiate.

THE STORY OF ART AND ARTIFACTS

Even in storytelling there is that tension about "telling," and in our writing and our talking, we are encouraged to "show" and not "tell." Even when successful, words that "show" would still appear to be a wall of words. We had committed to twelve panels of text in English alongside Chinese, arcs within the arc of the greater story. It was rather weighty in terms of text, but necessary and placed in a narrative relationship alongside the medical artifacts that were selected for display. While important, still, we wanted an exhibit that was an exciting "show," without the words, explanations, and background.

There was an amazing display of artifacts, some from within the museum archives and even some from my own family time capsule of first aid tools: herbal powders for poultices and herbal liniments that my grandfather had made in a big glass jug decades ago. A member of our advisory committee was both a Chinese medicine doctor and private collector of Chinese medicine artifacts who was enthralled both by antiquity and contemporary history. As such, his collection included the memorabilia that documented this evolution, including the colorful periodicals of the 1970s that captured dimensions of the West looking East through popular culture.

Still, we needed something to more visually punctuate the space, enhance the storytelling, and hold the experience that words alone could not describe. Art provided a third dimension. Specifically, the artwork of Zhang Hongtu, Cui Fei, Emily Mock, aaajiao, Guo Fengyi, Vincent Chong, and Robert Cipriano helped us expand the space to more fully explore complex concepts.

The work of aaajiao and Guo Fengyi provided a visual arts experience and representation of the oft-elusive construct of the Chinese medicine channel system and the foundational concept of "Qi" that flows through the body and all life-forms and experience (including that which is expressed through art). The medium encompassed the technology of art from pen and ink to computer simulation, much as the concepts transcended time. Illustrated in diagrams, models, and described in text—the ideas of the channels, Qi and the metaphysical—were elevated as a revelation through art and artistry beyond an intellectual process and into an experiential one.

To reconcile the variability of pictorial images of the people and practices that were to be featured and crossed millenia—from silk scroll painting to Kodachrome photographs—the museum invited two local artists, Robert Cipriano and Vincent Chong, to create the illustrations in woodblock print. The woodblock style would connect visually and stylistically to historical text and anatomical diagrams that were part of the medical artifacts on display. Further, woodblock prints would connect to the history of print and papermaking and would subtly echo the intent to bring these great innovations into the contemporary foreground. Likewise, the traditional papercut craft was brought to life by Emily Mock, who crafted papercut illustrations into a video storyboard that celebrated our maternal lineage and illuminated how Chinese medicine principles are naturally integrated into regional and traditional cuisines to harness the concept of "food as medicine," with roots deep in the foundation of home.

The acknowledgment of tension in the delineation between East and West was illustrated by the juxtaposition of two distinct anatomical archetypes: the 1928 Fritz Kahn print of *Man as the Industrial Palace* set alongside the plate rubbing of older *Nei Jing Tu*, where we see the body illustrated as a landscape that acknowledges our origins in nature. These anatomical illustrations were deliberately hung out of their timeline sequence to face each other—with the right-facing Kahn print on the left and the left-facing landscape print on the right. It felt controversial to hang these out of sequence, but in that tension, it was purposeful to position them poised for conversation.

Further resolution of this tension was shown through the art of master painter Zhang Hongtu. Mr. Zhang had paintings shown in a previous exhibit at MOCA, and he had a series in which he re-created classic Song Dynasty paintings in the style of European Impressionist artists. We selected two that were done in the style of van Gogh and another through which emerged the metaphysical concept of Yin Yang. The van Gogh style was distinct and recognizable and served to illustrate the layered effect of East *and* West together, with the additional dimension in the background for anyone familiar with van Gogh's study and collection of Japanese woodblock prints. This was a conversation between East and West that was multilayered and intergenerational.

The artist Cui Fei is known for utilizing materials found in nature such as leaves, twigs, seeds, or thorns that are then composed in a manuscript form—that is, in the traditional Chinese manuscript form where characters are written vertically from top to bottom and proceed horizontally from right to left. In her words, these manuscripts symbolize "the voiceless messages in nature that are waiting to be discovered and to be heard." Two of her pieces were selected to invite the viewer in to contemplate the seamless, mutual influence and expression of nature in the calligraphic art form of writing and to illustrate the nature of transformation that has been described through the metaphysical constructs of Yin Yang and Five Phase in the Chinese classics that infuse philosophical and medical concepts, perspectives, and practices.

THE STORY OF IDEAS, PEOPLE, AND PRACTICES

Narrowing the field of our presentation of Chinese medicine through "ideas, people, and practices" allowed us to work through a structural framework that prioritized those elements that were most emblematic, and in particular held contemporary relevance while connecting deeply to the historical and conceptual foundations of the medicine. The concept of "people" sat at the center in some respects, but as in a braid it is interwoven and connected to the expression of the medicine in its "ideas" and "practices."

Most relevant to the concepts of storytelling, it is perhaps the stories of people that are most impactful, not only as conduits of medical practice, but as these persons relate directly to us and reveal our human experience and potential. From archetypal mythological kings to whom canonical medical texts are attributed (but acknowledged to have been written by unnamed persons), to historical figures over the course of thousands of years of Chinese medicine history to the present day—we had more people to consider than we could count. Practically speaking, we started from the outside in, from either end of the timeline. We first contemplated the origins, particularly the origins and early foundations of medical thought. At the other end of the spectrum, we examined our more contemporary experience and selected those stories that reflected Chinese medicine history in America. Given MOCA's New York location, it seemed natural to highlight those people and experiences that were connected to this place wherever possible. These included Dr. Carl Shan Leung, who advocated on behalf of Chinese medicine professionals with government and regulatory authorities as herbal medicine practices came under scrutiny in the 1970s and 1980s. We told the story of Mutulu Shakur and the Black Panther Party's advocacy for grassroots community medicine and the use of acupuncture as a non-pharmacological intervention to support addiction recovery at the height of the heroin crisis. We told of traditional movement practices through the story of Sophia Delza, a modern dancer and choreographer who learned Tai Chi while her husband was stationed in Shanghai in 1948; she was among the first to perform and teach the art form to the world outside the Chinese community when she returned to New York.

The story of "Ing 'Doc' Hay, the China Doctor of John Day, Oregon," was highlighted in a dedicated exhibit in an adjacent space. Doc Hay's medical practice extended care beyond the Chinese to include non-Chinese in a community he served and was beloved by for more than fifty years. Titled *From the Shelves of Kam Wah Chung*, this exhibit disclosed the history and communities that were established by the Chinese sojourners as they built the transcontinental railroad, mined for gold, and faced isolation, racism, and discrimination. In 1974, Miriam Lee was arrested in California for practicing medicine without a license. Overwhelming numbers of her patients attended her trial to protest being denied access to the only medicine that helped them. This led to a legislative compromise that permitted acupuncture to be practiced as an "experimental procedure" in research, which ultimately resulted in California's legalization of acupuncture in 1976.

These challenges may be difficult to imagine today, given the availability of acupuncture at renowned medical establishments such as Memorial Sloan Kettering, the Cleveland Clinic, and within the Veterans' Administration. Nonetheless, these stories remind us to take nothing for granted and to understand how we have arrived and come to be. More than lessons as moves in a playbook, the stories create the frame for the movement and expression of our vitality, our humanity and history that allow us to reach forward into an untold future. Storytelling then, is essential and takes the threads of our experience into the fabric of legacy that both envelops us and reveals our nature and potential.

REFLECTION AND CONNECTION

As a noncuratorial professional, I was less accustomed to the routine ending of an exhibit run, and without the momentum of the next exhibit, I felt somewhat bereft but left to contemplate deeply what remains. Walls were broken down, art and artifacts were returned, and the space was repurposed. In the empty space of what remained, I revisited the origins of the exhibit and those first meetings with the curatorial team as we brainstormed through ideas and history through the lens of our individual experiences.

In the archeology of those first conversations, the first layers of stories we shared and connections that we made with one another and to the content of what would be the exhibit were personal. We reminisced about the foods that our families prepared, some seasonal and traditional, some specific to holidays and often attached to legends and lore. There were herbal soups that our grandmothers made that were part of the regular meal rotation. There were the "special" ones—and I remembered one in particular that was made just once a year that was so awfully bitter and came with rules not to take in anything sweet or sour for hours before or after. My grandmother would call it "muscle soup" to entice us beyond the bitter memory of our taste buds. We drank it dramatically with our noses pinched closed. There were powders mixed with hot water to gag down when we had a sore throat, powerful-smelling liniments poured from repurposed cough syrup bottles and rubbed vigorously on black and blues, and herbal pellets to choke down when we had stomach upset. There were mysterious references to hot or cold foods that had nothing to do with discernable temperature or spice. There was my grandmother's warning not to eat too many litchees or we would end up with mouth sores or a bloody nose, which just sounded like an "old wives' tale" or some device to ration the precious and costly summer fruit. She was vindicated in my adulthood during travel to China, where I had unlimited access to the fruit and ended up with a bloody nose. The rationale did not come until years later during my studies in Chinese herbal medicine and was the first in many arcs forged between the past and the present, tradition and scholarship, culture and science.

Our stories were just a little different, but the same. We each came from different generational and regional locations in our family's immigrant experience, rooted in different regional origins in China. The story of the medicine helped to make some sense of our cultural and human experience. That first spark informed and created the shape of the exhibit; the experience and telling of a story to share stories that bring each of us back around, in that spiral that time sometimes travels, to make connections, forge understanding, expand the depth of our experience of our origins, cross cultures, and connect us one to another in the world.

16

PRIVILEGING COMMUNITY VOICES

The Indian Arts Research Center

Elysia Poon

The Indian Arts Research Center (IARC), a division of the School for Advanced Research (SAR), is located on Tewa lands in O'gah'poh geh Owingeh (White Shell Water Place), also known as Santa Fe, New Mexico. Its goal is to bridge the divide between creativity and scholarship by supporting initiatives and projects in Native American creative expression that illuminate the intersections of the social sciences, humanities, and arts. Through its collection of over twelve thousand items of Native Southwest art and history and its work toward creating collaborative processes, the IARC functions as an important resource for Native communities, who are encouraged to take ownership over the collection and to promote and celebrate cultural learning and pride. It also serves as an ambassador between the general public and Southwest Native American communities to inspire learning about the Southwest's Indigenous peoples, arts, and cultures, in a culturally sensitive and inclusive manner.

The IARC actively serves as an institution for teaching and learning about Southwest Indigenous arts and history for people from kindergarten through PhD. These audiences not only include the many Pueblo, Navajo, and Apache communities that surround SAR, but also its broader local New Mexican communities. As a state that is highly dependent on the tourist industry, it also seeks to appropriately share the rich and complex Indigenous voices, arts, and histories with the many visitors drawn to this remarkable landscape.

As with many other "ethnographic" collections and institutions founded in the first decades of the twentieth century, what is today known as the IARC was established by a group of Santa Fe anthropologists, writers, and art patrons as the Pueblo Pottery Fund in 1922 in the context of Manifest Destiny, assimilationist policies, and salvage ethnography.[1] This set of circumstances created a power dynamic between the institution and the Indigenous communities represented in the collection that continues to this day. Understanding this, however, the IARC presently works to subvert these systems by working cooperatively with Native American Southwest communities, uplifting their stories and histories, and serving as a think tank for museology. Through conversation and practice, it actively seeks to create more equitable relationships with its surrounding communities and those represented within the collection. Because of the relatively small size of the IARC staff and collections, it is able to easily pivot and explore new processes and ideas, constantly critiquing, exploring, and revising the methodologies by which it functions.

IARC's programs and collections allow it to support the past (by preserving the collections themselves), present (by making the collection accessible to the public and initiatives such as its collections reviews and community-centered projects), and future of Native American arts (through artist fellowship and internship programs, which allow artists and young museum professionals to propel the legacy and spirit of Native American arts forward). In addition, its overarching policy-oriented *Guidelines for Collaboration* and *Core Standards* assist the IARC in creating space for Native voices, art, and histories. By touching on several of its core initiatives, the following sections provide examples of the ways in which the IARC supports community-based storytelling within the framework of an institution that stewards Native American cultural belongings. These examples might serve as models or jumping-off points for other institutions seeking ways to embrace a community-centered mission.

GUIDELINES FOR COLLABORATION AND *CORE STANDARDS*

The *Guidelines for Collaboration*[2] are a set of documents that call for a more equitable exchange and partnership between communities of origin and the utilization of museum collections. They were developed over a three-year period of collaboration between Native and non-Native museum professionals, cultural leaders, and artists. Since their publication, they have been employed by many institutions, including the Metropolitan Museum of Art, the Field Museum, and the Getty Conservation Institute.

The *Guidelines* are intended as a resource for community members as well as museums who are working in collaboration with each other. They are not a set of rules; instead, they offer ideas to consider when working together. As project creator and coordinator Landis Smith describes, the document helps to answer, "What does it mean to truly collaborate? How can we advocate for a collaborative model of museum work? How can museums build positive, long-term relationships with community members?"[3] For institutions with a singular focus like the IARC, the *Guidelines* formalized the process by which it conducted all of its collections-related programs, including its collections reviews and community-centered programs. Similarly, the guidelines can be applied to large-scale community projects by providing a pathway for potentially disparate communities to work together.

Realizing the need to extend the *Guidelines* beyond collections-focused areas, however, in 2019, the IARC embarked on a new journey with museum consultant Dr. Deana Dartt to develop the *Core Standards for Museums with Native American Collections*. Created with the support of the American Alliance of Museums, the *Core Standards* recognize that histories and stories can be told outside of traditional interpretive departments and are designed to help museums better work with and serve the communities they represent across all departmental lines. For example, standards are provided not only for education, curatorial, and collections, but also facilities, strategic planning, and organizational structure. Effectively, both the *Guidelines* and *Standards* work toward breaking down the traditional power dynamics that exist within museums and allow different and new stories to be told of the communities they serve.

COLLECTION REVIEWS

In Jim Enote's *Museum Collaboration Manifesto*, he notes:

> After working in museums for many years, we continue to see objects in collections disguised with mistaken and unsuitable interpretations. With so much error, many items gain false meaning and significance by the hand of outdated standards and practice. It is strange enough that objects separate from their local setting and context, now they are renamed and reframed in languages and systems foreign to the place and people from which they were born. How can these

> collections cultivate relationships and create more informed citizenry when crucial conversations about the stewardship and significance of the objects have not begun?[4]

As a long-standing initiative of the IARC, the collection reviews are a direct response to Enote's query and call to correct collection records through true collaboration with tribal communities. Since 2008, the IARC has worked with representatives from Pueblo communities to comprehensively review each piece from their community in the IARC collection, add new culturally appropriate information, correct inaccuracies, and share the newly improved records with the community.

Reviews are generally initiated by the IARC—although IARC also accepts requests from tribes—and it works with individuals appointed by the tribes to determine the appropriateness of multiple levels of access for the collection, including but not limited to research, loans, photography, and general viewing. Each session is audio-recorded to assist with notetaking; however, IARC always makes clear that participants can ask for the recorder to be turned off and/or the staff to leave the room to allow for private discussion at any time. Information garnered from each review session is documented by the registrar for cultural projects and then double-checked with participants for accuracy and appropriateness. Approved records are then transferred to the IARC's online catalog,[5] again in consultation with participants and restricting any sensitive information.[6] Recordings, information, photographs, and any other output resulting from the reviews are available to the tribe in whatever format they wish for whatever use they deem appropriate. All participants are paid honoraria for their shared knowledge and involvement in the project.[7]

The collection reviews are a way for communities to "set the record straight" as Zuni collections review participant and former A:shiwi A:wan Museum and Heritage Center director Jim Enote calls it. Over the years, the IARC has worked with Zuni Pueblo, Acoma Pueblo, and most recently Tesuque Pueblo on this process.

During one of the Zuni collections reviews, cultural leader Octavius Seowtewa and Enote examined a Ciwolo (buffalo) kokko from Zuni Pueblo. It was noted during the review that Ciwolo's accoutrements had become separated from him over time and the staff were unsure how to reattach them. A row of tinklers had, at some point, been placed across Ciwolo's chest as a bandolier, much to Seowtewa and Enote's amusement. They explained that the tinklers were meant to line the bottom of the kilt, so that they would make sounds as

Figure 16.1. Zuni Pueblo Ciwolo kokko we'ha (Buffalo kokko) before and after, 1895–1925, multimedia. Photo by Addison Doty. Image courtesy of the School for Advanced Research.

they hit Ciwolo's legs when he danced. Further, it was related that Ciwolo typically comes out in a group of five other kokko, consisting of Ciwolo, Girl, Warrior, Boy, and Ah-Na-Nu-Aya-Ha, and in fact, could be in a group as large as twenty or more other kokko. Finally, Enote and Seowtewa granted permission for Ciwolo to be viewed and researched by anyone who wished to access him.[8]

While lengthy—the Zuni collection reviews took just over seven years to complete—the aforementioned example and the reviews in general show how this process ensures that items from the IARC collection are represented as accurately as possible, and actively recognizes community knowledge as a primary source of information. It also prevents IARC from providing access to cultural belongings that might be considered sensitive to or inappropriate for certain demographics, such as non-Natives, non-Pueblo people, or even certain genders or uninitiated individuals. While this process inherently reduces access to a small portion of its collection, the reviews also make enormous areas of the collection far more accessible and their stories more rich, accurate, and complex.

COMMUNITY-CENTERED PROJECTS

The IARC facilitates a number of community-centered projects that derive from needs the communities we work with have expressed. Through close relationships the IARC has developed with members of the communities it serves, the IARC works to be responsive to these needs. For example, over the years the IARC has hosted many seminars relating to areas of its collection. The purpose of these seminars is to jointly advance the understanding of the collection and allow artists to talk shop and share their knowledge with each other. Themes and ensuing seminars have included micaceous pottery, Pueblo embroidery, moccasins, and textiles.

In contrast to the collection reviews, which primarily have internal-facing outputs, these gatherings generally result in some sort of external output, including public events and gatherings, publications, and museum exhibitions in cooperation with other local institutions.[9] Usually facilitated by the IARC director or curator of education, over the years the collections seminars have developed into a program that focuses heavily on community needs and input.

For example, from 2012 to 2015, the IARC hosted the San Felipe Pottery Project after a member of the community came to then IARC director Cynthia Chavez Lamar about the lack of knowledge and representation of San Felipe potters and pottery within their own community as well as in the Native art market. Seven San Felipe potters were brought together to discuss pottery making in their community. The potters met four times over the course of two years to define what they wanted out of this project and to grapple with various issues, such as how to define pottery from San Felipe and what it means to be a potter from the Pueblo. During their meetings, they also shared ideas, materials, and techniques related to creating pottery. These potters included Daryl Candelaria, Gerren Candelaria, Hubert Candelario, Ray Garcia, Joseph Latoma, Geraldine Lovato, and Ricardo Ortiz.

Since that time, SAR has worked with these potters to produce several outcomes. In August of 2013, the IARC facilitated the first public sale of San Felipe Pueblo pottery during Santa Fe Indian Market week at the La Fonda hotel. While many of the potters had sold at art markets previously, this event was a particularly poignant experience. It was noted by several participants that during other markets, they largely saw themselves as individuals representing themselves and a larger Pueblo community. This was the first time they had come together to represent themselves as specifically San Felipe Pueblo potters.[10]

Following this initial event, in June of 2014, a traveling banner exhibit, titled *Evolution in Clay at Katishtya*, was debuted during a community event at the

San Felipe Pueblo Head Start, a location chosen by community participants. The exhibit development was also overseen by community participants, who preferred that IARC staff take over the writing responsibilities but maintained control over their own narratives. Final approval was given by cultural leaders before the exhibit was shown to the public. The community event itself was open not only to community members, but also to the general public. These happenings served to fulfill the group's goal to celebrate pottery within the community as well as raise awareness for the general public. In addition, IARC also worked with the San Felipe Head Start and community potters to host six pottery workshops at their school.

Grounded in Clay: The Spirit of Pueblo Pottery

As the IARC collection approached its centennial anniversary, the IARC thought to develop an exhibition to celebrate this milestone. Around the same time, the Vilcek Foundation of New York approached IARC about the possibility of creating a traveling pottery exhibition. With its origins as the Pueblo Pottery Fund, the IARC could have simply developed an exhibit to showcase the long history the collection represents. It was the flexibility in funding and clear understanding of IARC's methodologies by the foundation, however, that allowed IARC to utilize the opportunity to demonstrate the community-centered methodologies it and other like-minded institutions have developed over the years.

This created a way for the IARC to more explicitly center the Indigenous communities by which SAR is surrounded, and provided it with a way to encourage other museums to critically examine their own curatorial processes. As such, in late 2019, IARC embarked on a community-curated exhibit with dozens of Pueblo writers and participants. *Grounded in Clay* challenged traditional methods of curatorial practice and notions of authority by creating space for over sixty Pueblo community members to have the freedom to choose and write about the works going into the exhibit. The goal was to uplift their voices and unique perspectives.

While general consultation with a few community members to produce an exhibit is becoming somewhat more common across the nation, it is still very rare and highly unusual to directly utilize the voices of the community as a group curatorial expression. Oftentimes, these voices still stand behind the voice of a singular or a few curators that tell a singular story and gloss over the complexities of said community. In this era of social change, the ways in which the voices of underrepresented communities, especially Native voices, have been muted are becoming more apparent. This revelation of past silences in the museum field has been helped through such works as *Decolonizing Museums: Representing Native America in National and Tribal Museums* by Amy Lonetree[11] and Chip Colwell's *Plundered Skulls and Stolen Spirits: Inside the Fight to Reclaim Native America's Culture.*[12] Thus, it is increasingly essential to demonstrate and enhance the ways in which multiple and complex community voices can speak without paternalistic oversight in a museum setting.

The *Grounded in Clay* project aligned with the tenants of the SAR *Guidelines for Collaboration*, utilized them, and took it to the next logical step, by acknowledging and embracing the complexities that arise out of community-based work.

In this exhibit, each community curator was given the option to choose one or two works for the exhibit and then asked to write about the piece. A small selection of works and write-ups were made by IARC staff to acknowledge their more recent collected history. General prompts were offered to assist with the writing process if needed, but curators were given the leeway to write however they wanted in relation to the piece in whatever format they wished. Staff offered editing, oral history recording, or transcription assistance when desired, but the content produced was entirely each curator's own. Each community participant was compensated both for choosing a piece and for writing an entry for the catalog.

From that point, IARC staff served as a liaison between host institutions and community curators to determine the essential takeaways for the exhibit and related programming based on the narratives of the curators. While most Pueblo pottery exhibits focus on the historic timelines and Western-derived concepts of fine art, this exhibit focused on concepts less explored in museums, the intangible aspects of pottery that are so intrinsic to the art and enduring culture of Pueblo people.

BUILDING COMMUNITY VIRTUALLY AND BEYOND

While the IARC always emphasizes the importance of in-person community building and continuing to grow relationships well ahead of and beyond any planned projects, the global COVID-19 pandemic became a lesson in how community building can happen at a distance. Almost exactly a century since another global pandemic dramatically changed the lives of Native Southwest communities, a second pandemic presented a new set of challenges. As the state of New Mexico went into a state of public health emergency, Native communities in the area began to shut their borders in a bid to protect their communities from the devastating effects of the pandemic. IARC also had to shift dramatically to accommodate a new way of existence and community building.

The collections reviews shifted to an online format with the help of upgraded technology in the form of better webcams, faster internet speed, and virtual meetings. Restricted grant funds meant to support new collection seminars were redirected with the help of our funders to create an artist relief initiative, *SAR Learns!* for former artist fellows who had more immediate needs and saw the ways in which intergenerational transfer of knowledge was threatened. *Grounded in Clay* began to host virtual community gatherings with less of an emphasis on business—although that was still happening in the background and by email—by incorporating wellness check-ins, encouraging community-centered conversations, and creating a support system.

A CALL FOR FLEXIBLE COMMUNITY-CENTERED FUNDING AND MUSEUM ACCOUNTABILITY

This new world in which the IARC found itself further solidified the importance of supporting community voices and clarified the ways that staff and funders could assist with community uplifting and history telling. It also taught staff that there were viable options outside of direct in-person contact[13] and gave them confidence that they and the people and communities they partner with could pivot and continue to push forward in the face of the most difficult challenges. In this new world, while not perfectly, the IARC was able to better understand its role more as a facilitator and less as a project developer, and reinforce that IARC should support and help develop community stories rather than create them.

To that end, IARC is now working with its funders to create initiatives that further expand IARC's role in assisting with the needs expressed by community members. Its COVID-relief program, *SAR Learns!* taught the institution that this litheness was possible. As a result, IARC has been working tirelessly with funders to create even more flexibility within its programs. For example, in *Grounded in Clay*, funding has been set aside to support community desires around the topic of pottery. While the broad theme is predetermined, the method by which that happens will be entirely determined by Native community members involved with the project. IARC will support projects presented by these community members or their tribes over a period of three years, and awardees will have the option for self-implementation, or in the cases where capacity is an issue, IARC will provide the needed support.

On an accounting level, this begs the question of whether the funds are awarded as a grant (in the case of self-implementation) or paid out as stipends (IARC supported or implemented). While this complicates matters, particularly for the funders, some funders have expressed a willingness to work with SAR[14] to ensure that the project is carried out successfully. This type of fluidity, however, is unusual and requires the direct support of the funders themselves.

In this new world we live in, the IARC hopes that, just as some of its funders have done, others will realize the need to create more flexibility within their requirements for budgeting and narratives and appreciate the essential role they play in ensuring that institutions can better support the communities they serve. From an institutional perspective, the IARC hopes that more museums recognize their colonial underpinnings and actively work to become more accountable to both the communities they serve within their collections and their geographic area. The IARC is no exception to these expectations, understands that there is so much more work to be done within itself, and looks forward to the long road ahead.

NOTES

1. For more about salvage ethnography, see Jacob Gruber's "Ethnographic Salvage and the Shaping of Anthropology," *American Anthropologist*, New Series, 72, no. 6 (1970): 1289–99, accessed August 13, 2021, http://www.jstor.org/stable/672848.

2. Indian Arts Research Center, *Guidelines for Collaboration* (website), accessed May 3, 2021. Facilitated by Landis Smith, Cynthia Chavez Lamar, and Brian Vallo (Santa Fe, NM: School for Advanced Research, 2019), https://guidelinesforcollaboration.info/.

3. School for Advanced Research, "A Brief History of the SAR *Guidelines for Collaboration*," accessed May 3, 2021, https://guidelinesforcollaboration.info/history-of-the-guidelines/.

4. Jim Enote, *Museum Collaboration Manifesto*, accessed May 17, 2021, https://guidelinesforcollaboration.info/wp-content/uploads/2019/11/sar_gl_museum_collaboration_manifesto_updated_nov_2019_v2.pdf.

5. School for Advanced Research, "Indian Arts Research Center eMuseum," accessed September 23, 2021, https://emuseum.sarsf.org/.

6. Restricted information can include anything from donor information to instructions for culturally appropriate care, or anything else that might not be suitable for public access.

7. For more about the IARC collection reviews, see Jennifer Day's "Record Keeping for a Long-Term Collaborative Project: The Acoma Collection Review at the Indian Arts Research Center at the School for Advanced Research," in SAR *Guidelines for Collaboration*, accessed August 13, 2021, https://guidelinesforcollaboration.info/improving-a-museums-information-about-its-collections/.

8. School for Advanced Research, "Zuni Collection Review: Zuni Tribe, Review 1," transcript of collection review, Santa Fe, New Mexico, April 6–7, 2009.

9. The Indian Arts Research Center does not have an exhibition space of its own.

10. Conversation with the author, August 15, 2013.

11. Amy Lonetree, *Decolonizing Museums: Representing Native America in National and Tribal Museums* (Chapel Hill, NC: University of North Carolina Press, 2012).

12. Chip Colwell, *Plundered Skulls and Stolen Spirits: Inside the Fight to Reclaim Native America's Culture* (Chicago: University of Chicago Press, 2017).

13. In-person contact is very much necessary and leads to more successful partnerships as relationships are being developed. That said, once relationships are established, virtual options are very much possible.

14. As IARC is a division of the School for Advanced Research (SAR), accounting occurs through SAR.

TRANSFORMATIVE INCLUSION IN EXHIBITION PLANNING

Michelle Grohe

In 2020, the Isabella Stewart Gardner Museum (ISGM) opened the exhibition *Boston's Apollo: Thomas McKeller and John Singer Sargent*. McKeller was a Black man who modeled for the painter as he prepared to create a mural cycle in the rotunda of the Museum of Fine Arts, Boston. McKeller's identity was erased in the murals; Sargent transformed the sketches of his body into white gods and goddesses in the final paintings. This chapter outlines the internal work by ISGM curators, educators, and staff and their collaboration with academic and community collaborators to center McKeller's story and frame the exhibition through multiple perspectives so that audiences of color would feel welcomed and see their own lived experiences reflected in the exhibition.

THIRTY-SIX MONTHS BEFORE THE EXHIBITION: AN UNEXPECTED REDISCOVERY

The Isabella Stewart Gardner Museum is the vision of the eponymous founder, a woman who boldly followed her dream of making a world-renowned museum in Boston that transported visitors to a different world. Inspired by Venetian palazzos and lush outdoor gardens, she spent decades building her collection focused on Italian Medieval and Renaissance paintings and sculptures, which she hung in galleries full of tapestries and other textiles, furniture, drawings, books, metalwork, stained glass, and ephemera.[1] Gardner was a patron for many young artists and scholars of her day, whose creative gifts line some of the smaller galleries. Her decades-long friendship with the painter John Singer Sargent is reflected in several portraits of Gardner on view throughout the museum.

In 2017, Nathaniel Silver, the William and Lia Poorvu Curator of the Collection, came upon a portfolio of charcoal and pencil studies by Sargent during an unrelated collections storage visit. These drawings, gifted to Gardner by Sargent himself in 1921, are of a Black, nude, male model and are not widely known; only two of the nine drawings had ever been publicly exhibited.[2] He discovered that the model was Thomas McKeller (see figure 17.1), a young man working as a bellman at the Hotel Vendome, where Sargent frequently stayed. Silver was fascinated and began researching the drawings and their subject, spending months searching records, including the census; McKeller's military service, employment history, marriage and death certificates; and correspondence about his work modeling for both Sargent and other artists. McKeller lived in the Roxbury neighborhood of Boston, next door to Gardner Museum, and he later worked for decades at the post office in the nearby Dorchester neighborhood of the city. The drawings were preparatory sketches for a mural cycle Sargent created for the Museum of Fine Arts (MFA), Boston in 1916.[3] However, in the murals, the figures are all white, and many were female as well. What was the story here? Who was Thomas McKeller and why was his involvement in this civic monument not widely known? Why were the drawings, which clearly depicted McKeller as a muscular, young, Black man, transformed into white gods and goddesses in the MFA murals? These questions would guide further work as the Gardner curators, educators, and community programmers prepared to tell the stories in the 2020 exhibition, *Boston's Apollo: Thomas McKeller and John Singer Sargent*.[4]

THIRTY MONTHS BEFORE THE EXHIBITION: THE STORY BEGINS TO UNFOLD

Focused exhibitions offer opportunities for deeper explorations into a collection. Due to their close friendship, Sargent is often associated with Gardner, and the museum has had many exhibitions of Sargent's work. He remains one of

Figure 17.1. John Singer Sargent (American, 1856–1925), *Study of Two Male Nudes for a Cartouche for the Rotunda of the Museum of Fine Arts*, Boston, 1917–1921. Charcoal on paper, 47.7 x 63.2 cm (18 3/4 x 24 7/8 in.). Isabella Stewart Gardner Museum, Boston. Isabella Stewart Gardner Museum. Photo: David Matthews.

the most well-known portrait painters of the late nineteenth and early twentieth century; his portraits of society's white elite in their finery, including his 1888 portrait of Isabella Stewart Gardner, conveyed power, wealth, and high upper class. However, this portfolio of drawings by the artist was unique in that it featured a male nude body, conveying not just beauty, health, and strength, but a different racial identity and vulnerability as well. While the Gardner Museum may inspire many visitors, it simultaneously presents challenges to other visitors who do not see themselves reflected in the permanent galleries. So, these images would need a different storytelling approach that centered McKeller's story in the exhibition, sharing discoveries made about his life and his contributions to the MFA murals, while also inviting questions about and reflection on how Black male bodies have been and continue to be treated in our society.

While this research and reconsideration of Sargent's drawings and McKeller's role in their interpretation was taking place, the Gardner Museum simultaneously began a rigorous year of work developing the values and framework for *Renewing the Promise: For the Public Forever, Strategic Plan 2019–24.*[5] The plan outlined four core values: "creativity is our legacy, community is our purpose, the collection is our catalyst, and diversity, equity, accessibility and inclusion (DEAI) are our commitments." As the first exhibition to open after the strategic plan's launch, *Boston's Apollo* would be the first exhibition that was approached with more intentionality than the Gardner previously had in exhibitions. Embodying all four strategic plan values, this exhibition featured a collaborative approach with multiple perspectives and differing opinions, as well as context from both the past and the present, encouraging personal connections and meaning-making.

Commitment to Different Perspectives: Academic Roundtable

The Gardner staff, who were predominantly white, recognized the need for input from Black and Brown stakeholders to understand a fuller range of responses to the nude studies of Thomas McKeller and his life story. To shape the next phases in planning, an academic roundtable was convened with art historians, historians, and artistic community stakeholders.

Following a brief review of the exhibition and the latest research findings, the consulting group reviewed the exhibition checklist: the Gardner's drawings were to be joined by additional, related drawings and an oil painting from the MFA depicting McKeller sitting on his knees, legs splayed, arms relaxed at his sides as he looks upward and to his right. The exhibition would also include primary source materials, including a check payment to McKeller for modeling, a letter written by Sargent asking McKeller to come to his studio to pose, and a letter written by McKeller to Sargent's dealer testifying that he was the main model for the murals.

The consulting group discussed the historical context, Sargent's working methods, the vulnerability of McKeller's pose in the oil painting, and the beauty of the drawings. There was a great deal of debate about Sargent and McKeller's relationship—was it as simple as artist and model, a more intense artist and muse dynamic, or possibly even something homoerotic, and what would be the implications of such a relationship, given the race and class distinctions between these men? Other questions emerged as well: Was McKeller's job as an elevator operator at a hotel in Boston's Back Bay a good job? What was life like for a young Black man at that time? What did it mean to erase McKeller's identity so completely in the final murals? Who decided to eliminate his identity, Sargent or perhaps the MFA? The discussion was transcribed and reviewed for further exploration. Many essays in the exhibition catalog and labels for the exhibition also intentionally pursued additional lines of inquiry discussed at the roundtable, including how the MFA acquired the oil painting of McKeller, how the impact of seeing that portrait in Sargent's studio as an art student likely inspired Black artist Beauford Delaney, who recalled the pose in a 1941 portrait he created of James Baldwin, and speculations about why the drawings were not on public display at the Gardner Museum.

TWELVE MONTHS BEFORE EXHIBITION OPENS: LAYING THE INCLUSION GROUNDWORK

While grappling with the complex issues of the exhibition, particularly of race and erasure, the Gardner staff also began in earnest to develop institutional cultural competency, working with the International Coalition of Sites of Conscience (ICSoC)[6] on a series of four key components of diversity, equity, accessibility, and inclusion (DEAI), including the following:

1. Institutional cultural assessment
2. Mandatory implicit bias training for all staff, volunteers, and board members
3. Train the trainer workshops to build our internal knowledge and skill to sustain the foundational DEAI trainings
4. Facilitated dialogues around challenging topics with the exhibition planning team and museum leadership

ICSoC were selected for their staff's experience with cultural organizations that had explored challenging histories and storytelling, including Thomas Jefferson's Monticello plantation, which had started to integrate more of the stories of the enslaved workers and their families into the institutional narrative. Implicit Bias workshops with lead trainer Dina Bailey provided essential definitions for DEAI:

> *Diversity* includes all the ways that people are different and the same at the individual and group levels. Even when people appear the same on the outside, they are different. Organizational diversity requires examining and/or questioning the makeup of a group to ensure multiple perspectives are presented.

> *Equity* refers to the fair and just treatment of all members of a community. It requires an intentional commitment to strategic priorities, resources, respect, and civility and ongoing action and assessment of progress toward achieving specific goals. It is, collectively, a step to recognizing past exclusion and accomplishing genuine inclusion.
>
> *Accessibility* refers to giving equitable access to everyone, along the continuum of human difference, ability, and experience.
>
> *Inclusion* refers to the intentional ongoing effort to ensure that diverse individuals fully participate in all aspects of the work, including decision making. Inclusion also refers to the ways that diverse participants are valued as respected members of an organization and/or community. While a truly inclusive group is necessarily diverse, a diverse group is not necessarily inclusive.

A framework called the Four Truths, which is grounded in the South African Truth and Reconciliation Commission, was introduced as a foundation for challenging internal conversations about race and lived experiences to which the museum had made an institutional commitment:[7]

1. Forensic Truth is the documents, dates, objects, and other sources that are more often considered "facts."
2. Personal Truth is the firsthand experiences or personal lived experience of people.
3. Social Truth is the major narrative largely accepted by societal groups.
4. Reconciliatory Truth is the narratives that contribute to remedying a perceived injustice.

For *Boston's Apollo*, the pressure was immense for interpretation, programming, and community outreach staff to support the curatorial scholarship while also creating relevancy with strategic growth audiences, which the Gardner Museum defines as local and between the ages of eighteen to thirty-four years old, including a focus on local Black and Brown audiences from the Roxbury community where Thomas McKeller had lived. Applying the Four Truths during a reflective group conversation, several staff members shared personal truths about a past exhibition very openly, including frustration that only curatorial authority seemed to drive exhibitions and the related work, which left little room for other, social narratives, or personal perspectives when engaging with the artwork. At this point in the exhibition planning, significant forensic truths about McKeller's life were revealed through the research; however, there was still a gap in social and personal truths so far in the exhibition planning.

TEN MONTHS BEFORE THE EXHIBITION OPENS: ROXBURY

Although McKeller's neighborhood of Roxbury is only a few blocks away from the Gardner, many community members had never heard of the museum, let alone visited or felt that it was a place for them. Could the predominantly white Gardner staff tell this story well in Roxbury—and would they be trusted to tell it well?

To tackle this very real question, the exhibition team had to learn to get comfortable with the uncomfortable, recognizing that each individual has their personal lens that informs their perspective. Through facilitated dialogues led by DEAI consultant Dina Bailey, exhibition planning team members developed the skills to better actively listen respectfully, which led to agreements on an approach to integrating multiple perspectives into the exhibition storytelling via a group of community stakeholders. With Dina's guidance, the team designed two community collaborator meetings, one at ISGM, the other in the Mattapan neighborhood of Boston, which was closer to where several of the collaborators lived and worked. In advance of the meetings, ISGM team members agreed through facilitated dialogue on a set of what exhibition components or levers were open for stakeholders' input. For example, there would not be a (Black or Brown) co-curator for the exhibition and the opening date was set, but the exhibition design was not yet final and was flexible to integrate various interpretation outputs. By adhering to the list of agreed-upon levers, the team members not only supported each other but also helped to frame the collaborators' expectations for the conversations to outcomes that the museum could practically offer.

Invitations were sent to thirty local BIPOC (predominantly Black, Indigenous, and people of color) community stakeholders who would be strong thinking partners, including artists, activists, cultural changemakers, and scholars. For the first meeting at the Gardner, eight community collaborators met with six ISGM staff, including the director, curator of the collection (and curator of this exhibition), curator of education, director of community engagement, director of public programs, and the collections assistant, who served as notetaker. After sharing the research for the exhibition, the main stories, artworks, and archival materials, collaborators were asked for honest, open feedback. The responses were visceral—ranging from deep anger and frustration, to confusion, to curiosity, to awe, admiration, and hope. The meeting originally had been planned to last for an hour—the group met for over three hours. To end the meeting, participants were asked what information was essential to make the interaction with the artwork as supportive as possible for Black and Brown visitors. Strong questions and suggestions around how to frame the story began to emerge: Had the museum considered a timeline of the many things happening in Boston during McKeller's lifetime? What resources and support would be provided to visitors who may be overwhelmed by the experience or need quiet space to unpack what they just explored? Could the exhibition design include space in which the public could share their responses?

Before the first community meeting, ISGM staff had started a list of anticipated questions for an initial interpretation outline, such as: Who was Thomas McKeller? Where was he from? What was it like to model for Sargent? What was Thomas McKeller's life like? Had he visited the murals at the MFA? This first community conversation yielded pages of ideas and thoughts to review; it also added further questions, including: If McKeller's identity was never intended to be known publicly, what does it mean for his identity to be the focal point of this exhibition? What other artworks did McKeller model for, and was his identity erased in those artworks too? How was his body parceled into pieces? What is the difference between muse, model, subject, and object? Was McKeller present at the MFA murals' unveiling ceremony? Were Blacks allowed to visit the MFA in the 1920s? Would the museum consider integrating Black artists' creative responses to this material into the exhibition?

After the first community meeting, the internal team debriefed and collaboratively outlined next steps. Questions that surfaced during this conversation were integrated into the interpretation platform grid, identifying where these issues or questions would be addressed within the exhibition design; programmers considered what balance of program format would invite a range of entry points into the exhibition content, and the curator considered if there were a way to add a Black artist's artwork that had been inspired by the drawings into the show. The team also agreed with the collaborators' suggestion for a response space inside the exhibition.

Two months later, the second meeting with community collaborators met at the Mattapan Branch of the Boston Public Library.[8] After reviewing the exhibition materials again, takeaways and key themes that had emerged in the first meeting were shared. This meeting included a few new community collaborators who asked different questions, such as: Were Sargent and McKeller lovers? What was the agency for a Black man in the 1910s when modeling for a world-famous painter? How much was McKeller paid to model, and how much was Sargent paid for this mural commission? Lastly, there was a lengthy discussion about the treatment of Black bodies in the eighteenth and early nineteenth centuries and now, and how nude models have been depicted over time. Participants' responses were very different, depending on their lived and learned truths. What truths should be included in this exhibition's story, and who would tell them?

EIGHT MONTHS BEFORE EXHIBITION OPENS: INTEGRATING MULTIPLE PERSPECTIVES

The community conversations crystallized the importance of weaving together different points of view to tell the exhibition's story and identified the need for three main interpretation approaches.

The first was a timeline[9] to provide historical context, using Thomas McKeller's birth and death years (1890 and 1962) as end points. Key moments for the timeline were created by a small working team of the curator, two educators, and two community collaborators. In addition to highlighting McKeller's pivotal life experiences, such as the first time he met John Singer Sargent in the elevator of the Hotel Vendome in 1916, the timeline also featured key dates for Isabella Stewart Gardner and Sargent's friendship as well as the years of their deaths. The majority of the timeline shared key moments in Black history, including the white supremacist coup in Wilmington, North Carolina, in 1898,[10] where McKeller lived until emigrating north to Boston and New York as a young man; the introduction of Jim Crow laws in the late nineteenth century; the 1915 formation by Black musicians into American Federation of Musicians Union Local 535 in Boston's South End neighborhood, registering well-known local and national jazz artists; the formation of the Brotherhood for Sleeping Car Porters, a predominantly Black union in 1925; and the story of Joseph L. Walcott, the first African American to own a jazz nightclub, Wally's Paradise in Boston in 1948, which is still in operation today. These historical points helped narrate the evolution of Boston and illustrated both the opportunities for and limitations on Black Americans like Thomas McKeller. The names of the community contributors were listed just below the timeline title.

The second interpretive resource was a series of thematic and personal response labels[11] written by community collaborators and academic roundtable participants. Each of the six essential themes had a label written from a different perspective:

1. Class dynamics and power
2. Erasure
3. Queerness
4. Historical context
5. Agency and power
6. Model/Muse

ISGM staff asked the collaborator who spoke with the greatest passion about and/or who had the lived or learned experience to author the corresponding label. The collaborator's thematic text panels were displayed on one main wall in the exhibition, anchoring the exhibition in these key issues.

In addition, several collaborators were asked to write personal responses to a drawing of their choosing. That group of contributors spent time with the drawings, selecting the drawing that resonated the most personally. Some contributors wrote poems while others critiqued the treatment of Black bodies—both in the art and within art museums. These personal responses were displayed on the left side of the drawings; the ISGM curator's label appeared on the right.

The oil painting of McKeller, which had elicited such a wide range of deeply personal and emotional responses in planning meetings, had four labels: one by the curator and three by collaborators. In sharing a range of responses, we hoped that visitors would not only see their own lived experiences reflected but also other perspectives that would encourage new ways of seeing the painting. Lastly, although the Gardner Museum was unable to secure the loan of the 1941 Beauford Delaney portrait *Dark Rapture (James Baldwin)* for the exhibition, it was important to share an example of how Sargent's painting influenced other artists, including Delaney, who may have seen this painting as a young Black man. A large text panel featuring an image of the painting was paired with a response by a collaborator who himself is an artist. All of the collaborators' labels were only minimally edited by the ISGM curator of education and director of interpretation so as to encourage the most creative responses. Similar to the timeline, the community authors were identified by name on their labels.

The third interpretive element was a response wall placed at the end of the exhibition as a space for visitors to pause and reflect. Several of the mural segments were painted to look like roundels in the MFA's ceiling. Using the circle as a design inspiration, the ISGM studio projects manager designed an interactive station where visitors could respond to the prompt, "*Boston's Apollo* celebrates the accomplishments of Thomas McKeller. His story is one of many that deserve to be told. We invite you to share images of individuals whose achievements, like McKeller's, have been overlooked by posting a photo or drawing of them on Instagram. Tag us with #BostonsApollo." Circular-shaped paper and pencils were provided, and visitors shared both writing and drawings. ISGM team members took turns reviewing the responses daily and saved them for consideration and analysis.

ONE WEEK BEFORE THE EXHIBITION OPENS: COMMUNITY COLLABORATOR ADVANCE PREVIEW

As the final installation touches went into place, the community collaborators joined the ISGM exhibition planning team for a sneak peek at the exhibition. Collaborators walked around the galleries, read the interpretation, posed in front of their labels, shared favorite moments of the planning and writing, and hugged each other and ISGM staff as they witnessed the collaborative storytelling come to life (see figure 17.2). Afterward, a group photograph was taken and installed on the exhibition's introduction text panel, along with the list of community collaborators and a description of their role as co-creators of the interpretation, which introduced visitors to the lenses through which they would experience the exhibition.

THE EXHIBITION OPENS, THE WORLD CLOSES, BUT THE EXHIBITION REMAINS OPEN ONLINE

Boston's Apollo opened to the public on Thursday, February 12, 2020. That opening week, the Gardner hosted three evenings of opening receptions and

Figure 17.2. ***Boston's Apollo: Thomas McKeller and John Singer Sargent community collaborator preview of the exhibition,*** **Isabella Stewart Gardner Museum, Boston. Photo: Carlie Febo.**

three days of public and community programming. The exhibition's approach to storytelling, which centered on Thomas McKeller and his life, as well as the collaborator's involvement, piqued the curiosity of many first-time visitors and generated interest among audiences already familiar with the Gardner.

As the COVID-19 virus began to impact public safety, the Boston art museums mutually decided to close to the public on March 12, 2020, a month after *Boston's Apollo* opened.[12] The museum experimented with new ways of engaging the public at home by sharing the labels and timeline via a "gallery guide" online. The exhibition webpage also included a carousel of profile pictures and brief biographies of the collaborators, as well as a description of the collaborative storytelling process.

The public programs that had been paused due to COVID-19 launched as an online program series, and a virtual tour with the curator, the education curator, and community collaborator, artist, and art educator Chanel Thervil[13] walked visitors through the exhibition. In describing the collaborative approach to the exhibition storytelling, curator Nathaniel Silver explained, "together, these many voices opened up new avenues of inquiry and new perspectives that we alone [as staff] would not have brought to this exhibition. And we're very grateful to all of them for sharing their thoughts and ideas with us." After Chanel read her response next to the drawing she had selected, she reflected:

> When I was first presented with the idea to join in as a community collaborator, I'm not going to lie, I was a little skeptical. There tends to be a very weird history between Black and Brown communities [and artists] and arts institutions in Boston . . . my immediate thought was, I hope it gets done right, and I hope that they're honest. I was really excited to find throughout the process that the honesty was there, which also meant that there could be real conversation about important issues. One of the things that impressed me about collaborating with the Gardner in this way was really seeing how they truly valued my expertise . . . and not only my lived experience but what I bring to the table as an arts professional. And I'd love to see more arts institutions in Boston continue that trend of not only thinking about Black and Brown artists as experts but also paying them for their time, acknowledging their labor, crediting their work, and continuing to modify their own processes internally based on the feedback they receive through collaboration.

Later, in May 2020, the community collaborators and ISGM team members reflected on this shared journey via video webchat. Appreciations from collaborators included the freedom of not having their label text edited by ISGM staff, which demonstrated an openness to both creative and critical writing by collaborators; acknowledging how rare it was to have time and space with a museum curator to discuss and debate ideas and reactions to a body of work, and then to see and hear where that feedback is applied to curatorial decisions; recognizing that museum staff regularly checked in, asking if the approach was working for the participants, and the pivots the museum staff made in response; and also appreciating the opportunity to express their responses to the drawings through writing labels as well as through programming.

Challenges and areas to improve included better, more consistent communication after the project, including more support for the collaborators at opening events and activities, and checking with collaborators individually to ensure the museum was creating opportunities for them to reflect honestly about all of their experiences. All three of these points directly connect to a question heard early in the process, "How will the Gardner Museum engage Black and Brown communities and artists after this exhibition closes?" *Boston's Apollo* and this collaborative work was just the beginning of the Gardner's relationship-building with local communities, and the museum is committed to improving its systems to ensure the relationships with community members are sustained effectively in future projects.

Integrating multiple perspectives is an approach the Gardner Museum has already continued into planning future exhibitions and projects. To ensure a consistent planning vocabulary and level of staff resources needed for different types of work with external perspectives, the Gardener's exhibition team members created a collaboration rubric to define levels of community involvement: consultation, contribution, collaboration, and co-creation (see table 17.1).

Boston's Apollo is an example of collaboration because our community conversations led to the creation of several exhibition interpretation outputs, including many authored by the collaborators or collaborators and staff together. This collaboration rubric has now become a required component for each exhibition proposal, helping the exhibition team to start with a shared understanding of the work, a guide to determining the appropriate level of community involvement to best meet the audiences, collaborators, and ISGM team's needs. The following recommendations encapsulate what the museum learned from this experience.

RECOMMENDATIONS FOR INCLUSIVE EXHIBITION STORYTELLING

1. Catalyze institutional leadership commitment to this inclusive approach that is supportive of risk-taking and acknowledges this way of working will take more staff time and resources to achieve.

Table 17.1. Community Involvement with Exhibition Development Rubric

Commitment Level	*Type of Participation*	*Description*	*Example*
Light touch	Consultation	Community members are asked to give feedback on specific concepts, proposed platforms, etc. These usually take the form of convenings, academic roundtables, community conversations, or focus groups.	Focus group on general wayfinding and experience for Mandarin-speaking visitors.
	Contribution	Community members are solicited to provide limited and specified objects, actions, or ideas to an institutionally controlled process.	Select local poets are commissioned to create poems about gender in response to an exhibition.
	Collaboration	Community members are invited to serve as active partners in the creation of institutional projects that are originated and ultimately controlled by the institution.	*Boston's Apollo* community conversations lead to the development of timeline, visitor response station, and community labels.
Deep touch	Co-Creation	Community members work together with institutional staff members from the beginning to define the project's goals and to generate the program or exhibit based on community interests.	External curator co-curates an exhibition with ISGM Contemporary Curator.

Source: Created by author and Elizabeth Gardner, ISGM Educators

2. Determine if external perspectives are needed for the exhibition to be successful. If collaboration is desired, decide what level of community and/or scholarly input would be most useful and at what point(s) in the exhibition planning process. It is essential that all internal and external team members are updated if and when the depth of collaboration changes over time.
3. Agree on the goals and outputs for the external collaborators. Will they co-curate, collaborate, contribute, or consult, and for which platforms—labels, films, audio content, digital resources, programming? Will the perspectives be filtered or edited by the museum, and for what purpose? Why this level of involvement? Will the museum voice be separate from these voices, and how will each be clearly identified in the exhibition? How does this level of collaboration further your goals for the exhibition and the stories you will tell?
4. Clearly communicate the collaborators' roles to all staff, including front-line teams. It is crucial for the collaborators to feel welcome, respected, and supported throughout all of the work on-site—not just by the exhibition team. If they are not, they will not be comfortable or set up for success in the work.
5. Build shared purpose and commitment to the inclusive approach through transparency with other staff and stakeholders as you progress through major exhibition benchmarks. Share quotes from collaborators about how they are responding to the material, share what you and the team have learned, and outline upcoming activity—both visible and behind the scenes.
6. Move authentically and purposefully through the work. Museum culture is hard for outsiders to understand—not just the collaborators, but our coworkers as well—especially those from outside of the sector. Ensure that all involved understand the process.
7. If the museum asks for feedback, it must commit to using it in some visible and meaningful way. This builds trust with collaborators and honors their time, their lived and learned experiences, as well as their contributions to the exhibition.
8. When telling the story of the exhibition, or the "what," also be sure to share the "why" and "how" this working approach embodies the institutional values. This approach may be very different from how the institution has presented exhibitions in the past. Why focus on these stories, what is central to the exhibition themes and why? Why is this approach important and necessary to be successful?

9. Set achievable outcomes, and reflect often both during and after the project. Reflection is not limited to just staff—continue the collaborative process by also reflecting with all key stakeholders. Adjust the key performance indicators as needed along the way.
10. Share what you have learned, including challenges, successes, and unexpected responses, as well as next moves the organization will make in response to what was learned.

Boston's Apollo was the first major exhibition to start the Gardner Museum's inclusive exhibition storytelling. By the time this book is published, the learnings and processes from *Boston's Apollo* will have been applied to several more projects, including audio content generated by several community members on sixteenth-century paintings that delve into issues of sex, lust, violence, and love; a contemporary art exhibition co-curated by the Gardner's curator of contemporary art and a *Boston's Apollo* community collaborator and scholar; academic and community roundtables to examine the language that will be used to compare and contrast travel and cultural experiences in the nineteenth-century with today; and an exhibition designed to emphasize the needs of families' multigenerational visitor experiences. In each, the Gardner will experiment with methods of inclusive storytelling so that more visitors experience the Gardner Museum as community collaborator Valerie Stephens said she felt after *Boston's Apollo* opened: "after spending time with you all . . . I really wish I had met Thomas . . . To know this man. I think if a museum can do that, show me an avenue to see a painting of someone, and I want to know that person, that says a lot to me . . . It's been a joy."

NOTES

1. Christina Nielsen, Casey Riley, and Nathaniel Silver, *Isabella Stewart Gardner Museum: A Guidebook* (New Haven and London: Yale University Press, 2017), 10.
2. https://www.gardnermuseum.org/experience/collection/18174.
3. https://collections.mfa.org/objects/31933/apollo-and-the-muses?ctx=f68356f4-3cea-4096-bb8a-532c7d89f5a9&idx=15.
4. https://www.gardnermuseum.org/calendar/exhibition/bostons-apollo.
5. https://www.gardnermuseum.org/organization/executive-summary-2019.
6. See https://www.sitesofconscience.org/en/home/.
7. https://www.justice.gov.za/trc/index.html.
8. https://www.bpl.org/locations/30/.

9. https://www.gardnermuseum.org/sites/default/files/uploads/files/BostonsApolloTimeline_06FebRev.pdf, accessed October 8, 2021.

10. https://www.theatlantic.com/politics/archive/2017/08/wilmington-massacre/536457/, accessed October 8, 2021.

11 https://www.gardnermuseum.org/sites/default/files/uploads/files/bostonsapollolabels_forweb_v2.pdf.

12. https://www.bostonglobe.com/2020/03/12/arts/bostons-biggest-art-museums-will-close-after-today/.

13. https://www.gardnermuseum.org/experience/virtual-bostons-apollo.

18

HONORING THE ANCESTORS

Descendant Voices at Montpelier

Iris Carter Ford, Patrice Preston-Grimes, and Christian J. Cotz

The commitment at James Madison's Montpelier in central Virginia to develop meaningful relationships with descendants of people who were once enslaved there has grown significantly, year after year, for more than two decades. Including and involving the many voices of the Montpelier Descendant Community was critical to the success of the award-winning exhibition *The Mere Distinction of Colour* (2017) and to the effectiveness of the *Rubric on Engaging Descendant Communities* (2018). In the same spirit of collaboration, this chapter presents three distinct points of view that relay and recount some of the processes, experiences, and emotions of that engagement. Iris Carter Ford and Patrice Preston-Grimes are both members of the Montpelier Descendant Community and have been involved with the museum in different ways for more than fifteen years. Christian Cotz was Montpelier's manager of student programs from 2000 to 2011 and director of education and visitor engagement from 2011 to 2020. He was the project director for both the exhibition and the rubric mentioned above.

WHO WERE THEY, TO INVITE ME HOME?
IRIS CARTER FORD

Montpelier is among my earliest memories. But never did I—or certainly my ancestors—believe that those memories would be a part of America's official narrative on slavery, however ineffectual that might remain.

My mother and her siblings were born and raised on family land across the road from Marion duPont Scott's Montpelier. My mother's father built the family home, which is described in the National Register of Historic Places as "eclectic early twentieth century," one of only two in the area built of concrete block, and the only one with a mansard roof. He also built and remodeled structures at Montpelier, from horse barns to the famed art deco trophy room. His father, born enslaved, taught him how to do all of that—and sold him the land for the farm! And his father's father owned Bloomfield, the work camp literally next door to James Madison's Montpelier that afforded neighborly transactions from witnessing Madison's will to transferring land. I didn't know any of this until I reached adulthood.

My mother's family, the Jacksons, were uncompromisingly communicative about their achievements, but compromisingly uncommunicative about slavery and the legacy that influenced them—for better and worse. But some things you just come to know without words. When I was a small child, in the 1950s, my family moved north, away from Montpelier, but I spent summers "down south" acquiring a visceral awareness of segregation—north and south.

With that awareness, a history class here and there in high school (more revealing by what was left out), gradual family revelations (including a suspected lynching and a documented rape), and graduate studies in anthropology (a discipline with roots in pernicious social Darwinism), in 2007, by invitation, I traveled to Montpelier, with a lot of baggage, for a reckoning.

Montpelier orchestrated a sit-down with in-house public historians, genealogists, archaeologists, outside experts, and a community of descendants to re-frame the narrative. The event was a milestone for James Madison's Montpelier: There were scores of descendants from across the nation in attendance, whose family histories were collected and videotaped. There were historians, notably the incomparable John Hope Franklin, and other experts who delivered keynotes and interacted with descendants. Every descendant was offered DNA testing by the nation's leading expert. And all of this took place against a backdrop of ancestral landscape, excellent Virginia cuisine, and the vibrant sights and sounds of African ceremony. It represented years of historical, archaeological, and genealogical research, but to my mind (and I had been involved with

Montpelier before this event), this was the first time staff developed a strategy to help ensure substantive and sustained involvement of descendants.

The very definition of "descendant" was a part of that strategy. Even now, most plantation museums working toward descendant involvement embrace a narrow definition based on DNA, other indicators of direct descent, and, importantly, the physical landscape. You belong if you can trace your "blood" to the property owner—or to the soil, as the owner's property.

Montpelier expanded that understanding well before the 2007 event, culminating in the 2018 Rubric of Best Practices Established by the National Summit on Teaching Slavery, developed by an interdisciplinary cadre of experts convened at Montpelier in partnership with the National Trust for Historic Preservation. According to the rubric,[1]

> In its most fundamental form, a "descendant community" is a group of people whose ancestors were enslaved at a particular site, but it can transcend that limited definition. A descendant community can include those whose ancestors were enslaved not only at a particular site, but also throughout the surrounding region, reflecting the fact that family ties often crossed plantation boundaries. A descendant community can also welcome those who feel connected to the work the institution is doing, whether or not they know of a genealogical connection.

This definition is consistent with folklorist Barbara Allen's "genealogical landscape," a conceptual framework essential to the goal of engaging descendants to understand slavery in a more engaging and inclusive manner. According to Allen, the landscape is much more than merely physical dimensions, it includes a complex structure of dense kinship networks—including non-kin neighbors through marriage, fictive kinship, and a deep knowledge of local heritage.[2] These networks and practices transform physical space into cultural place. It is that cultural place that is the key element in Montpelier's success in working with and translating the intellectual wealth of its descendant community and the resulting richer and more diverse narrative. No small feat when one considers the narrative of many plantation museums that focus almost exclusively on the landowner and the land.

Before the 2007 milestone event, my involvement with Montpelier was welcoming, productive even. But in terms of my investment in narrative-building, I felt more like a sharecropper than an owner. The event itself was by invitation from a bunch of museum folks with no real connection to the place other than their professional mandates. Who were they to invite me home? My family had been around for generations—building social capital through intellect, emotional intelligence, and spirituality. I still marvel at their hard work rooted in intellectual proficiency, their boundless joy in spite of endless suffering, their exceptional creativity, like my grandfather's eclectic mansard roof. And given the ubiquitous stereotyping and devaluing of African American people, I wondered if any museum could do those achievements proud.

Moreover, I believed the museum professionals held allegiance first and foremost to the carefully crafted image of James Madison as preeminent statesman, but not slaveholder (the confounding contradiction of the Constitution),[3] and Dolley Madison as preeminent first lady, but not slave trader (the case of Ellen Stewart White and the Pearl).[4] An example of this perceived allegiance occurred at the 2007 descendants' event during a tour of the restored mansion and grounds, which I learned cost twenty-four million dollars. I stepped out onto the second-floor terrace of the mansion overlooking the South Yard, where the domestic servants lived and worked. I saw nothing but, as I am quoted as saying, "dead grass and railroad ties." As a child, I knew very little about the legacy of slavery, but as an adult I knew enough to ask why so much money was pumped into the big house, but not the South Yard. And it was a rhetorical question. I knew the answer.

I felt resentment, as did some of my family members. Some wondered why I would even bother to work with Montpelier. Others wondered why I would actually pay for a membership when my ancestors were not compensated for the work that resulted in the well-crafted story of Montpelier and the nation's founding myth—with scant mention of the prolific contributions of Africans and African Americans. While James Madison was writing to transform the political landscape, and Dolley Madison was entertaining to transform the diplomatic landscape, the enslaved were transforming the economic, social, and cultural landscapes as the bedrock of American democracy—even as they were excluded. And I have to spend my time working to convince white people that my ancestors were essential to the founding of America? I should be satisfied as supporting cast? As I write this, I realize there is still some resentment, but it is not paralyzing.

FINDING THE POWER OF PLACE
PATRICE PRESTON-GRIMES

On a cold, overcast Sunday afternoon in 2006 I drove from my home in Charlottesville, Virginia, to the Fine Arts Center in Orange to see a Black History Month exhibit, featuring works by local student artists. As a new professor at the University of Virginia, I was eager to explore the spaces and sites in the

Commonwealth that most of my students called home. On that weekend drive, I didn't pay attention to the sign that I passed on Virginia Route 20, marking the entrance to James Madison's plantation home, Montpelier—and I missed completely seeing the small white cabin across the road. Thanks to an amazing person whom I was soon to meet, that was the last time that either of those sites would go unnoticed.

As I entered the Arts Center, a very petite, well-dressed, silver-haired woman greeted me with a warm smile and pointed to the gallery at the back of the main floor. Rebecca Gilmore Coleman then was whisked away to greet others after encouraging me to mingle and chat with the guests. She later reappeared and directed me to a new photography display created especially for the occasion featuring the lives of Black Orange County residents. As she gestured to highlight the exhibit, she beamed with pride, pointing to a poster of an old, whitewashed homestead that belonged to her grandfather, George Gilmore. Born into slavery, Gilmore became a farmer after Emancipation, and by the turn of the century, owned the cabin and the adjacent land, where he raised his family.

By spring 2007, I was redesigning a master's-level university course, "Teaching Social Studies in the Elementary School," and seeking ways to impact my undergraduate students' learning. Trying to move students beyond being satisfied with a good grade for digesting educational theory and writing term papers, I wanted them to finish the course with the knowledge, skills, and dispositions to teach with confidence diverse populations of children, from kindergarten through middle school.

Impacting student dispositions was a key course outcome, as the class was tasked to reflect in end-of-course evaluations. The profile of my typical student was so diametrically different from my own—white, young, and female, with varying degrees of exposure to ideas and people different from their social class and upbringing. I wondered: As an African American, older professor transplanted from urban spaces to this "college-plus town," would my teaching style and perspectives be dismissed? In designing a new series of lessons, how could I motivate students to embrace historical thinking and understanding and not just regurgitate facts? In a time when the political and social climate on campus (and the nation) was increasingly polarized, how could I keep the historical themes centered through difficult conversations that were a part of the instruction?

The recurrent elephant in the classroom was the influence of the university's founder, Thomas Jefferson, whose visions of learning, leadership, and citizenship resonate in every aspect of academic and civic life on "the Grounds." The contradiction of Jefferson as a master orator, statesman, author of the Declaration of Independence—and slaveowner continues to create dissonance for many students and faculty at the University of Virginia, whether voiced or unspoken. Years later, my five years of service on the President's Commission on Slavery and the University helped me greatly to wrestle with the complex and evolving interpretations of Jefferson's life and legacy, that at times were painful for me to confront and process.[5]

Then, I recalled the words of educator Parker J. Palmer, who said, "whoever our students may be, whatever the subject we teach, ultimately, we teach who we are."[6] How did I learn best? What were the lessons that stuck with me? How did my most memorable teachers make history come alive? What are the issues that have challenged me in the past? To reframe the course, I needed to break free from the classroom walls and go into the field. What better way to embark on this experiment and "do history" than to explore a nearby site, like Montpelier, and to study the rich, yet often overlooked, African American community that surrounded it. Grounded in the understandings of my own personal heritage and identity that were planted at sites in Philadelphia, West Virginia, and now, Central Virginia, I crafted a blueprint for what is now a seminal element of my collegiate teaching that highlights the *power of place*.

For the next ten years, I took a group of teachers-in-training to Orange each semester for a field study led by Montpelier's staff. Matthew Reeves, director of archeology for the Montpelier Foundation, suggested resources, and members of the Orange County African-American Historical Society were sounding boards as I crafted grade-appropriate lessons that aligned with the Virginia Standards of Learning (VA-SOL)[7] in civics, economics, geography, and history. The themes of freedom and slavery anchored interdisciplinary lessons that featured visits to public archeological excavation sites around the plantation and tours of the Gilmore cabin, the adjacent Montpelier Civil War Trail encampment, and the Jim Crow–era Train Depot. Each site offered a unique window into nineteenth-century rural life and the vestiges of legalized racial segregation.

During the planning stage, I realized that touring a historic site is not a neutral experience—we enter these spaces with our own notions and beliefs that form the basis of how we make meaning of what we see and interpret.[8] When arriving at the Train Depot, for example, most white students usually flock first to enter the "colored" side of the Depot and touch the artifacts of a bygone era. Some struggle visibly to interpret the tight space, stark furnishings, and bulletin board notices that offer a glimpse into the second-class legal status of its rail passengers. Until that moment, the privilege of unfettered movement by white passengers traveling through the Jim Crow South had been an abstract fact in their history texts. Yet my initial entry into the same waiting room, with its potbelly stove and hard wooden benches, reminded me of my father's recollections of his first train ride to visit relatives "up North," and his vivid description of how the family prepared for the daylong journey. Then, my emotions flared as I noted the ways in which the physical space perpetuated a caste system based on race, and its subliminal messages to its travelers. Our varying responses entering the same site aligned with experiences of other Depot visitors, according to Price Thomas, former director of marketing and communications for the Montpelier Foundation. He explained, "The stories become more salient when you can experience how small the rooms were, or how far families had to walk to see each other. You can't get that from a book. You can't get it from a podcast."

No one could have predicted the change over time in Montpelier's landscape or the degree of stakeholders' engagement. In hindsight, I was fortunate to be involved in many stages of the transformation. During each seasonal visit, my University of Virginia classes would learn of a new archeological discovery from one of Montpelier's Field School interns or meet descendants from around the country searching for clues to their past, which led them through Montpelier's gates. The teachers-in-training were also becoming adept information detectives and were delighted to share their class research about Madison, and especially Dolley, with the house tour guides.

At the same time, the concerted efforts of the Orange County African American Historical Society (OCAAHS) to engage Montpelier with the local community were taking root. For generations, African Americans in and near Orange viewed James Madison's "house on the hill" as a site where its owners were interested only in their labor, and not in their kinship ties. In 2005, the completion of the restoration of the Gilmore cabin by the Montpelier Foundation board of directors was a key step in publicly recognizing the contributions of the Gilmore family and descendant community.

The time was ripe for descendants to come together. With the Commonwealth of Virginia poised to celebrate its four-hundreth anniversary, and Montpelier embarking on major restoration of the mansion and grounds, OCAAHS became a co-sponsor of the 2007 Montpelier Slave Descendants Reunion. The three-day summer celebration on-site would not only honor the contributions of African Americans to Montpelier, but also recognize their role in building Virginia and the nation, before and after Emancipation. The convening of the descendants and their supporters was a turning point, giving voice to a people who had sustained Montpelier but had long been silenced.

As Montpelier's physical site grew, so did the descendants' input and footprint on the land. In 2010, for example, the Montpelier Train Depot was restored and dedicated to support the public's awareness of racial segregation during the turn of the nineteenth century. In 2012, timber frame silhouettes of the slave cabins were built in the South Yard, based on findings of the Montpelier archeological team. A breakthrough came at a 2014 Descendants dinner meeting, when keynote speaker Rex Ellis endorsed the descendants' mandate that the timber frame structures and surrounding landscape be re-created with the same detail as the main house and grounds. Shortly thereafter, a donor's gift to the foundation enabled the transformation of the South Yard and mansion cellar, with an advisory committee of archeologists, descendants, educators, and historians giving input every step of the way.

WHY WOULD WE DO THE SAME THING?
CHRISTIAN J. COTZ

On June 4, 2017, years of hard work came to fruition. On that day, James Madison's Montpelier opened a new exhibition called *The Mere Distinction of Colour* that was located throughout the cellar level of the fourth president's plantation home and in the four newly recreated dependencies nearby. Some eight hundred people, the majority of them people of color, the majority of them people who were still connected to the communities that resided nearby, some of them even descended from the people who were once enslaved on or near Montpelier, sat or stood under a tent on the back lawn that afternoon and celebrated a sea change. For the first time, "the slavery exhibit" at a presidential plantation home was elegant, honest, relevant, and told from the point of view of the enslaved, rather than from the enslaver.

The *Wall Street Journal*'s Ed Rothstein gave the exhibition a lukewarm review and mostly lamented the fact that it was not about Madison the Constitution-maker. Dozens and dozens of visitors wrote angry or disappointed letters and emails to the leadership and board of Montpelier over the following months and years. Some promised never to come back. Some promised never to donate again. Some called for the heads of the responsible staff. Many visitors complained loudly to the interpretive and visitor center staff, and anyone else within earshot. And many more tested the waters of the exhibit with a toe, decided it was too uncomfortable, and walked away without a word.

The exhibition also instigated some two-dozen positive media stories in its first two years of life from such news outlets as PBS, NPR, Buzzfeed, and the *Washington Post*. It received six awards from the museum field: two AAM Muse awards for two separate media productions; SEMC's Technology award; AASLH's Award of Merit and AASLH's History in Progress Award; and NCPH's Outstanding History Project award. Over the next two and half years, it generated dozens and dozens and dozens of tours requested by other museum and nonprofit staff and boards, introspective university faculty groups, law enforcement training classes, and teacher development programs. It became an anchor for projects determined to redesign social studies curricula in Charlottesville and Albemarle County area schools. And it led to Montpelier convening a national gathering that created *The Rubric for Engaging Descendant Communities.*

The Mere Distinction of Colour was a $1.6 million exhibition that was *funded* by a larger gift from David Rubenstein, and it was created over a two-year period between 2015 and 2017. But *The Mere Distinction of Colour* was not *made possible* by David Rubenstein. *The Mere Distinction of Colour* was made possible by an incredible network of people that had developed, often unknown to each other, and over decades, that included staff, advisors, professional colleagues, community members, friends of friends, and, most important of all, the Montpelier Descendant Community.

The $10 million gift from David Rubenstein was intended to achieve three goals: to finish the archaeology of the South Yard area near the mansion where archaeologists knew six dependencies to be (three slave quarters, two smokehouses, and a kitchen house); to rebuild and interpret those six structures; and to finish furnishing the interior of the mansion, which included about a third of the spaces on the first and second floors, as well as the entire cellar level, all of which were then fairly empty. Upon getting the news that Rubenstein was seriously considering making a gift and required a rough but fairly accurate budget, we convened a hastily organized meeting to work out the numbers. What would the archaeology cost? What would rebuilding the structures cost? What would furnishing the mansion's main passage, three guest rooms, and Mother Madison's suite of rooms cost? Finally, the conversation turned to what furnishing the cellars would cost. But I interjected and asked, "Do we have to furnish them?" and suggested that building a modern exhibition in the cellars about the enslaved community, rather than populating it with crates, barrels, spinning wheels, and pots and pans, would allow us to tell a bigger and more important story. The curatorial representatives argued that we would miss the opportunity to show two very different kitchen spaces—one, early nineteenth-century posh, and the other, late eighteenth-century practical. Visitors can see kitchens at any number of historic houses, I suggested. We have a blank slate and empty space to create a unique experience—why would we do the same thing you can see at any number of other historic house museums?

After he committed to funding us, we clarified the question about the cellars with Rubenstein. Unlike many donors, he thought it best to leave the decision making to the professionals. As director of education and visitor engagement, I was tasked with pursuing this interpretive path, though I had no idea what that should look like. But there was something I knew I didn't want, and I began to explore that notion in my own head. What was it that I was pushing back so hard against? What was it that I didn't want to see happen in those cellars? I wasn't sure, but I started visiting as many plantation museums, African American sites, and museums that were utilizing out-of-the-box exhibition design to start thinking about it. On a trip to Manhattan to visit the African Burial Ground Memorial, the Museum of Jewish Heritage, the New-York Historical Society, and the 9/11 Museum and Memorial, I met Frank Vagnone, author of *The Anarchists Guide to Historic House Museums*, for cocktails and to chat about the project. Put simply, his advice was to flip visitors' expectations on their head. It was advice I would take deeply to heart over the next two years of design work.

Over the fall of 2014 and into the spring of 2015, with the guidance of Engaging Places principal, Max van Balgooy, and with the added strength on staff of the newly arrived Dr. Elizabeth Chew, we continued to familiarize ourselves with unique museum experiences, and who was creating them, and to seek out the design team we wanted. After an intense interview process, we hired Proun Design in partnership with Northern Light Productions and quickly got down to work on a concept design for the spaces. Between May and September of 2015, we churned through meeting after meeting, painfully pushing the boundaries of our creativity, honing the focus of the exhibit's content, zeroing in on its aesthetic, and finding its authentic voice.

In October of 2015, the concept design process culminated with a gathering of the African American Advisory Committee, sixteen people from the museum field and descendant community who reviewed the concept design up to that point. We were painfully aware of the lack of diversity on the Montpelier and Proun teams (we started out as all-white teams, though that improved somewhat over the course of the exhibition's creation). The meeting was led by consultant Tanya Bowers, who had facilitated previous gatherings of the Montpelier Descendant Community. Over the course of a contentious day, the creative team of staff and designers listened while the advisory group brought to our attention aspects of the design they liked or didn't. There was agreement, there was disagreement, there was approval, consensus, and frustration. The major takeaways from that advisory committee meeting were: Treat the narrative of our ancestors' stories with as much importance and dignity as the white narrative; emphasize the humanity of the ancestors; and do not leave the story in the past—trace the historical dots that connect the institution of slavery to today.

We continued to keep members of the advisory committee engaged during the remainder of the design process, but the exact same group did not meet in person again. Through the next year and a half of content creation, we asked select members to weigh in on select items—a panel here, a room there, a particular video—and we asked more descendants and other friends in the field to contribute as well. In July of 2016, shortly before their own museum's opening, a group of colleagues from the *Smithsonian National Museum of African American History and Culture* (NMAAHC) led by Rex Ellis, John Franklin, and Nancy Bercaw graciously responded to our request to review schematic designs and the rough draft of content by providing us several hours of their time and written commentary from their team. And at conferences from Riverside to Detroit, I met colleagues in hotel lobbies and bought anyone a drink or two if they would comment on the designs as I scrolled through them on my laptop.

Through the spring and summer of 2016, many members of the descendant community came to Montpelier to be photographed, interviewed, and recorded for the multiple exhibit elements that spotlighted them or utilized their voices. This included twenty-four unique recordings that play on listening stations found in two rooms in the cellars, which convey oral histories and responses to open-ended subjective questions about history and race. Descendant voices are also found in the multiscreen video montage *What Is Slavery?* as well as in the award-winning video *Legacies*, which is the capstone of the exhibition, and in the main interpretive panels in the dependencies.

COLLABORATION WAS KEY . . .
IRIS CARTER FORD

With innovative ideas about who descendants are, an immeasurable value placed on descendant knowledge, and the culmination of years of research, Montpelier positioned itself to develop the groundbreaking *The Mere Distinction of Colour*. And with resentment as motivation, when invited to participate in the conception and creation of the exhibition, I accepted with alacrity. My motivation was sufficient to alleviate any lingering paralysis. I no longer viewed the invitation as an affront. The invitation was an opportunity to challenge and dispel wordless untruths rooted in the stories we tell ourselves, our mythologies—falsehoods that are so ingrained that we never for a moment stop to think we should interrogate them. The invitation was an opportunity to dismantle and transform the power differential that allows one group of people to select, value, and display the practices and products of another to meet their racist-laden proclivities, their Eurocentric standards of taste, their essential mythologies. The invitation was an opportunity to resolve the cognitive dissonance that characterizes *America's* big house and *its* South Yard.

We were ready to do the work—and we did it. Not in a perfect way (just how much context and comprehension can we expect from a museum?), but in a way that had no precedence. Through a series of face-to-face meetings, descendants, Montpelier staff, and a cadre of public historians and museum professionals painstakingly developed the collaboration, content, and technology required for an award-winning exhibition on slavery at Montpelier.

There were important questions to address:

- How do we represent enslaved people, widely thought to be timeless and without history?
- How do we ensure that the economic context of slavery and its role in the development of democracy and the nation are highlighted?
- What must be excluded due to space, time, focus?
- What are the different perspectives from which the story can be told? How will we make the space for an inclusive telling?
- How do we guard against white supremacy creeping into the narrative?

We didn't always agree. The exhibit is housed in the work rooms beneath the mansion, which was a point of contention for some descendants. But in the end, we made peace with the location and tackled the big question: Does the exhibit provide room for complexities—the political, economic, and religious domination of African people, the story of their in-spite-of immanence, and the founding of a nation?

Collaboration was key to the success of including descendant voices in addressing these questions. Our meetings were engineered by Christian Cotz, Montpelier's then director of education and the exhibit point person, to help ensure such collaboration. We listened closely to the experts and each other. We celebrated one another as equals. We held space for our differences—which were many. We spoke from our own experiences, our own truths. We avoided assumptions about others. We avoided the tendency to "fix" others. We remained open to the process and steadfast about the potential to move the African American story from the periphery to the core.

Towards that end, descendants played the major role in providing the substance and intellect to interpret the African and African American experience at Montpelier. We toured the landscape, the historic structures, the archaeology labs. We were involved firsthand in the genealogical and archaeological research. We were photographed, interviewed, and recorded. We were feted and fed throughout the consultative process. Our experience over the development of the exhibit can be best characterized as immersive—a kind of participant observation, the process by which anthropologists learn about other cultures, and themselves. And in doing so, we merged our newfound understanding of the potential of the museum as institution, with a deep understanding of African American heritage, to provide an unparalleled expertise in building *The Mere Distinction of Colour*.

It must be noted that the foundation of effective collaboration was rooted in the tireless, visionary work of Montpelier archaeologist Dr. Mathew Reeves and his team. Matt has been a persistent, resolute advocate of descendant involvement for over twenty years—well before widespread acceptance of community engagement at the museum. He was there at the founding of the Orange County African American Historical Society. He was the force behind the reclamation of the South Yard and the 2007 descendants' event—both of which were pivotal in the transformation of Montpelier. He developed research and archaeology expeditions to engage descendants, resulting in interpretative richness. He relentlessly mentored staff and leadership to advance an understanding of the essential role of descendants in forging a more inclusive narrative. He remains one of the most steadfast proponents of the Montpelier Descendants Committee in its work to achieve organizational and structural parity. When working for change, the commitment of people like Matt cannot be overvalued.

. . . THAT METHODOLOGY NEEDED TO CHANGE CHRISTIAN J. COTZ

We set out in the content creation stage of our work to tell the truth, push boundaries, and flip expectations. To do that we had to define a starting point. What were our visitors expecting that we did not want to re-create? After a lot of reflection, we realized that when we visit plantation museums, we expect to see an exhibition about slavery, and we have a pretty good idea of what it will look like before we see it. It will likely be in the cellars or outbuildings. It will likely utilize an earth-tone color palette. It will convey anecdotes about labor processes and tool use, long hours and poor living conditions, and it will probably relate a personal story of a "celebrity slave"—a story with a happy ending that visitors won't be upset by. Mostly museums talked about the processes of labor that visitors viewed as both fascinating and childishly outdated ("Can you imagine they did things that way?") and the log walls and dirt floors of the cabins slaves lived in ("that doesn't look comfortable" or more frequently, "that doesn't look that bad"). If we celebrated anything about the enslaved themselves, it was their skilled hands, their "loyalty" to their owners, and their good-natured endurance of suffering.

Museums did this, whether consciously or unconsciously, because it is easier for visitors to think about slavery as a monolithic experience that happened to tens of millions of people, hundreds of years ago. It is easier for human brains to comprehend slavery in these terms because it is nonspecific and nonpersonal—it's too large a number of people to really comprehend and long enough ago to know that it's all over now, anyway. Visitors are not forced to imagine, consider, or empathize with individual stories of pain and suffering that they will find unbearable, nor to assign responsibility for those experiences. Montpelier's team understood that methodology needed to change. We needed to make visitors come face-to-face with the stories of the individuals who were enslaved at Montpelier and recognize that enslavement itself was actively forced upon hundreds of individuals by the Madisons. We needed to convey those experiences in terms that modern visitors could relate to and empathize with. And we needed to ensure our visitors realized that those stories and experiences have a direct bearing on people today.

Few of our visitors will ever know what plowing a field with draft animals is like. Few people will ever work uncompensated. Few people will ever cook over a fire for their family, much less for someone else. Few people will ever spend time in an uninsulated home with dirt floors. Though none of these things are the truly devastating conditions of slavery, they are the aspects of slavery that museums focused their interpretation on for decades. On the other hand, most of us do know what being someone's child is like. We know how it feels to have a parent or a sibling, grandparents, a spouse, a child, or even friends. But most of us can only imagine the horror of being forever separated from a loved one, of having a person taken or sold away from us, of seeing a loved one physically tortured, or knowing a loved one is being raped. Can we ask visitors to imagine those things? Will museumgoers be able to process those conditions and empathize with those historical experiences? If they can, might they have a better idea of the trauma that was inflicted on some ten million people in the United States, and stand a better chance of understanding that trauma's legacy on generations of their descendants?

For many museum visitors, it is both natural and easy to turn away from such painful truths that may challenge the way we perceive our own American identity, especially when those stories are conveyed through an institutional voice. Most humans are not preprogrammed to be introspective and self-critical. Though museums are still considered a trustworthy authority by most Americans, the air of dispassionate neutrality that many museums adopt is easy for visitors to blow off simply because it lacks the magnetism that passion demands. On the other hand, most of us *are* preprogrammed to be empathetic and *will* pay attention when a real person delivers a real story that demonstrates a real impact on the real world that we live in. So, who better to convey the history of the enslaved, and to display the legacy of trauma, perseverance, survival, and resistance than the descendants themselves?

The descendant voice empowers *The Mere Distinction of Colour* and authenticates Montpelier. It demands attention in the exhibit in a way that an institutional voice never could. Perhaps there is no better example of that sort of power than the scene in the *Legacies* video, when octogenarian Rebecca Gilmore Coleman identifies on screen as being only "three generations removed from being enslaved here at Montpelier" (her great-grandfather was enslaved there). A few seconds later, speaking of the different shades of people's skin, in a moment of barely suppressed rage, she says, "and how did they become lighter? . . . Well, they were raped." That sort of mic-drop moment can't be replicated on a two-dimensional panel and commands attention and respect.

The descendant voice also provided the authority of the Black community that has long been absent from many other museum experiences. It provided legitimacy for Montpelier among skeptical Black audiences and liberal-educated white audiences. It also demonstrated an institutional alliance with the descendants that was harder to ignore for those who would nay-say and protest the more inclusive narrative. It also evidenced a commitment on the part of Montpelier to not only include the descendant community as co-creators of the exhibit, but also as stakeholders in the institution, an effort the museum had been working on for nearly two decades.

"HARD HISTORY DOES NOT HAVE TO BE IGNORED." PATRICE PRESTON-GRIMES

When students see *The Mere Distinction of Colour* they divide into smaller groups and descend into the cellar through two separate doors at the rear of the house, entering the compact spaces that feature media and interactive exhibits. Many are quick to notice the names of the enslaved men, women, and children etched into the plastered walls—a sampling of the dozens of known and unknown who were owned by James and Dolley Madison. Kiosks with seats in the corners of the cellar room display black-and-white images of living descendants, who bring to life the oral history accounts of their ancestors with chilling descriptions of the enslaved community's daily hardships, determination, and hopes for a better life in freedom. A student commented as she came up from the cellar, "There were lots of reflective moments and the weight of the atmosphere was immense."

As the group boarded the bus to return to Charlottesville, students had more questions than answers, with varying degrees of attention. Within five minutes of passing through the gates, silence envelops the bus for the rest of the ride to Grounds. At this moment, I shifted my thoughts from logistics manager to teacher educator, exhaled, and wondered in the quiet, "What will they remember? What will they choose to forget? Did they sense the power of place, and if so, where? How might this later affect their teaching when they are soon in their own classrooms?"

We referred often to the Montpelier experience throughout the semester. The class comments varied and resurfaced at unexpected moments. From journaling, essays, class activities, and informal discussions, four themes emerged that captured their thoughts and experiences. The first was the importance of *including multiple perspectives* in studying and interpreting our past, and its influence on the present and the future. As one student commented on the tour, "I think it's important to go past that [slavery is an event that ends after the Civil War] to dig deeper. Definitely, what I learned [at Montpelier] will help me in the future to dig deeper with my students." Another was moved by the site experience when she reflected in class that "So many people's stories happened in that place . . . it's remarkable." This introduction to different narratives was her eye-opening moment. The second theme was identifying and giving *value to the descendant voice*. A student noted, "Listening to a reenactment of Paul Jennings' letter detailing Madison's death puts African American freedom into perspective and allows for time to stand still for a moment." (Jennings was Madison's enslaved personal servant. When Madison died, the enslaved community was well aware that their futures and their families' now rested upon the shoulders and whim of Dolley Madison and her son Payne Todd, neither of whom valued Montpelier in the same way that the late president had.) The third theme captured the impact of a *place-based learning experience to engage students*. Overwhelmingly, students expressed emotion in what they saw, heard, and touched on-site. In the South Yard, a student observed that, "archeologists can be critical in studying history because they can put all of the small pieces together." Another commented in her essay that, "I learn history best when the information is tangible and/or surrounding me." One student echoed the sentiment when she journaled, "Looking out his [Madison's library] window in the same room that he came up with so many of the ideas that are in the Constitution is a surreal experience." The fourth theme underscored the significance of *a museum as a unique site of connection, engaging visitors and communities in unique ways*. In one student's words, "The artifacts that are found are a major way that historians figure out where buildings are, where people lived, and how they lived. Because artifacts are what people really used in the past." One student shared on her class exit card, "hard history does not have to be ignored." The power of being in the historical space where events occurred provided a new way to hear and think about past events.

Perhaps the most significant and long-lasting takeaway was that the field experience should be a more central part of all students' learning, from kindergarten through college. One student captured the spirit of the experience at the end of the course when she wrote:

> The most memorable takeaway from our visit to Montpelier was the *Mere Distinction of Colour* exhibit. I found it extremely impactful that it honored the lives of the enslaved peoples at Montpelier in a way that was a little bit easier to digest. Although discussing these topics is difficult, I feel more confident in my ability to have these discussions in my classroom after this visit.

Site-based learning experiences can help students to develop new knowledge and provide a powerful catalyst to spark deeper thinking and understanding. At the end of the course, some students were motivated to take informed action about a local history issue in Charlottesville (for example, the Confederate monument debate); others planned to seek professional development opportunities to learn how to address challenging topics that will arise in their classrooms. For many descendants, the power of place is more personal. Unearthing the stories of family ties at Montpelier (or any historical site) can confirm, as was the case for my ninety-year-old mother, that, "we were here . . . we belonged . . . we mattered," and we are connected forever to a past that is still being discovered.

#CHARLOTTESVILLE
CHRISTIAN J. COTZ

It's important to remember that the exhibition's opening, June 4, 2017, took place just two months prior to August 12, 2017—a date that has changed the nation's perception of #Charlottesville. To this day, any time a white supremacist event occurs anywhere in the country, and sometimes in other countries, the reporters always compare it to what happened "at the Unite the Right event in

Charlottesville." That event and Montpelier's proximity to it, plus the new exhibition and its recent publicity, positioned Montpelier to become a strong voice in the conversations that were taking place around race in the local community, in education, and in the museum field.

Shortly after the exhibition opened, an impressed donor approached Montpelier's CEO, Kat Imhoff, who is due enormous credit for blocking and tackling innumerable roadblocks to this project that we haven't even acknowledged in this chapter, and suggested that she would fund the writing of a book for the museum field about how to do what we had done. Thinking that a bit presumptuous, we suggested that perhaps she could fund a collaborative gathering that could discuss the best ways to go about interpreting slavery and building relationships with descendants, resulting in a guide for other sites to utilize. With that understanding we partnered with the National Trust for Historic Preservation's African American Cultural Heritage Action Fund to host an event at Montpelier in early 2018 that brought fifty people together for three days of collaborative brainstorming, writing, and rubric-making. The group included academics, museum professionals, and descendants of enslaved people from all over the country. Every person we invited was a rock star, and not one single person we invited said no. The collective willingness to leave egos at the door, to listen, to make space, to collaborate, and to do the work, was unlike any process I think most of us had ever witnessed before or since. Afterward, three separate committees continued to write and edit, and the rubric was complete and available to the public by September. It was published as a technical leaflet in *History News* (AASLH's quarterly magazine) in their Winter 2018 edition. Since then, dozens and dozens of groups have contacted Montpelier to let them know they are utilizing it.

"SHARING POWER & VOICE"
PATRICE PRESTON-GRIMES

Of the many gatherings at Montpelier that I participated in through the years, the National Summit on Teaching Slavery in 2018 was a different meeting from the start. Unlike invitations to other events that focused on discovery and celebration, the charge to participants for this weekend conference from Montpelier President and CEO Kat Imhoff was specific: "create[ing] a rubric for public historians to work with descendants."[9] This was a clear, but unheard of, request within museum and foundation circles at that time. Work with—not for, or through, or on behalf of—and lay the foundation for, in the words of our esteemed colleague Michael Blakey, "sharing power and voice with descendants."

I was no stranger to creating and using a range of assessments in the educational arena. I also understood the crucial role that evaluation plays in determining the effectiveness of a product or service. I was honored to be invited to engage with some of the most experienced scholars, museum professionals, and members of the descendant community, whom I had come to know and care about through my many visits to Montpelier.

I questioned if the desired outcome was too lofty to complete within the time frame, knowing that this would be our only opportunity to work in person on such an important task. But I never doubted that this approach was a fair one to guarantee equitable representation for all stakeholders and to retain the hard-earned trust and commitment to authenticity that had developed among Montpelier's descendants, executives, and staff over the past two decades. Then, I heard the still, small voices of the ancestors in my head, saying, "Patrice, we've waited our lifetimes to have a seat at the table. Get to work!" Guided by Kat Imhoff's stated premise that summit attendees would be on equal footing to weigh in on the interpretation of slavery, I tossed my concerns to the wind and dug in.

The working sessions were lively and sometimes intense. We worked in pairs, in small focus groups, and engaged as a general audience. There were differences of opinion on every element of the benchmarks, from how many categories to include, and how to list, group, and label criteria, to making meaning of the mountains of datapoints. Although we were weary after a full day of critical thinking, debating, and listening to dozens of ideas from a variety of perspectives, we continued to wrestle with the task over meals and, for a few hearty souls, into the night. We returned early the next morning to work another full day. When it was clear that the weekend would not produce an initial draft, over twenty participants committed to work with the Montpelier team to create a user-friendly product by the end of the summer. The published document describes specific standards for doing multidisciplinary research, relationship-building, and interpretation, using a five-point scale with criteria for each benchmark.

I have participated in dozens of these sessions in corporate and nonprofit think tank settings in recent years. What made this summit different? How were we able to walk away from the weekend confident that the reams of sticky notes and easel papers generated would not end up in an obscure closet never to be seen again? Our outcome was the result of *years of relationship-building* that created trust in four ways:

1. taking risks, whether financial, emotional, professional, or personal, to imagine an outcome that had not ever been achieved,

2. communicating consistently in all interactions with transparency and a spirit of reciprocity,
3. anticipating and navigating the emotions possible that can surface when different interpretations of histories emerge and collide, and
4. setting shared goals for outcomes that are specific, measurable, and lofty, in other words, dreaming *Big*.

These elements were foundational to Montpelier's transformation to tell a more complete narrative of the roots and consequences of slavery in our nation's history. This is hard work that occurs over time, yet is essential, to produce a more inclusive history that is truthful, informative, and authentic. Stakeholders cannot assume that because the opportune climate exists today to engage in this work, that it will remain. Like any valued relationship, museums and descendants must work constantly to support the building blocks of trust, even as the context and climates in which they operate shift over time.

To this end, the museums and historic sites that consider a model of best practices must confront the power dynamic of who sets and who controls the narratives at their institutions. To be sure, generous donors and altruistic stakeholders must make room for one (or more) descendants' chairs in the board room, but that alone is insufficient. For institutional stakeholders willing to change their paradigms of self-governance, the *Rubric of Best Practices* could become a significant tool to guide the process toward actions that are, "ethical, meaningful, and effective," with empathy that is evident "for the enslaved, their descendants and the learner." Whether motivated to act because it is the right thing to do, or to engage in shared governance as a consequence of interest convergence, historical museums have a responsibility to move past well-intended conversations about topics such as slavery and engage descendants in ways that affirm the humanity of all.[10]

One outcome of the National Summit on Teaching Slavery was the realization that the tasks, issues, and challenges that all Montpelier stakeholders face in the future will be more complex. The growth of the descendants' community in recent years is also requiring more formalized structures of communication, operations, and possibly fundraising. In late 2018 and early 2019, the discovery of multiple burial sites adjacent to the current boundaries of the existing African American cemetery at Montpelier posed another opportunity to consider how to memorialize descendants, with the same fidelity and care that was given to *The Mere Distinction of Colour* and the South Yard. The Montpelier Descendants Committee (MDC) was formed as an independent organization in partnership with James Madison's Montpelier to participate actively in future decision making. It is described on its website as,

> An independent, tax-exempt, 501(c)3 organization representing the Montpelier Descendants Community as an equal co-steward of James Madison's Montpelier. that seeks to identify and create bridges to living descendants of the African American women and men who were enslaved at Montpelier and elsewhere in Orange County, Virginia. Beyond this, Montpelier researchers and scholars wish to expand the local, regional, and national African American community whose members identify and connect with the history of James Madison's Montpelier.[11]

In November 2019, the MDC hosted its first Memorialization Workshop at Montpelier. The weekend event brought together archeologists, architects, descendants, educators, and researchers to explore the possibilities for expanding memorialization at Montpelier and to consider its next steps.

IS IT ENOUGH . . . ?
IRIS CARTER FORD

The Mere Distinction of Colour is widely proclaimed a success—certainly from the perspective of the museum world. But is that enough? It provides an opportunity for Montpelier's descendants to be seen through image and heard through word—not just to talk for our ancestors, but to talk through them. But who's seeing? Who's listening? There is documented resistance from the very visitors who perhaps stand to learn the most. Even in the face of glowing reviews from the majority of visitors, we have to contemplate the efficacy of the museum in educating consumers. And in turn, we have to ask ourselves how effective education is in addressing the exigencies of race, in advocating for social justice, in practicing anti-racist activism. It may not be the panacea we think. James Madison knew that slavery was wrong and lamented "that there could be property in men," but he wrote a "slavery-protecting constitution."[12]

Racial injustice was at the heart of the matter when Montpelier was founded. It was the heart of the matter when the Constitution was drafted. And it remains the heart of the matter today. This may be one of the most challenging of all the legacies we must confront: even educated people who think themselves well-meaning may harbor implicit bias and embrace systemic white privilege that precludes them from making right what they know to be wrong. Like Madison, even educated people place social comfort and unjust laws over moral conscience.

Museums like Montpelier have a unique responsibility. They must commit to actively challenging racism through the research they conduct, the educational initiatives they develop, and the communications they disseminate. They must commit to actively engaging voices in communities of color to both inform and promote their work. They must commit to identifying practices within their organizations that reproduce systemic oppression and to developing strategies that counter them. They must root out bias and privilege that compromise social justice in all its forms—from among their own and the programs they develop, from among their visitors, and from among the widespread communities that they serve on their digital platforms. They must hold themselves accountable.[13]

The Mere Distinction of Colour is rooted in accountability. It bears witness to Montpelier's unprecedented partnership with descendants to tell a more complete American story and to interrogate the truth behind James Madison's words at the Constitutional Convention in 1787: "We have seen the mere distinction of colour made in the most enlightened period of time, a ground of the most oppressive dominion ever exercised by man over man."

POSTSCRIPT

Amid the turmoil of the global pandemic in 2020 and 2021, conversations between the Montpelier Foundation, the Montpelier Descendants Committee, and the National Trust for Historic Preservation were shaping Montpelier's future. On June 16, 2021, one day before President Biden declared Juneteenth a federal holiday, the institutions agreed to structural parity as described in the rubric:

> Exemplary structural parity occurs when members of the descendant community are represented and empowered at every level of the institution—board, senior leadership, supervisors, junior staff, and volunteers. Representation goes beyond tokenism; these positions are invested with power and authority.

According to the announcement on Montpelier's website:

> *The vote on bylaws on June 16, 2021, during the week of Juneteenth, followed a resolution passed by the Board of TMF on May 27 which stated, "The Board of The Montpelier Foundation affirms its commitment to collaborate with the Montpelier Descendants Committee (MDC) to achieve structural parity with descendants at all levels of the organization." James*

French, Montpelier Descendants Committee founding chair, later stated, "This vote to grant equal co-stewardship authority to the Descendants of those who were enslaved is groundbreaking . . . The decision moves the perspectives of the Descendants of the enslaved from the periphery to the center and offers an important, innovative step for Montpelier to share broader, richer and more truthful interpretations of history with wider audiences."

—https://www.montpelier.org/learn/montpelier-board-restructure-parity

NOTES

1. National Summit on Teaching Slavery, "Engaging Descendant Communities in the Interpretation of Slavery at Museums and Historic Sites," in History News: The Magazine of the American Association of State and Local History 74, no.1 (Winter 2019): 2.

2. Barbara Allen, "The Genealogical Landscape and the Southern Sense of Place," in Sense of Place: American Regional Cultures, ed. Barbara Allen and Thomas J. Schlereth (Lexington: University Press of Kentucky, 1990), 152–63.

3. http://www.montpelier.org/learn/6-ways-that-understanding-slavery-will-change-how-you-understand-american-freedom, accessed April 10, 2021.

4. https://www.montpelier.org/learn/the-women-of-montpelier, accessed April 10, 2021.

5. https://slavery.virginia.edu/wp-content/uploads/2021/03/PCSU-Report-FINAL_July-2018.pdf, accessed April 24, 2021.

6. Parker Palmer, The Courage to Teach: Exploring the Inner Landscape of a Teacher's Life (San Francisco: Josey-Bass, 1998).

7. Virginia Department of Education (VDOE), "History and Social Science Standards of Learning," retrieved April 8, 2021, https://www.doe.virginia.gov/testing/sol/standards_docs/history_socialscience/.

8. Christine Baron et al., "What Teachers Retain from Historic Site-Based Professional Development," Journal of Teacher Education (Newbury Park, CA: Sage, 2020), 1–17, DOI: 10.1177/0022487||984|889.

9. National Summit on Teaching Slavery, "Engaging Descendant Communities in the Interpretation of Slavery at Museums and Historic Sites," in History News: The Magazine of the American Association of State and Local History 74, no.1 (Winter 2019): 16.

10. The late law professor Derrick Bell created the term interest convergence to describe an idea that a majority will only support the interests of the minority if their

interests align. Open Education Sociology Dictionary, https://sociologydictionary.org/interest-convergence/, retrieved April 24, 2021.

11. https://montpelierdescendants.org/, retrieved April 24, 2021.

12. Noah Feldman, The Three Lives of James Madison, Genius, Partisan, President (New York: Random House, 2017).

13. Adapted from Montpelier Descendants Committee Statement, 2020.

ACKNOWLEDGMENTS

The seeds of my thinking on this topic were planted between 2006 and 2015 via numerous conversations with colleagues and friends from the National September 11 Memorial & Museum, New York University, and Oberlin College. In addition, my editorial colleagues at the National Council on Public History and co-conspirators on the Southeastern Museums Conference Equity and Inclusion Action Team have contributed much to shaping my thinking and refining my writing and editing skills over the years.

What became this book began with an open call on Twitter in 2015 for participation in a "talk show" session at the American Alliance of Museums (AAM) conference in Washington, DC, about enlisting personal stories to serve larger narratives. I am grateful to Miriam Bader, Rachel Feinmark, Margaret Middleton, Paul Bowers, and Amy Weinstein for their interest in the idea and their contributions to the 2016 AAM session.

When AAM press accepted the book proposal in 2020, Dina Bailey was invaluable in suggesting additional contributors, and Susan Greenberg found me a gem from her diverse and wonderful network of lifelong friends. To all the authors who ultimately agreed to share their perspectives—Benjamin Filene,

Corey Timpson, Amy Weinstein, Anna E. Tucker, Marcy Breffle, Mary Margaret Fernandez, Miriam Bader, Deitrah J. Taylor, Rebecca Melsheimer, Jose Santamaria, Lois E. Carlisle, Samir El Azhar, Judy Goldberg, Meredith Schweitzer, Margaret Middleton, Sarah Litvin, Donna M. Mah, Elysia Poon, Michelle Grohe, Iris Carter Ford, Patrice Preston-Grimes, and Christian J. Cotz—my heart is full. For my chapter on Holocaust museums, Mindy Langer reached out to Linda Milstein, who kindly connected me with Dale Daniels and Sara Brown, who provided their excellent Western and Northeastern perspectives to compliment my Southeastern regional experience. The content of that chapter was refined with input from my stellar colleagues at Kennesaw State University: Jennifer Dickey, Catherine Lewis, and Andrea Miskewicz. The whole team at the Museum of History and Holocaust Education continues to inspire me every day.

For their editorial review of the complete manuscript, I am indebted to Priya Chhaya, Calinda Lee, and Modupe Labode. Micah and Mindy Langer both provided essential feedback on the preface, and Mindy Langer's eagle eye caught many a typo and grammatical error. Charles Harmon and Erinn Slanina at Rowman & Littlefield kept everything on schedule; their consistent and clear communications were much appreciated.

To my husband, Matthew DeAngelis, thank you for your willingness to discuss and debate every aspect of this book's premise, structure, word choice, and thematic organization. You are the better half of my brain and the rock on which I hone my thinking. Thank you for your patience, love, and support (often in the form of increasingly delicious bread products).

And finally, to my children, Leo and Ilana DeAngelis, the stories we tell are for you.

BIBLIOGRAPHY

"10 Stages of Genocide." Accessed June 25, 2021. http://genocidewatch.net/genocide-2/8-stages-of-genocide/.

"$3,500 in 1908 → 2021 | Inflation Calculator." Official Inflation Data, Alioth Finance, August 10, 2021. https://www.officialdata.org/us/inflation/1908?amount=3500.

Adair, Bill, Benjamin Filene, and Laura Koloski. *Letting Go? Sharing Historical Authority in a User-Generated World.* Philadelphia: Pew Center for Arts & Heritage/Left Coast Press, 2011, 174–93.

Adichie, Chimamanda. The Danger of a Single Story. TED video (filmed July 2009, posted October 2009), 18:49. Accessed March 28, 2016.

Alexander, Edward P., Mary Alexander, and Juilee Decker. *Museums in Motion: An Introduction to the History and Functions of Museums* (third edition). Lanham, MD: Rowman and Littlefield, 2017, 23–27.

Allen, Barbara. "The Genealogical Landscape and the Southern Sense of Place." In *Sense of Place: American Regional Cultures*, edited by Barbara Allen and Thomas J. Schlereth, 152–63. Lexington: University Press of Kentucky, 1990.

American Alliance of Museums. "Excellence in Label Writing Competition." https://www.aam-us.org/programs/awards-competitions/excellence-in-exhibition-label-writing-competition/.

American Library Association. "Issues and Trends," April 12, 2020. Accessed May 10, 2021. http://www.ala.org/news/state-americas-libraries-report-2020/issues-trends.

"Artificial Intelligence Project Lets Holocaust Survivors Share Their Stories Forever." Accessed June 25, 2021. https://www.cbsnews.com/news/artificial-intelligence-holocaust-remembrance-60-minutes-2020-04-03/.

Association for Holocaust Organizations. "Membership." Accessed July 21, 2021. https://www.ahoinfo.org/membership.

Atlanta History Center IMPACTS Experience, National Awareness, Attitudes, and Usage Study, 2019.

"Atlanta History Center Shares Similarities between 1918 Spanish Flu and COVID-19." WSB-TV, People2People. https://www.wsbtv.com/community/people-2-people/atlanta-history-center-shares-similarities-between-1918-spanish-flu-covid-19/LOLHGCWKHZJGF7M2W3NPALENWY/?fbclid=IwAR3cOzIyzIdf9KcUWP_mb3gGJgGh_L6oozwSWW7GSxoWnfLu-zTuopWt7uU.

Atlanta History Center. "When You Work at a Museum." Accessed July 1, 2021. https://www.atlantahistorycenter.com/blog/when-you-work-at-a-museum/.

Bailey, Dinah. "Finding Inspiration Inside: Engaging Empathy to Empower Everyone." In *Fostering Empathy Through Museums*, edited by Elif M. Gokcigdem. Lanham, MD: Rowman and Littlefield, 2016.

Baron, Christine, Sherri Sklarwitz, Hyeyoung Band, and Hanadi Shatara. "What Teachers Retain from Historic Site-Based Professional Development." In *Journal of Teacher Education*, 1–17. Newbury Park, CA: Sage, 2020. DOI: 10.1177/0022487||984|889.

Bedford, Leslie. "Storytelling: The Real Work of Museums." *Curator: The Museum Journal* 44, no. 1 (2001): 27–34. https://doi.org/10.1111/j.2151-6952.2001.tb00027.x.

Bell, Kenton, ed. "interest convergence." In *Open Education Sociology Dictionary*. Accessed April 25, 2021. https://sociologydictionary.org/interest-convergence/.

Berenbaum, Michael. *The World Must Know: The History of the Holocaust as Told in the United States Holocaust Memorial Museum* (revised edition). Baltimore, MD: Johns Hopkins University Press, 2006.

Berger, Jenna. "Review Essay: Teaching History, Teaching Tolerance—Holocaust Education in Houston." *Public Historian* 25, no. 4 (2003): 125–31. https://doi.org/10.1525/tph.2003.25.4.125.

Bilali, Rezarta, and Rima Mahmoud. "Confronting History and Reconciliation: A Review of Civil Society's Approaches to Transforming Conflict Narratives." In *History Education and Conflict Transformation*, edited by Charis Psaltis, Mario Carretero, and Sabina Čehajić-Clancy. London: Palgrave Macmillan, 2017.

Birmingham Times. "The Iconic Wales Window inside 16th Street Baptist Church." Accessed July 1, 2021. https://www.birminghamtimes.com/2018/10/the-iconic-wales-window-inside-16th-street-baptist-church/.

Bishop, Rudine Sims. "Mirrors, Windows, and Sliding Glass Doors." *Perspectives: Choosing and Using Books for the Classroom* 6, no. 3 (1990).

Borowsky, Larry. "Telling a Story in 100 Words: Effective Label Copy." *History News* 62 (Autumn 2007), Technical Leaflet #240: 1–8.

Bourguignon, Erika. "Bringing the Past into the Present: Family Narratives of Holocaust, Exile, and Diaspora: Memory in an Amnesic World: Holocaust, Exile, and the Return of the Suppressed." *Anthropological Quarterly* 78, no. 1 (2005): 63–88.

Bower, Michelle. "Is Your Brand a Painkiller, Vitamin, or Candy?" Dalziel & Pow. https://www.dalziel-pow.com/news/is-your-brand-a-painkiller-vitamin-or-candy.

Brock, Julia et al. "Exploring Identities: Public History in a Cross-Cultural Context." *Public Historian 34*, no. 4 (2012): 9–29.

Brooklyn Museum. "Kehinde Wiley: A New Republic." Accessed July 1, 2021. https://www.brooklynmuseum.org/opencollection/exhibitions/3312.

brown, adrienne m. *Emergent Strategy: Shaping Change, Changing Worlds*. Chico, CA: AK Press, 2017.

Brown, Brené. *Daring Greatly: How the Courage to Be Vulnerable Transforms the Way We Live, Love, Parent, and Lead*. New York: Avery, 2012.

Brown, Jeffrey, and Leah Nagy. "Henry Louis Gates Jr. on His New Series 'The Black Church.'" Accessed July 1, 2021. https://www.pbs.org/newshour/show/henry-louis-gates-jr-on-his-new-series-the-black-church.

Brown, Sara. Discussion with CHHANGE Executive Director on the Future of Storytelling in Holocaust Museums. Interview by Adina Langer. Zoom, June 9, 2021.

Bruhm, Steven, and Natasha Hurley. "Introduction." In *Curiouser: On the Queerness of Children*, ix. Minneapolis: University of Minnesota Press, 2004.

"Building Bridges Chhange: The Center for Holocaust, Human Rights & Genocide Education." Accessed June 24, 2021. https://www.chhange.org/programs/educators/building-bridges.

Carter G. Woodson Center. "The Power of Sankofa: Know History." Accessed July 1, 2021. https://www.berea.edu/cgwc/the-power-of-sankofa/.

Caswell, Michelle, and Marika Cifor. "From Human Rights to Feminist Ethics: Radical Empathy in the Archives." n.d., 22.

Chang, Ailsa, Rachel Martin, and Eric Marrapodi. "Summer of Racial Reckoning." NPR, August 16, 2020. https://www.npr.org/2020/08/16/902179773/summer-of-racial-reckoning-the-match-lit.

Colwell, Chip. *Plundered Skulls and Stolen Spirits: Inside the Fight to Reclaim Native America's Culture*. Chicago: University of Chicago Press, 2017.

Cooley, John K. "A 'Black Saturday' Shadows the Future of Hassan's Morocco." Accessed March 2, 2021. https://www.washingtonpost.com/archive/politics/1981/08/25/a-black-saturday-shadows-the-future-of-hassans-morocco/8a5cb6ce-39b4-42b9-bb48-f3a196706961/.

Dalrymple, G. Brent. "The Age of the Earth in the Twentieth Century: A Problem (Mostly) Solved." In *The Age of the Earth: From 4004 BC to AD 2002*, edited by C. L. E. Lewis and S. J. Knell, 205–21. London: Geological Society of London, 2001.

Daniels, Dale. Discussion of the Evolution of CHHANGE with Its First Executive Director. Interview by Adina Langer. Zoom, June 9, 2021.

Day, Jennifer. "Record Keeping for a Long-Term Collaborative Project: The Acoma Collection Review at the Indian Arts Research Center at the School for Advanced Research." In SAR *Guidelines for Collaboration*. Accessed August 13, 2021. https://guidelinesforcollaboration.info/improving-a-museums-information-about-its-collections/.

Dichtl, John. "Most Trust Museums as Sources of Historical Information." *AASLH* (blog). Accessed January 31, 2022. https://aaslh.org/most-trust-museums/.

Dickey, Jennifer, and Catherine Lewis. "Introduction: The Museums and Community Collaboration Abroad Project." In *Crossing Borders: A Transatlantic Collaboration*, edited by Samir El Azhar. Casablanca: Force Equipment, 2010.

Dierking, Lynn. "What Is Family Learning?" *Engage Families*. Accessed May 10, 2021. https://engagefamilies.org/family-learning-101/what-is-family-learning/.

Diner, Hasia R. *We Remember with Reverence and Love: American Jews and the Myth of Silence after the Holocaust, 1945–1962* (first edition). New York: New York University Press, 2009.

"Disability Impacts All of Us." Centers for Disease Control and Prevention, last updated September 16, 2020. https://www.cdc.gov/ncbddd/disabilityandhealth/infographic-disability-impacts-all.html.

Dungey, Azie Mira. *Ask a Slave: The Web Series*. 2013. http://www.askaslave.com/.

Eckmann, Monique, Doyle Stevick, Jolanta Ambrosewicz-Jacobs, and International Holocaust Remembrance Alliance, eds. *Research in Teaching and Learning about the Holocaust: A Dialogue beyond Borders*. IHRA Series, vol. 3. Berlin: Metropol, 2017.

El Azhar, Samir. "The Ben M'sik University Museum: The Necessity to Preserve the Collective Memory of the District and the City" (in Arabic). In *Plural Morocco: Multiculturalism and Identity*, edited by Samir El Azhar. Casablanca: Force Equipment, 2020.

El Azhar, Samir. "The Ben M'sik Community Museum: Beyond Cultural Boundaries." In *Museums in a Global Context: National Identity, International Understanding*, edited by Jennifer W. Dickey, Samir El Azhar, and Catherine M. Lewis. Washington, DC: AAM Press, 2013.

El Azhar, Samir. "Ben M'sik: Creating Community in Casablanca." In *Bassamat* 4. Casablanca: Best Imprimerie, 2010.

ElShafie, Sara J. "Making Science Meaningful for Broad Audiences through Stories." *Integrative and Comparative Biology* 58, no. 6 (2018): 1213–23. doi.org/10.1093/icb/icy103.

Endacott, Jason L., and Christina Pelekanos. "Slaves, Women, and War! Engaging Middle School Students in Historical Empathy for Enduring Understanding." *The Social Studies*, no. 106 (2015): 1–7.

Enfin un Master muséologie à Rabat. Accessed February 26, 2021. https://www.etudiant.ma/articles/enfin-un-master-museologie-a-rabat (in French; S. El Azhar, Trans.).

Engouement des Marocains pour les musées nationaux, selon Mehdi Qotbi [Interview]. Accessed February 25, 2021. https://www.yabiladi.com/articles/details/53798/engouement-marocains-pour-musees-nationaux.html (in French; S. El Azhar, Trans.).

Enote, Jim. *Museum Collaboration Manifesto*. Accessed May 17, 2021. https://guidelinesforcollaboration.info/wp-content/uploads/2019/11/sar_gl_museum_collaboration_manifesto_updated_nov_2019_v2.pdf.

Erdman, S., N. Nguyen, and M. Middleton. *Welcoming Young Children into the Museum: A Practical Guide*. New York: Routledge, 2021.

Faber, Eli. *Jews, Slaves, and the Slave Trade: Setting the Record Straight*. New York: New York University Press, 1998.

Feldman, Noah. *The Three Lives of James Madison, Genius, Partisan, President*. New York: Random House, 2017.

Ferentinos, Susan. *Interpreting LGBT History at Museums and Historic Sites*. Lanham, MD: Rowman and Littlefield, 2015.

Filene, Benjamin. "What Finland Taught Me about Doing History in Public." In Museum Studies: Bridging Theory and Practice, edited by Nina Robbins. Finland: ICOM International Committee for Museology, 2021.

Filene, Benjamin. "History Museums and Identity: Finding 'Them,' 'Me,' and 'Us' in the Gallery." In *Oxford Handbook of Public History*, edited by James B. Gardner and Paula Hamilton, 330–31. New York: Oxford University Press, 2017.

Filene, Benjamin. "Listening Intently: Can StoryCorps Teach Museums How to Win the Hearts of New Audiences?" In *Letting Go? Sharing Historical Authority in a User-Generated World*, edited by Bill Adair, Benjamin Filene, and Laura Koloski, 174–93. Philadelphia: Pew Center for Arts and Heritage/Left Coast Press, 2011.

"Fondation Nationale des Musees." Accessed February 25, 2021. http://www.fnm.ma/fondation/presentation-de-la-fnm/ (in French; S. El Azhar, Trans.).

Freund, Alexander. "Under Storytelling's Spell? Oral History in a Neoliberal Age." *Oral History Review* 42 (2015): 97, 108.

Frisch, Michael H. *A Shared Authority: Essays on the Craft and Meaning of Oral and Public History*. Albany: State University of New York Press, 1990.

Georgia College. "Student Places First in National Costume Design Contest for 60s Inspired Garb." *Georgia College Arts and Sciences Newsletter*, Spring 2018, page 21. https://www.gcsu.edu/sites/files/page-assets/node-2046/attachments/spring_2018.pdf.

Gill-Peterson, Jules. Histories of the Transgender Child. Minneapolis: University of Minnesota Press, 2018. 2.

Gokcigdem, Elif M., ed. *Designing for Empathy: Perspectives on the Museum Experience*. Lanham, MD: Rowman and Littlefield, 2019.

Graesser, Arthur C., Brent Olde, and Bianca Klettke. "How Does the Mind Construct and Represent Stories?" In *Narrative Impact: Social Cognitive Foundations*, edited by Melanie C. Green, Jeffrey J. Strange, and Timothy C. Brock, 229–62. Mahwah, NJ: L. Erlebaum Associates, 2002.

Grant, Melissa Gira. "The Right-Wing War on Trans Youth Was Hiding in Plain Sight." *New Republic*, May 4, 2021.

Green, Stephanie J., Kirsten Grorud-Colvert, and Heather Mannix. "Uniting Science and Stories: Perspectives on the Value of Storytelling for Communicating Science." *Facets* 3 (2018): 164–73. doi.org/10.1139/facets-2016-0079.

Greenesmith, Heron. 2019. Best Interests: How Child Welfare Serves as a Tool of White Supremacy. Political Research Associates, November 26, 2019. https://politicalresearch.org/2019/11/26/best-interests-how-child-welfare-serves-tool-white-supremacy.

Gruber, Jacob. "Ethnographic Salvage and the Shaping of Anthropology." Accessed August 13, 2021. *American Anthropologist*, New Series, 72, no. 6 (1970): 1289–99. http://www.jstor.org/stable/672848.

Heath, C., and D. vom Lehn. "Interactivity and Collaboration: New Forms of Participation in Museums, Galleries and Science Centres." In *Museums in a Digital Age*, edited by Ross Parry, 266–80. Milton Park: Routledge, 2009.

Heimlich, J., and J. Koke. "Gay and Lesbian Visitors and Cultural Institutions: Do They Come? Do They Care? A Pilot Study." *Museums and Social Issues* 3, no. 1 (2009): 93–104.

Hein, George E. *Learning in the Museum*. New York: Routledge, 2000 (1998).

Hein, George E., and Mary Alexander. *Museums: Places of Learning*. Washington, DC: American Association of Museums, 1998.

Herman, Judith L. *Trauma and Recovery: The Aftermath of Violence—from Domestic Abuse to Political Terror* (1R edition). New York: Basic Books, 2015.

HG&Co. *Your Story, Our Story Final Summative Evaluation Report*, 2020.

Horton, James Oliver, and Lois E. Horton, eds. *Slavery and Public History: The Tough Stuff of American Memory*. New York: New Press, 2006, 49–53.

Human Right Watch. *Morocco's Truth Commission: Honoring Past Victims during an Uncertain Present*. Accessed March 2, 2021. https://www.hrw.org/sites/default/files/reports/morocco1105wcover.pdf.

Humphries, Steve. "Unseen Stories: Video History in Museums." *Oral History* 31, no. 2 (2003): 75–84.

IfThen. "Case Study|Atlanta History Reimagined." https://www.ifthen.com/case-study/atlanta-history-center.

Indian Arts Research Center. *Guidelines for Collaboration* (website). Facilitated by Landis Smith, Cynthia Chavez Lamar, and Brian Vallo. Accessed May 3, 2021. Santa Fe, NM: School for Advanced Research, 2019. https://guidelinesforcollaboration.info/.

International Museum Theatre Alliance. Accessed July 1, 2021. http://www.imtal-us.org/.

"Interview: Fierce Pussy." *Curve Magazine* 31, no. 1 (2019). Accessed June 30, 2021. https://www.curvemag.com/blog/art/interview-fierce-pussy/.

Isabella Stewart Gardner Museum. *Boston's Apollo: Thomas McKeller and John Singer Sargent*. Accessed June 25, 2021. https://www.gardnermuseum.org/calendar/exhibition/bostons-apollo.

Isabella Stewart Gardner Museum. "*Boston's Apollo*: Virtual Exhibition Tour and Events." Accessed June 25, 2021. https://www.gardnermuseum.org/calendar/exhibition/bostons-apollo.

Isabella Stewart Gardner Museum. *Renewing the Promise: For the Public Forever, Strategic Plan 2019–24.* Boston: Isabella Stewart Gardner Museum, 2019. https://www.gardnermuseum.org/organization/executive-summary-2019.

Jackson, James H. "Alltagsgeschichte, Social Science History, and the Study of Migration in Nineteenth-Century Germany." Accessed March 1, 2021. https://www.cambridge.org/core/journals/central-european-history/article/abs/alltagsgeschichte-social-science-history-and-the-study-of-migration-in-nineteenthcentury-germany/C073E7B7D14F838F1A535391680F7734.

Johannesson, Åsa, and Claire Le Couteur. "Nonbinary Difference." In *Museums, Sexuality, and Gender Activism,* edited by Joshua G. Adair and Amy K. Levin, 167–79. New York: Routledge, 2020.

Karp, Ivan, Steven Lavine, and Rockefeller Foundation. *Exhibiting Cultures: The Poetics and Politics of Museum Display*. Washington, DC: Smithsonian Institution Press, 1991.

Keenan, Harper, and Lil Miss Hot Mess. "Drag Pedagogy." *Curriculum Inquiry* 50, no. 5 (2021): 440–61.

Kinsley, R., M. Middleton, and P. Moore. "[Re]Frame: The Case for New Language in the 21st Century Museum." *Exhibition* 36, no. 1 (2016): 56–63.

Kirby, David A. *Lab Coats in Hollywood: Science, Scientists, and Cinema*. Cambridge, MA: MIT Press, 2015, 97–103.

Koh, David. "The 4th Person Perspective: The Emergence of the Collective Subjective." *Medium*, February 20, 2020. https://medium.com/@CellestialStudios/the-4th-person-perspective-the-emergence-of-the-collective-subjective-5bb10302dd14.

Koster, Emlyn. "Forward." In *Fostering Empathy Through Museums*, edited by Elif M. Gokcigdem. Lanham, MD: Rowman and Littlefield, 2016.

Krause, P. Allen. *To Stand Aside or Stand Alone: Southern Reform Rabbis and the Civil Rights Movement*, edited by Mark Bauman and Stephen Krause. Tuscaloosa: University of Alabama Press, 2016.

Kreps, Daniel. "Al Abrams, Motown Records Pioneer, Dead at 74." *Rolling Stone*. Accessed July 1, 2021. https://www.rollingstone.com/music/music-news/al-abrams-motown-records-pioneer-dead-at-74-161907/.

Laaboudi, Jalil. "Casablanca: Dernier jour du bidonville Kariane Ben M'sik." Accessed March 1, 2021. https://www.bladi.net/casablanca-bidonville-kariane-ben-msik,43011.html (in French; S. El Azhar, Trans.).

Lakoff, George, and Mark Johnson. *Metaphors We Live By* (first edition). Chicago: University of Chicago Press, 2003.

Langer, Adina. "Holocaust History—The Inclusive Historian's Handbook," November 4, 2019. https://inclusivehistorian.com/holocaust-history/.

Langer, Adina. "Report | Qualtrics Experience Management: Assessing the Content and Quality of Traveling Historical Exhibits." Accessed June 25, 2021.

Les émeutes de Casablanca. Accessed February 27, 2021. https://www.lemonde.fr/archives/article/1981/06/24/les-emeutes-de-casablanca_2729314_1819218.html (in French; S. El Azhar, Trans.).

Lewis, Catherine. "Museums, Archives, and Rare Books 2018–2019 Overview." Kennesaw State University, October 14, 2019.

Lindquist, David H. "Avoiding Inappropriate Pedagogy in Middle School Teaching of the Holocaust." *Middle School Journal* 39, no. 1 (2007): 24–31.

Lindquist, David H. "Meeting a Moral Imperative: A Rationale for Teaching the Holocaust." *Clearing House* 84, no. 1 (2011): 26–30.

Literary Managers and Dramaturgs of the Americas (LMDA). "The Role of the Dramaturg." Accessed July 1, 2021. https://lmda.org/dramaturgy.

Lonetree, Amy. *Decolonizing Museums: Representing Native America in National and Tribal Museums*. Chapel Hill: University of North Carolina Press, 2012.

Lord, Gail, and Ngaire Blankenberg. *Cities, Museums, and Soft Power*. Washington, DC: American Alliance of Museums, 2016.

Mark, Joshua. "Ancient Egypt." In *World History Encyclopedia*. Accessed November 1, 2021. https://www.worldhistory.org/egypt/.

Master en Politiques culturelles et Gestion culturelle: Appel à candidatures à l'Université Hassan II. Accessed February 26, 2021. https://lematin.ma/journal/2020/appel-candidatures-luniversite-hassan-ii/339253.html (in French; S. El Azhar, Trans.).

Mehrabian, Albert. *Nonverbal Communication*. New Brunswick: Aldine Transaction, 1972.

Middleton, Margaret. "Mimi's Family: One Family's Story of Transition and Unconditional Love." *Museums & Social Issues* 1, no. 2 (2016): 147–55.

Middleton, M. "Museum Leaders as Allies for Queer Inclusion." In *The Inclusive Museum Leader*, edited by C. Catlin-Legutko and C. Taylor, 183–89. Lanham, MD: Rowman and Littlefield, 2021.

Middleton, Margaret, and Alicia Greene. "Trans Narratives in Children's Museums." *Journal of Museum Education* 43, no. 3 (2018): 220–27.

Middleton, Margaret. "Queer Possibility." *Journal of Museum Education* 45, no. 4 (December 2020): 426–36.

Middleton, Margaret. "The Queer-Inclusive Museum." *Exhibition* (Fall 2017): 81.

"Mission: Museum of History and Holocaust Education." Accessed August 17, 2021. https://historymuseum.kennesaw.edu/about/mission.php.

"Mission Statement and History Chhange: The Center for Holocaust, Human Rights & Genocide Education." Accessed June 24, 2021. https://www.chhange.org/about/history-of-chhange.

"Mohammed VI Museum Hosts Exhibition of 115 Picasso Works." Accessed February 25, 2021. https://www.moroccoworldnews.com/2017/05/216465/mohammed-vi-museum-hosts-exhibition-115-picasso-works/.

"Moroccan King Visits Restored Bayt Dakira in Essaouira." Accessed March 3, 2021. https://middle-east-online.com/en/moroccan-king-visits-restored-bayt-dakira-essaouira.

"Morocco's First National Photography Museum Opens in Rabat." Accessed March 3, 2021. https://www.moroccoworldnews.com/2020/01/291459/morocco-photography-museum-rabat/.

"Museum Connect." Accessed February 27, 2021. http://ww2.aam-us.org/about-us/grants-awards-and-competitions.

Museum of Fine Arts, Boston. "John Singer Sargent, Apollo and the Muses." Accessed June 25, 2021. https://collections.mfa.org/objects/31933/apollo-and-the-muses?ctx=f68356f4-3cea-4096-bb8a-532c7d89f5a9&idx=15.

"Museums of Morocco." Accessed in 2010. http://www.maroc.net/museums/.

My Jewish Learning. "Jewish Refugees during and after the Holocaust." Accessed June 25, 2021. https://www.myjewishlearning.com/article/jewish-refugees-during-and-after-the-holocaust/.

National Council on Public History. "What Is Public History." Accessed July 1, 2021. https://ncph.org/what-is-public-history/about-the-field/.

National Museum of African American History and Culture. "Ten Shards." Accessed July 1, 2021. https://nmaahc.si.edu/object/nmaahc_2010.71.1.1-.10.

National Museum of African Art. "Egungun Masquerade Dance Constume: Ekuu Egungun." Accessed July 1, 2021. https://africa.si.edu/exhibits/resonance/44.html.

National Summit on Teaching Slavery. "Technical Leaflet #285: Engaging Descendant Communities in the Interpretation of Slavery: A Rubric of Best Practices." In *History News: The Magazine of the American Association for State and Local History* 74, no. 1 (Winter 2019): 1–8. Note: You can also find the rubric at https://savingplaces.org/african-american-cultural-heritage#; https://www.montpelier.org/learn/tackling-difficult-history; and https://montpelierdescendants.org/rubric/.

Neiman, Susan. *Learning from the Germans: Race and the Memory of Evil*. New York: Farrar, Straus and Giroux, 2019.

Nelson, Mary Chellis. "Suzy Post: The Last Interview." *Louisville Magazine*, January 2019.

Nevins, Elizabeth. "On Relevance." November 2016. http://www.museumedu.org/on-relevance/.

Niedwiecki, A. "Save Our Children: Overcoming the Narrative That Gays and Lesbians Are Harmful to Children." *Duke Journal of Gender Law & Policy* 21 (2014): 125–75.

Nielsen, Christina, Casey Riley, and Nathaniel Silver. *Isabella Stewart Gardner Museum: A Guidebook*. New Haven and London: Yale University Press, 2017.

Norbert Friedman Interview, 2013-11-11, Legacy Series Oral History Program, 2013, KSU/14/05/03/001. Museum of History and Holocaust Education, Kennesaw State University.

"Number of Smartphone Users in the United States from 2018 to 2025 (in millions)." Statistica, last updated March 19, 2021. https://www.statista.com/statistics/201182/forecast-of-smartphone-users-in-the-us/.

Olson, Randy. *Houston, We Have a Narrative: Why Science Needs Story*. Chicago, IL: University of Chicago Press, 2015, 33–52.

Palmer, Parker. *The Courage to Teach: Exploring the Inner Landscape of a Teacher's Life*. San Francisco: Josey-Bass, 1998.

Perks, Robert, ed. *The Oral History Reader* (third edition). London; New York: Routledge, 2015.

Perry, Gillian Walnes. *The Legacy of Anne Frank*. Yorkshire: Pen and Sword History, 2018.

Pieprzak, Katarzyna. "Introduction." In *Art and Modernity in Postcolonial Morocco: Imagined Museums*. Minneapolis: University of Minnesota Press, 2010.

Przybysz, Jane. "The Victorian Crazy Quilt as Comfort and Discomfort." *Quilt Journal* 3, no. 2 (1998).

Psaltis, Charis, Mario Carretero, and Sabina Čehajić-Clancy, ed. *History Education and Conflict Transformation: Social Psychological Theories, History Teaching and Reconciliation*. London: Palgrave Macmillan, 2017.

Rand, Judy. "Write and Design with the Family in Mind." In *Connecting Kids to History with Museum Exhibitions*, edited by D. Lynn McRainey and John Russick, 266. Walnut Creek, CA: Left Coast Press, 2010.

Rector and Visitors of the University of Virginia. *President's Commission on Slavery and the University: Report to President Teresa A. Sullivan*. Accessed April 24, 2021. Charlottesville: University of Virginia Press, 2018. DOI: https://slavery.virginia.edu/wp-content/uploads/2021/03/PCSU-Report-FINAL_July-2018.pdf.

Reed, Annette Gordon. *On Juneteenth*. United Kingdom: Liveright, 2021, 71.

Ritchie, Donald A. *Doing Oral History: A Practical Guide*. New York: Oxford University Press, 1995.

Robinson, Kerry H. "In the Name of 'Childhood Innocence': A Discursive Exploration of the Moral Panic Associated with Childhood and Sexuality." *Cultural Studies Review* 14, no. 2 (2008): 113–29.

Rosenbaum, Alan S. *Is the Holocaust Unique? Perspectives on Comparative Genocide* (third edition). Boulder, CO: Routledge, 2009.

Rothberg, Michael, and Jared Stark. "After the Witness: A Report from the Twentieth Anniversary Conference of the Fortunoff Video Archive for Holocaust Testimonies at Yale." *History and Memory* 15, no. 1 (2003): 85–96. https://doi.org/10.2979/his.2003.15.1.85.

Rowe, Shawn M., James V. Wertsch, and Tatyana Y. Kosyaeva. "Linking Little Narratives to Big Ones: Narrative and Public Memory in History Museums." *Culture & Psychology* 8, no. 1 (March 1, 2002): 96–112. https://doi.org/10.1177/1354067X02008001621.

Rumbaut, Rubén G. "Ages, Life Stages, and Generational Cohorts: Decomposing the Immigrant First and Second Generations in the United States." *International Migration Review* 38, no. 3 (2004): 1160–1205. JSTOR 27645429.

Schiele, Bernard. "Science Museums and Science Centres." In *Handbook of Public Communication of Science and Technology*, edited by Massimiano Bucchi and Brian Trench, 27–39. New York: Routledge, 2008.

School for Advanced Research. "A Brief History of the SAR *Guidelines for Collaboration*." Accessed May 3, 2021. https://guidelinesforcollaboration.info/history-of-the-guidelines/.

School for Advanced Research. "Indian Arts Research Center eMuseum." Accessed September 23, 2021. https://emuseum.sarsf.org/.

School for Advanced Research. "Zuni Collection Review: Zuni Tribe, Review 1." Transcript of collection review, April 6–7, 2009. Santa Fe, NM.

Schulz, Laura E., and Elizabeth B. Bonawitz. "Serious Fun: Preschoolers Engage in More Exploratory Play When Evidence Is Confounded." *Developmental Psychology* 43, no. 4 (July 2007): 1045–50.

Serrell, Beverly. *Exhibit Labels: An Interpretive Approach* (second edition). Lanham, MD: Rowman and Littlefield, 2015. https://rowman.com/ISBN/9781442249028/Exhibit-Labels-An-Interpretive-Approach-Second-Edition.

Sheffield, Sarah L., Meghan L. Cook, Victor J. Ricchezza, Guixella A. Rocabado, and Fenda A. Akiwumi. "Perceptions of Scientists Held by U.S. Students Can Be Broadened Through Inclusive Classroom Interventions." *Communications Earth & Environment* 2, no. 83 (2021). doi.org/10.1038/s43247-021-00156-0.

Sheppard, Beverly, Marsha Semmel, and Carol Bossert. "'Think with Me': David Carr's Enduring Invitation." *Curator: The Museum Journal* 59 (April 2016): 113–19.

Silver, Nathaniel, ed. *Boston's Apollo: Thomas McKeller and John Singer Sargent.* New Haven, CT, and London: Yale University Press, 2020.

Simon, Nina. *The Participatory Museum*. Santa Cruz, CA: MUSEUM, 2010.

"Social Studies Georgia Standards of Excellence (GSE)." Accessed July 21, 2021. https://www.georgiastandards.org/georgia-standards/pages/social-studies.aspx.

Sourgo, Youssef. "Making Change: Making History." In *Ben M'sik Community Museum: Building Bridges*, edited by Samir El Azhar. Casablanca: Force Equipment, 2012.

Sullivan, Nikki, and Craig Middleton. "Warning! Heteronormativity." In *Museums, Sexuality, and Gender Activism*, edited by Joshua G. Adar and Amy K. Levin. London and New York: Routledge, 2020.

"Supporting Survivors of Trauma: How to Avoid Re-Traumatization." Accessed October 7, 2021. https://www.onlinemswprograms.com/resources/social-issues/how-to-be-mindful-re-traumatization/.

Sweet, Natalie, and Adina Langer. *The Southeastern Museums Conference Equity and Inclusion Survey Report*, 2019.

Switek, Brian. *My Beloved Brontosaurus: On the Road with Old Bones, New Science, and Our Favorite Dinosaurs*. New York: Farrar, Straus and Giroux, 2013.

"Teacher's Guides—Museum of History and Holocaust Education." Accessed October 7, 2021. https://historymuseum.kennesaw.edu/education/digital-education/teachers-guides.php.

Tervalon, M., and J. Murray-Garcia. "Cultural Humility Versus Cultural Competence: A Critical Distinction in Defining Physician Training Outcomes in Multicultural Education." *Journal of Healthcare for the Poor and Underserved* 9, no 2 (1998): 117–25.

"The 17 Goals." United Nations, adopted by all United Nations Member States in 2015. https://sdgs.un.org/goals.

Thorne, John. "A Community Museum Records Real Moroccan Life." Accessed March 1, 2021. https://readingmorocco.blogspot.com/2009/12/community-museum-records-real-moroccan.html.

Tilden, Freeman. *Interpreting Our Heritage*, edited by R. Bruce Craig. Chapel Hill: University of North Carolina Press, 2007.

Timpson, Corey. "Intangible Museum Collections and Dialogic Experience Design." In *Museum ID*, edited by Gregory Chamberlain, issue 20 (2017): 67–75.

Tosia Schneider Interview, 2014-07-08, Legacy Series Oral History Program, 2013, KSU/14/05/03/001. Museum of History and Holocaust Education, Kennesaw State University.

Trevor Project. "Strategic Plan and Mission." Accessed August 17, 2021. https://www.thetrevorproject.org/about/strategic-plan-mission/.

Tschopp, Emmanuel, Octavio Mateus, and Roger B. J. Benson. "A Specimen-Level Phylogenetic Analysis and Taxonomic Revision of Diplodocidae (Dinosauria, Sauropodia)." *PeerJ* 3 (2015): e857. doi.org/10.7717/peerj.857.

University of Massachusetts Boston. "The Ancient Egyptian Theatre." Accessed November 1, 2021. https://www.faculty.umb.edu/gary_zabel/Courses/Phil%20281b/Philosophy%20of%20Magic/Arcana/Neoplatonism/theatre.htm.

USC Shoah Foundation. "Collecting Testimonies." Accessed December 14, 2020. https://sfi.usc.edu/collecting.

U.S. History.org. "Mother Bethel AME Church." Accessed July 1, 2021. https://www.ushistory.org/tour/mother-bethel5.htm.

Virginia Department of Education (VDOE). "History and Social Science Standards of Learning," 2015. Retrieved April 8, 2021. *Standards of Learning (SOL) and Testing*. DOI: https://www.doe.virginia.gov/testing/sol/standards_docs/history_socialscience/.

Warfield, DL. "I Wanna Be Where You Are." Accessed July 1, 2021. https://dlwarfield.com/.

Wargo, Jon M., and James Joshua Coleman. "Speculating the Queer (In)Human: A Critical, Reparative Reading of Contemporary LGBTQ+ Picturebooks." *Journal of Children's Literature* 47, no. 1 (Spring 2021): 84–96.

Wellenbach, Patricia D. "Museum CEO: 'At No Time Did We Consider Canceling' Pride Events, Even after Backlash." *Philadelphia Inquirer*, June 11, 2018. Accessed August 17, 2021. https://www.inquirer.com/philly/opinion/commentary/philadelphia-pride-please-touch-museum-drag-queen-storytime-lgbtq-gay-diversity-programming-20180611.html.

"What Is Narrative Theory? | Project Narrative." Accessed January 7, 2022. https://projectnarrative.osu.edu/about/what-is-narrative-theory.

Wiley, Kehinde. "Stained Glass." Accessed July 1, 2021. https://kehindewiley.com/works/stained-glass/.

Wiley, Kehinde. "Madonna and Child." https://www.alamy.com/stock-photo-stained-glass-window-entitled-madonna-and-child-2016-by-african-american-131522630.html.

Wilkening Consulting. "Curiosity: A Primer." American Alliance of Museums, October 13, 2020. http://www.wilkeningconsulting.com/uploads/8/6/3/2/86329422/curiosity_primer_ds.pdf.

Woolley, S., T. Quinn, and E. Meiners. "The Gender, Sexuality, and Queer Milieu." In *The SAGE Guide to Curriculum in Education*, edited by M. Fang He, B. D. Schultz, and W. H. Schubert, 351–57. Los Angeles: SAGE, 2015.

Wright, Tiffany E., and Nancy J. Smith. "A Safer Place? LGBT Educators, School Climate, and Implications for Administrators." *Educational Forum* 79, no. 4 (2015): 394–407.

Youth.gov. "Behavioral Health." Accessed August 17, 2021. https://youth.gov/youth-topics/lgbtq-youth/health-depression-and-suicide.

Youth.gov. "Homelessness & Housing." Accessed August 17, 2021. https://youth.gov/youth-topics/lgbtq-youth/homelessness.

INDEX

ABOUT THE EDITOR AND THE CONTRIBUTORS

ABOUT THE EDITOR

Adina Langer has served as the curator of the Museum of History and Holocaust Education at Kennesaw State University in Kennesaw, Georgia, since 2015. A 2009 graduate of the MA program in archives and public history at New York University, she has focused her career on interpreting traumatic historical events for diverse audiences while emphasizing the dignity and individuality of the people who experienced them. Langer has publications in *History@Work*, *The Inclusive Historian's Handbook*, and *The Public Historian*, among others, and has curated more than eighteen exhibits. Follow her on Twitter @Artiflection and find her on the web at www.artiflection.com.

ABOUT THE CONTRIBUTORS

Samir El Azhar is a full professor in Hassan II University of Casablanca, Faculty of Letters & Humanities, Ben M'sik, Casablanca, Morocco. He has authored numerous articles about Moroccan literature, art, and culture. Previous publications include "The Ben M'sik Community Museum: Beyond Cultural Boundaries" in *Museums in a Global Context: National Identity, International Understanding* published by the AAM Press (2013) and *Plural Morocco: Multiculturalism and Identity* published by Faculty of Letters & Humanities, Ben M'sik (2020). He presently occupies the post of director of the Ben M'sik Community Museum and Secretary General of the Moroccan Association for Cultural Policies.

Miriam Bader is a learning designer with expertise developing dynamic programming that facilitates reflection, connection, and leadership development. She is passionate about creating innovative content that elevates our shared humanity and celebrates our diversity. As director of program design at JDC Entwine, Miriam designs content that engages leaders in making a difference internationally. She also serves as a consultant in the field of museum education. Her experience includes work at the Tenement Museum, Museum at Eldridge Street, Jewish Museum, Guggenheim Museum, and National Park Service. She received her master's degree in Museum Education at Bank Street College.

Marcy Breffle, education manager at Historic Oakland Foundation, develops programming to illuminate the multifaceted history of Atlanta's Oakland Cemetery and its residents. Since beginning work at Oakland in 2015, Marcy has created programs to educate and engage visitors of all ages and backgrounds, including an annual Juneteenth celebration, photography workshops, a homeschool program, and after-hours thematic tours. She studied history at the University of Georgia and received a graduate degree in public history from Georgia State University.

Lois E. Carlisle is a writer and historian living on the unceded territory of the Muscogee (Creek) Nation in Atlanta, Georgia. She studied history and art history at the University of South Carolina and the University of Warwick. Lois has taught in and developed curriculum for schools and institutions on two continents. She is passionate about elevating undertold stories and breaking complex ideas into their constituent parts. She is assisted by Orla Carlisle, to whom all typos and stray cat treats belong.

Christian J. Cotz became the CEO of the First Amendment Museum in Augusta, Maine, in January 2020. He spent the first two decades of his career at James Madison's Montpelier, where he was eventually given charge of historic interpretation for visitors, whether via two-dimensional, audio/video, or in-person interpreters. At the forefront of building relationships with Montpelier descendants as early as 2004, he pushed to make Montpelier's narrative more inclusive. He was the project director for *The Mere Distinction of Colour* exhibition and the *Rubric on Engaging Descendant Communities*. Cotz received undergraduate and graduate degrees from James Madison University.

Mary Margaret Fernandez holds the position of director of special events, special projects and volunteers at Historic Oakland Foundation, overseeing Oakland Cemetery's large-scale programming and managing over three hundred active volunteers. She has been involved in museum work, the arts, and nonprofit organizations for over a decade, with a professional focus on BIPOC representation at historic sites. Fernandez received her master's degree in Latin American Art History from Rutgers University. In her spare time, she can be found salsa dancing and eating copious amounts of Indian food. She enjoys a codependent relationship with her dog, Alfalfa, and a healthy relationship with her partner, Christian.

Benjamin Filene is associate director for curatorial affairs at the National Museum of American History (NMAH). Filene came to NMAH from the North Carolina Museum of History in Raleigh, where he served as chief curator. Previously he was director of public history and professor of history at University of North Carolina at Greensboro; prior to that, he served as senior exhibit developer at the Minnesota Historical Society. Filene co-edited the book *Letting Go? Historical Authority in a User-Generated World*. He recently published a new critical edition of a 1939 children's photobook about African American life: *Tobe: New Views on a Children's Classic*.

Iris Carter Ford is associate professor emerita at St. Mary's College of Maryland, The Public Honors College at Historic St. Mary's City. She serves as vice chair of the Montpelier Descendants Committee Board of Directors and is a current fellow and former board member at Sotterley, the only Tidewater plantation in Maryland open to the public with a full range of visitor activities and educational programs. Ford earned undergraduate and graduate degrees at Howard University and her PhD in cultural anthropology from The American University.

Judy Goldberg is an educator, media producer, and story facilitator; strengthening community alliances, nurturing dialogue, and inspiring activism. Judy designed and implemented "Drawing from the Well: Connecting School to

Community," an interdisciplinary curriculum with the Museum of New Mexico; founded and directed the nonprofit *Youth Media Project* and the student-directed *Audio Revolution!* radio broadcasts; and produced/hosted *Back Roads Radio*, a narrative radio series. She works as an independent consultant, orchestrating programs with regional museums, colleges, and nonprofits to further the craft of digital storytelling and the art of listening for a more just and sustainable world.

Michelle Grohe is the Esther Stiles Eastman curator of education at the Isabella Stewart Gardner Museum in Boston, Massachusetts. She works with other senior leaders to advance the Gardner as a distinctive provider of innovative, inspiring cultural experiences that broaden and diversify the museum's audiences and expand its network of community and academic partners, artists, and affinity groups. Grohe has a BFA in studio art from Millikin University and MA in art and design education for museums at Rhode Island School of Design and served as the museum education division director on the board of the National Art Education Association.

Sarah Litvin is director of the Reher Center for Immigrant Culture and History, a new museum and cultural center in Kingston, New York. She has worked as a curator and educator for the New-York Historical Society, the National Museum of American Jewish History, and the Lower East Side Tenement Museum. She completed her PhD in US women's history in 2019 at the Graduate Center, City University of New York (CUNY) with a dissertation focused on how the upright parlor piano expanded women's roles at the turn of the twentieth century. Follow the Reher Center on Instagram @ReherCenter and on facebook @ ReherBakery.

Donna M. Mah served as guest curator for the Museum of Chinese in America's 2018 exhibit *Chinese Medicine in America: Converging Ideas, People, and Practices*. Through a series of twelve narrative arcs punctuated by art and artifacts, the exhibit explored Chinese medicine through the historical, philosophical, and clinical lenses of its ancient origins and modern expression. Donna is a New York State–licensed acupuncturist, providing patient care in private practice and research, and in her faculty role in Chinese medicine and Integrative Health Education, she works to connect Chinese medicine principles to the health of individuals, families, organizations, and processes.

Rebecca Melsheimer has been the assistant exhibit developer at Tellus Science Museum in Cartersville, Georgia, since 2017. After receiving an MS in anthropology from the University of New Mexico in 2003, she has worked to share her love of science with audiences of all ages and backgrounds.

Margaret Middleton is an independent exhibit designer working at the intersection of design and social justice. They have a degree in industrial design from the Rhode Island School of Design and over fifteen years of experience in the museum field. Middleton developed the Family Inclusive Language Chart and consults with museums on implementing family inclusive practice. Other books they have contributed to include *The Inclusive Museum Leader*, *Welcoming Young Children into the Museum: a Practical Guide*, and *Feminist Designer: On the Personal and the Political in Design*. See Middleton's work at www.margaretmiddleton.com.

Patrice Preston-Grimes is associate professor emerita at the University of Virginia, where she was a member of the President's Commission on Slavery and the University. She has been a scholar-consultant on several Teaching American History Grants and to the Jefferson School African-American Heritage Center in Charlottesville, Virginia). She earned her undergraduate degree from Northwestern University (IL) and her masters and doctoral degrees in educational studies from Emory University. Her email is pgrimes@virginia.edu.

Elysia Poon is director of the Indian Arts Research Center (IARC) at the School for Advanced Research. With two decades experience in the museum field, her career has demonstrated a commitment to collaborative programming and community-based collections care. Under her leadership, the IARC continues to be at the forefront of the national conversation around how collecting institutions and Native American communities can work together to foster and promote cultural heritage and further contemporary art practices. She received her MA in art history from the University of New Mexico.

Jose Santamaria has been director of Tellus Science Museum, formerly the Weinman Mineral Museum, since 1996. Born in Cuba, Jose grew up in Atlanta, where he earned a degree in visual arts at Georgia State University. His lifelong interest in geology, minerals, and science in general led him to his current position at Tellus. Among his publications are *The 50 Coolest Things at Tellus* (2015, co-author), *Minerals of Georgia* (2016, editor), and *Baryte Microcrystals from the Cartersville Mining District* (2021, co-author). He and his wife, Maia, now live in Rome, Georgia, in a renovated 1929 craftsman bungalow.

Meredith Schweitzer is a communications consultant based in New Mexico with over a decade of experience in cultural institutions in the areas of curating, exhibition management, public programs, and communications. She believes that powerful stories and meaningful gatherings can bring any cultural non-profit's mission and vision to life.

Corey Timpson is an active collaborator and thought leader in the experience design and digital media discourses within the museum and cultural industries. As vice president, exhibition, research, and design, at the Canadian Museum for Human Rights (CMHR), Corey was responsible for the direction and oversight of all exhibition programs, research and curation, design and production. As the project director for the design-build of the CMHR, his focus was on interpreting difficult knowledge and presenting it through a multisensory, transmedia storytelling approach. Corey also championed the creation of the museum's internationally recognized inclusive design and accessibility practices.

Deitrah J. Taylor is a freelance public historian, dramaturg, and playwright with thirteen years of experience serving active learners of all ages. She is also a scholar who believes that history is active, accessible, and enjoyable. Deitrah is a native Georgian with roots in the red clay of central Georgia and the sand of coastal Georgia, where her maternal Geechee ancestors resided. Deitrah would like to dedicate her portion of this work to her late mother, E. Delean Smith Taylor, a retired high school English teacher who told her many stories and took her on her first museum and theater adventures. Deitrah's website is https://www.joyefultimetraveler.com/.

Anna E. Tucker is the curator at the newly opened Museum of the Southern Jewish Experience (MSJE) in New Orleans, Louisiana. She graduated from the history programs at Berry College (BA) and Georgia State University (MA) and has over a decade of experience in the museum field. Prior to joining the MSJE, she served as the special projects curator for the Department of Museums, Archives and Rare Books at Kennesaw State University and was a member of the executive team overseeing the Museum of History and Holocaust Education, Bentley Rare Book Museum, and Zuckerman Museum of Art.

Amy Weinstein is senior curator of oral history and vice president of collections at the National September 11 Memorial & Museum. Part of the team that created the museum, she works with 9/11 responders, survivors, family members, journalists, artists, and others affected by the terrorist attacks to record oral histories, acquire artifacts, and interpret the museum's collection. Previous publications include essays for *The Stories They Tell: Artifacts from the National September 11 Memorial Museum* (Rizzoli, 2013) and *Once Upon a Time* (Princeton Architectural Press, 2005), reflecting a lifelong interest in children's books.